ANCIENT ISRAEL'S NEIGHBORS

ESSENTIALS OF BIBLICAL STUDIES

Series Editor
Patricia K. Tull, Louisville Presbyterian Theological Seminary

ANCIENT ISRAEL'S NEIGHBORS
Brian R. Doak

SIN IN THE NEW TESTAMENT
Jeffrey Siker

READING HEBREW BIBLE NARRATIVES
J. Andrew Dearman

THE HISTORY OF BRONZE AND IRON AGE ISRAEL
Victor H. Matthews

NEW TESTAMENT CHRISTIANITY IN THE ROMAN WORLD
Harry O. Maier

WOMEN IN THE NEW TESTAMENT WORLD
Susan E. Hylen

Ancient Israel's Neighbors

BRIAN R. DOAK

OXFORD
UNIVERSITY PRESS

OXFORD
UNIVERSITY PRESS

Oxford University Press is a department of the University of Oxford. It furthers
the University's objective of excellence in research, scholarship, and education
by publishing worldwide. Oxford is a registered trade mark of Oxford University
Press in the UK and certain other countries.

Published in the United States of America by Oxford University Press
198 Madison Avenue, New York, NY 10016, United States of America.

© Oxford University Press 2020

Library of Congress Cataloging-in-Publication Data
Names: Doak, Brian R., author.
Title: Ancient Israel's neighbors / Brian R. Doak.
Description: New York : Oxford University Press, [2020] |
Includes bibliographical references and index.
Identifiers: LCCN 2020000039 (print) | LCCN 2020000040 (ebook) |
ISBN 9780190690595 (hardback) | ISBN 9780190690601 (paperback) |
ISBN 9780190690625 (epub) | ISBN 9780190690632
Subjects: LCSH: Bible. Old Testament—History of Biblical events. |
Iron age—Middle East. | Bronze age—Middle East. |
Jews—History—To 586 B.C. | Middle East—History—To 622.
Classification: LCC BS1197 .D593 2020 (print) |
LCC BS1197 (ebook) | DDC 221.9/5—dc23
LC record available at https://lccn.loc.gov/2020000039
LC ebook record available at https://lccn.loc.gov/2020000040

CONTENTS

List of Figures   vii
Series Introduction   ix

1. Israel's Neighbors and the Problem of the Past   1

2. The Canaanites   22

3. The Arameans   51

4. The Ammonites   74

5. The Moabites   98

6. The Edomites   122

7. The Philistines   146

8. The Phoenicians   170

    Conclusion: History and Identity   194

    Sources and Research Tools   *199*
    Index   *207*

FIGURES

All maps produced using GoogleMaps; Images and map data © 2019 Google, satellite view with contemporary labels and borders stripped away, with new labels and text added by the author; see https://www.google.com/permissions/geoguidelines/attr-guide/. All other line drawings produced by the author, modeled after the sources listed, except for Fig. 8.3 by Nora Clair.

1.1. Map of ancient Israel's neighbors.   8

2.1. Map of Canaan.   25

2.2. "Standing stone" from Hazor; 1300s–1200s BCE.   28

2.3. Ivory plaque from Megiddo with image of king and procession; c. 1200s BCE.   30

2.4. Three examples of early "Canaanite"-style writing, from top to bottom: (1) Wadi el-Hôl early alphabetic inscription; early second millennium BCE. (2) Inscription on a bronze arrowhead (front and back); c. eleventh century BCE; (3) Inscription on a bowl from Qubūr Walaydah; c. 1200 BCE.   32

3.1. Map of Aram.   52

3.2. Stele of a weather/storm god figure; Aleppo;
ninth century BCE.   58

4.1. Map of Ammon.   75

4.2. Ammon Citadel Inscription; ninth century BCE.   79

4.3. Stone statues of male and female figures;
Iron Age Ammon.   86

5.1. Map of Moab.   100

5.2. Limestone altar from Khirbat al-Mudayna
(ath-Thamad); eighth century BCE.   109

5.3. At left, the Baluʿa Stele; at right, the basalt Shihan
Warrior Stele from Rujm al-ʿAbd (twelfth–eighth
century BCE?).   110

6.1. Map of Edom.   124

6.2. Three-horned clay head from Hurvat Qitmit;
sixth century BCE.   130

6.3. Front and side view of a clay figure from Hatzeva;
seventh–sixth century BCE.   131

6.4. Examples of Edomite pottery decoration from
Kadesh Barnea; Iron Age.   132

7.1. Map of Philistia and selected cities.   148

7.2. Philistine "Ashdoda" figure.   157

7.3. Examples of Philistine pottery (kraters/mixing bowls)
and bird motif on pottery.   158

7.4. Philistine clay "musicians stand" from Yavneh.   160

8.1. Map of Phoenicia.   172

8.2. Phoenician alphabet, compared with Greek and
Latin alphabets (capital letters); Phoenician alphabet
as represented by the Ahiram sarcophagus
(c. 1000–975 BCE).   180

8.3. Three examples of Phoenician iconography.   180

SERIES INTRODUCTION

The past three decades have seen an explosion of approaches to study of the Bible, as older exegetical methods have been joined by a variety of literary, anthropological, and social models. Interfaith collaboration has helped change the field, and the advent of more cultural diversity among biblical scholars in the West and around the world has broadened our reading and interpretation of the Bible. These changes have also fueled interest in Scripture's past: both the ancient Near Eastern and Mediterranean worlds out of which Scripture came and the millennia of premodern interpretation through which it traveled to our day. The explosion of information and perspectives is so vast that no one textbook can any longer address the many needs of seminaries and colleges where the Bible is studied.

In addition to these developments in the field itself are changes in the students. Traditionally the domain of seminaries, graduate schools, and college and university religion classes, now biblical study also takes place in a host of alternative venues. As lay leadership in local churches develops, nontraditional, weekend, and on-line preparatory classes have mushroomed. As seminaries in Africa, Asia, and Latin America grow, particular need for inexpensive, easily available materials is clear. As religious controversies over the Bible's origins and norms continue to dominate the airwaves, congregation members and even curious nonreligious folk seek reliable paths into particular topics. And teachers themselves continue to seek guidance in areas of the ever-expanding field of scriptural study with which they may be less than familiar.

A third wave of changes also makes this series timely: shifts in the publishing industry itself. Technologies and knowledge are shifting so rapidly that large books are out of date almost before they are in print. The internet and the growing popularity of e-books call for flexibility and accessibility in marketing and sales. If the days when one expert can sum up the field in a textbook are gone, also gone are the days when large, expensive multiauthored tomes are attractive to students, teachers, and other readers.

During my own years of seminary teaching, I have tried to find just the right book or books for just the right price, at just the right reading level for my students, with just enough information to orient them without drowning them in excess reading. For all the reasons stated above, this search was all too often less than successful. So I was excited to be asked to help Oxford University Press assemble a select crew of leading scholars to create a series that would respond to such classroom challenges. Essentials of Biblical Studies comprises freestanding, relatively brief, accessibly written books that provide an orientation to the Bible's contents, its ancient contexts, its interpretive methods and history, and its themes and figures. Rather than a one-size-had-better-fit-all approach, these books may be mixed and matched to suit the objectives of a variety of classroom venues as well as the needs of individuals wishing to find their way into unfamiliar topics.

I am confident that our book authors will join me in returning enthusiastic thanks to the editorial staff at Oxford University Press for their support and guidance, especially Theo Calderara, who shepherded the project in its early days, and Dr. Steve Wiggins, who has been a most wise and steady partner in this work since joining OUP in 2013.

1

Israel's Neighbors and the Problem of the Past

NEIGHBORS FIGHT EACH OTHER

I recently spoke with a colleague who teaches political science and asked her about research literature that might shed light on the question of "national neighbors," that is, groups that share a border. How do they interact with one another? Are there patterns? Is there research on this? Her immediate response: "Oh, there have been many studies, and this is what we know for sure: *neighbors fight each other.*" Indeed, research bears this out: people who share a border engage in constant conflict. This conflict does not always negate the cooperation that occurs between neighbors, of course. For nations sharing boundaries, conflict and cooperation function as alternating modes, and sociologists who study the idea of a "neighbor" and "neighborhood" have highlighted the ways neighbors can organize and achieve common goals. But even at the personal level, as many of our anecdotal experiences tell us, to have a neighbor is to have a *problem* that needs constant attention. Again, from my political science colleague: "Humans seem to be ridiculously attached to territory." We care immensely about our boundaries and spend a lot of time fretting about them.

The ancient Israelites who produced the Hebrew Bible / Old Testament occupied a geographical territory with complex, uneven, and changing borders. The people situated on the other side of

Ancient Israel's Neighbors. Brian R. Doak, Oxford University Press (2020). © Oxford University Press.
DOI: 10.1093/oso/9780190690595.001.0001

Israel's immediate borders constitute what I am calling in this book "Israel's nearest neighbors": specifically the Canaanites, Arameans, Ammonites, Moabites, Edomites, Philistines, and Phoenicians. Readers of the Bible often wonder: Who are these people, exactly? Knowing their identity makes a big difference, because nations surrounding Israel appear very frequently throughout the Bible and a play a crucial role in Israel's story. In fact, these smaller surrounding nations form the most critical, immediate crucible in which Israel forged its identity.

The most frequently mentioned nation outside of Israel in the Bible, Egypt or ("Egyptian[s]"), appears just under 750 times in the Hebrew Bible, while the Babylonians, who destroyed the Temple in the year 586 BCE, appear a little over 300 times. These were both fearsome and large empires in the ancient Near Eastern world. The Assyrians—another massively sophisticated and sizeable empire whose activities influenced the shape of the biblical texts in major ways and dominated the politics of the entire ancient Near East for a century—appear around 125 different times in the text. The Hittites, whose empire was based in central Anatolia and who also vied for control of the ancient Near Eastern world and flourished periodically from around 1600 to 1200 BCE, are mentioned around 60 times. (Israel's relationship to some of these larger empires will be covered in other volumes in the Essentials of Biblical Studies series.)

Now, consider Israel's nearest neighbors—those groups sharing a direct boundary with Israel: the Philistines appear most, at 265 references (all these are rounded numbers), followed by Moab/Moabites (185), Aram/Aramaeans (135), Ammon/Ammonites (130), Edom/Edomites (125), various Phoenician cities (100), and Canaanites (maybe around 100). All told, these smaller, direct-border-sharing groups get nearly as much attention as the three dominant empires of Assyria, Babylon, and Egypt, and indeed, several of these smaller neighboring groups individually feature more frequently in the Bible than the mighty Assyrians. These numbers tell us that Israelite authors and their audiences were frequently engaged with their bordering neighbors. The story Israel has to tell about itself deeply involves these smaller, lesser-known nations. In fact, we can only understand Israel's story of itself by understanding Israel's place among these groups.

AN OVERVIEW OF THIS BOOK

My purpose in this book is to tell the story of Israel's nearest neighbors—not only discovering what the Bible has to say about them but also what we can know from archaeology, ancient inscriptions, and other sources. To say that this task is complicated is putting it lightly. For one thing, the Bible itself presents these neighbors in nuanced and conflicting ways; sometimes they are friends or even related to Israel at a family level, and sometimes they are enemies, spoken of as though they must die in order for Israel to live. The Moabites, for example, violently confront the escaped Hebrew slaves on their way out of Egypt yet also provide the great-grandmother of King David in the person of Ruth, a Moabite refugee. The Edomites, reviled in the Bible as participators in the sacking of Jerusalem in 586 BCE, have familial ties with Israel in the book of Genesis, and the Aramaeans, political enemies of Israel in the book of Kings, occupy a mysterious place near the heart of Israel's own journey in Deuteronomy 26:5, where the individual Israelite is to recite a short historical creed that begins, "A wandering Aramaean was my ancestor. . . ." Moreover, the biblical story never presents the identity of these groups as pure "history," but rather as a complex mix of legend, storytelling, political invective, and memory. We are left wondering how the biblical portrayal might have affected our thinking about these people as historical groups. How would an Aramaean have described her own religion? How would an Edomite have described conflict with Israel?

In this book, then, I explore the biblical portrayal of the smaller groups surrounding Israel as well as what we can know about these groups through their own literature, archaeology, and other sources. Learning what we can about these various peoples in their own right will deepen our awareness of Israel's close neighbors. By uncovering the identity of the Philistines as settlers along the coast at the same time that early Israel carved out its place in the land, for example, we can better understand the social turmoil and political maneuvering that lies just beneath the surface of the biblical narrative—and we can see more clearly just how the authors of the Bible saw themselves in the face of others.

We could order the presentation in ways other than how these chapters now appear, and my hope is that the book can function just as well if the chapters are taken completely out of order. I begin with the Canaanites because their identity is so central to the biblical imagination, and these Canaanites often dwell within Israel's borders. From there, I proceed roughly in the order that each of the neighbors appears in the Bible's first book, Genesis: Aram (note Abram's connection to Haran, an Aramaean city, in Gen 11–12); Ammon and Moab (named descendants of Lot in Gen 19); Edom (the Esau narrative in Gen 25–28 and 32–36); Philistia (which becomes prominent in 1 Samuel, but is already significant in Gen 21 and 26); and finally, the Phoenicians, represented by major cities such as Sidon and Tyre, which appear more frequently in Samuel–Kings and the later prophetic books. Moreover, each chapter is organized around a uniform set of headings:

> *Archaeology*: What do we know about this group from archaeology, which includes inscriptions, material culture of all kinds, religious structures, and texts outsi-de the Bible? I begin each chapter with archaeology not because this field is totally objective, but in order to establish a material identity for each group in question that is not first filtered through the Bible.

> *Biblical Representation*: Where does this group appear in the Bible, and how does the Bible represent this group's identity? I review specific instances where Israel seems to identify with or against the other group's practices and identity. Each case must be taken

on its own, with care to affirm any differences between the way the Bible presents this group's history, culture, or religion versus what we know from other sources.

What Happened to the Neighbor: How does the identity of this group evolve in the later periods represented by the biblical narrative—past the end of "Israel" as a putatively independent nation in the Iron Age (around 1200–500 BCE) and into the Second Temple period and the New Testament and early Christian era (around 500 BCE–200 CE)? The New Testament deals with these groups sparsely, but what references we do have to these groups sometimes provide a useful endpoint to the discussion, insofar as the treatment in this book is broadly biblical in its scope. And in some cases, the historical identity of the neighbor has resonances even today.

As with other books in the Essentials of Biblical Studies series, the primary intended audience comprises students in undergraduate and seminary classrooms, but in every case I have attempted to write as though some readers are approaching this book outside any formal setting. There may even be a stray professional scholar who ends up reading the book, not to mention professors who may use it in their own classrooms as a text. To the specialists in the various academic fields represented here, all introductory or survey discussions come off as lacking nuance—as indeed they are. For that reason, my goal here will be to never pretend that we are more confident about the evidence that we do have. Nevertheless, scholars need to understand that repeated marks of hesitancy and ponderous overqualification make for a bad general reading experience and belong in peer-reviewed technical journals.

Nevertheless, students and more casual readers must understand that when they wade into the world of biblical scholarship, archaeology, and history, they are proceeding into very deep waters. You may find yourself wanting clearer answers on a given point, and those answers simply may not exist given our current state of knowledge—or those answers may be frustrating or even disconcerting. At the end of this book, I provide a list of Sources and Research Tools in which readers can find more information to take their studies further. Within the chapters themselves, I selectively use endnotes to cite sources and point the astute reader toward further debate and more complex presentations.

SOME TERMS, PROBLEMS, AND DEBATES . . .

Before we proceed, a few clarifications are in order. Where are these neighbors exactly, and what land did they occupy alongside Israel, and when? Can we call all of these surrounding groups "nations"? How might these other nations function as a social, religious, or political foil to ancient Israel, and how does this process affect the way we think about these other groups and our views of ancient Israel itself? Finally, how do we know anything at all about the past? Where does our information come from, and to what extent can we trust it?

Where Is Israel, and Where Are These Neighbors?

The region in question has contemporary political boundaries that do not map onto ancient realities. By looking at a map of the Middle East today, we can see Israel bordered by several entities. Directly to the north of the modern state of Israel/Palestine along the coast, there is Lebanon, and to the north and northwest, Syria. To the east, spanning from the Gulf of Aqaba in the south nearly all the way to the Sea of Galilee, across the Jordan River, lies the country of Jordan. To Jordan's south along the Gulf of Aqaba, Saudi Arabia shares a border with Jordan (but not Israel), and then to the east of Jordan itself is the far western portion of Iraq. To the south of Israel/Palestine we have the Sinai Peninsula, part of Egypt. Within Israel itself, various spaces have been marked out as the so-called Palestinian territories, including the West Bank (and East Jerusalem), Golan Heights, and Gaza Strip, controlled by Israel since the Six-Day War of 1967. The status of these territories has provoked massive international debate, and most of us are familiar with the near-constant state of conflict that characterizes the region.

These contemporary political divisions, however, did not exist in the ancient world of the Bible, even though some geographical features such as deserts, mountain ranges, and rivers play the same border roles today that they played in the past. Whereas present-day researchers can consult many maps, news reports, photographs, and books to track precisely Israel's changing borders in the twentieth century CE, those of us looking to the past cannot speak with the same kind of certainty. An ancient religious text may make a claim that this or that nation inhabited this or that place—but did they, actually, in history? Moreover, just as borders change in the contemporary world, they did so in the ancient world—and borders could not be policed or defined in a manner that allows us to make a very confident map of this region in the ancient world generally at all. Archaeologists who carefully study settlement patterns frequently debate the identity of people living in a particular place. Nevertheless, the map displayed in Figure 1.1 can serve as a starting point for thinking generally about Israel's ancient neighbors in a broader geographic region sometimes called "the Levant," a portion of territory defined in various ways historically but which is often used to designate the western part of the so-called Fertile Crescent—a region now territorially occupied by nations like Syria, Jordan, Lebanon, and Israel/Palestine.

To the north of Israel along the coast were powerful cities involved with Mediterranean trade networks, including Tyre, Sidon, and Byblos—cities grouped under the heading "Phoenician." To the north and northeast of Israel were the Aramaeans (Aram), sometimes also called "Damascus" in the Bible after the name of a prominent city there. South of Aram, the Ammonites (Ammon) carved out a space, and directly to west of the Dead Sea lived the Moabites in Moab. Farther south in the desert region was Edom. Though

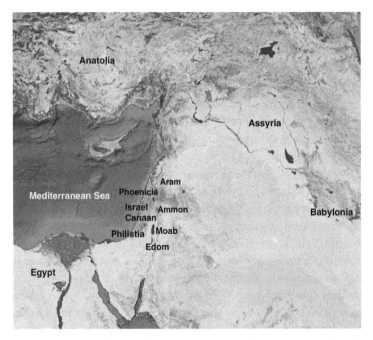

FIG. 1.1 Ancient Israel's neighbors (by region). Map data ©2019 Google, with text added by the author.

contemporary Egypt shares a political border with Israel, and though ancient Egypt made many incursions north into the area, Egypt was not a close neighbor with biblical Israel, nor were the Assyrians in the north, though their territory came close to the far northern parts of Israel. Along the southern coast, the Philistines lived clustered around key cities such as Gaza, Ashkelon, Ashdod, Gath, and Ekron.

Interspersed throughout all of these formally named areas, many tribal groups and smaller entities existed and flourished in different ways and time periods. As today, local communities in the region often identified themselves more strongly (or even completely) within a tribal network not easily subsumed under any larger political framework or national name. Indeed, in some cases, one may begin to get the impression that these surrounding "nations" were not really nations at all, at least in some historical periods—and the same would be true for biblical Israel as well.

Nations and Identity in the Ancient World

What exactly defines a nation (or people, state, country, or polity)—and should we be calling any of the people groups in this book "nations," including Israel? Modern scholars have explored multiple dimensions of this question, and I do not provide a definitive answer in this volume.[1] Political theorists sometimes describe nations as people living in defined territory, with a name, who have a clear leadership structure, and who are oriented by or toward some common language and goals. Alternatively, "nation" may describe the country or the land and not the people, or some mix of people and land. A group may function as a nation, even if the group does not have or agree upon a name for that nation.

However, we may speak of "nations" in more complex terms. Nations are ideas just as much, or more, than they are places or even people. The nation truly exists in the ideological conceptions of those who talk about the nation—in their hopes, dreams, needs, and projections. Perhaps nations bear primarily economic meanings and came about as the product of industrialization and

---

1. See, for example, classic studies like Benedict Anderson, *Imagined Communities*, 2nd ed. (1983; London: Verso, 2006), and Eric Hobsbawm, *Nations and Nationalism since 1788*, 2nd ed. (Cambridge: Cambridge University Press, 1990). For thinking about the ancient Near East specifically, see Rainer Kessler, Walter Sommerfeld, and Leslie Tramontini, eds., *State Formation and State Decline in the Near and Middle East* (Wiesbaden: Harrassowitz, 2016), and Bruce Routledge, *Archaeology and State Theory: Subjects and Objects of Power* (London: Bloomsbury, 2013).

its needs.[2] Nations are not natural, in this way of thinking, but *created*; the rise of world exploration, sophisticated mapmaking techniques, and faster travel facilitated new ideas of national identity. Empires have been known to redraw maps and create nations out of thin air for purposes of taxation or military control. True, everyone lives somewhere, and we all speak certain languages and group ourselves together for purposes of convenience or shared goals—but does this make us a "nation"? Putting a finger on exactly what a nation should be is not easy.

We also have other categories related to and often conflated with the idea of a nation but that are now considered in their own right:[3] "tribes," often discussed in terms of common genealogical descent (whether real or fictive); "race" and "ethnicity," which also evoke notions of descent; and "culture," which, among other things, may describe the particular institutions related to one's way of life, such as food and the arts. We might also consider markers of identity such as religion, values, language, among others. Most of us are familiar with contemporary debates about multiculturalism, identity, and race, but are far less familiar with what we mean when we use words like "culture" and "race." How do these notions interact with the idea of a "nation"? Very often, the way we use group designations and markers of identity show that we possess an amazing ability to misunderstand others in the service of some argument or strategic purpose we might have.[4]

2. Ernest Gellner, *Nations and Nationalism*, with an introduction by John Breuilly, 2nd ed. (Ithaca, NY: Cornell University Press, 2006).

3. George W. White, *Nation, State, and Territory: Origins, Evolutions, and Relationships*, vol. 1 (Lanham, MD: Rowman and Littlefield, 2004), 21–64.

4. Charles Taylor, ed., *Multiculturalism: Examining the Politics of Recognition*, ed. and introduced by Amy Gutmann (Princeton, NJ: Princeton University Press, 1994), and Edward Said, *Orientalism*, 25th anniversary ed., with a new preface by the author (New York: Random House, 1994).

The obvious problem for our purposes here, then, involves the question of our terminology for these people groups surrounding Israel. Were they nations? Not always, and certainly not in the modern sense. As we explore the ancient biblical world, we are going to find that definitions of named nations and the character of their leaders and people living in those nations are determined by very specific purposes—religious and political. Let us consider, as a very brief case study anticipating a chapter later in this book, the example of the Phoenicians. Biblical authors such as the prophet Ezekiel (chs. 27–28) speak of Phoenicians, such as the king of Tyre, as utterly drunk on power, even considering themselves divine, arrogantly sailing about the Mediterranean trading, and selfishly amassing wealth for themselves. Is this what the nation of Phoenicia was actually like, historically and fundamentally? Were most Phoenicians like this? Biblical authors had specific rhetorical reasons for labeling people under various national rubrics or titles by city. As it turns out, scholars today are engaged in contentious debate about whether anyone at all called themselves "Phoenician" in the ancient world or considered Phoenician cities as we know them—such as Sidon, Tyre, or Byblos—under any common term. Using broad-brush labels falls flat and may wrongly color our thinking about thousands of people and diverse practices.

If or when we choose to use the word "nation" or other terms to describe entities such as Moab, Ammon, Israel, or any other ancient group, we need to use the term with at least implicit "scare quotes" around it, knowing that history is complicated and people are hard to define. We must consider not only geography, borders, and names of kings, but also effects, consequences, and practices— not only texts but also the material objects that archaeologists uncover for us. Identity is complicated.

How Do We Know Anything about the Past?

All of this leads us to another crucial question: How do we know what we know about the past? Defining "history" itself proves difficult, but the task is important because one of my goals in this book is to explore not only what the Hebrew Bible says about the nations immediately surrounding it but to determine, as possible, what those people were actually like. Such terminology reminds professional historians of a famous phrase by the nineteenth-century German scholar Leopold von Ranke, who in his major historical work declared his goal to be showing *wie es eigentlich gewesen* (how it really was). Interpreters of von Ranke take the meaning of that phrase in various ways—perhaps to mean history "on the ground," that is, in the lives of normal people and not just kings and elites, or possibly indicating some other kind of value-neutral assessment of the past. To know the past as it really was probably sounds like a noble goal to most of us. Who intentionally aspires to distortion and unreality?

Yet the trajectory of modern history writing teaches us that knowing the past completely objectively requires an impossible interpretive situation—one in which we could really know anything without bias, perspective, or goal. History is not just what happened, though events certainly happened in time and space, but rather *a particular way of talking about what happened.* To quote a famous definition of history by Johan Huizinga, "History is the intellectual form in which a civilization renders account to itself of its past." We talk to ourselves about history—and about what we want and who we are. All history is, in the words of yet another famous intellectual, Claude Lévi-Strauss, *history-for*, that is, history for a certain group, from a perspective. If taken down a certain path, all of this no doubt threatens us with a type of relativism. If everything is just your perspective, and no one's perspective is better than anyone else's perspective, then no one can ultimately say they are correct and another person is wrong about, say, history. You say a thing happened; I say it didn't. The powers of mere assertion, on the one hand, and blanket denial, on the other, prove again and again to be really powerful.

But the tools of history in the enlightenment mode introduce us to ways of knowing outside of bald assertions, superstitions, and tradition. I can point to a vacant lot beside my house and declare that no house ever stood there, but you could move away some of the grass and reveal a crumbled foundation of a basement, and remains of a fireplace, and artifacts of various kinds. Now the conversation gets more difficult for me. Critical historical inquiry of all kinds, based on certain rules of argumentation and material evidence, asks us to engage in a different way of talking. An ancient inscription by a particular king proclaims he enacted thus and such a reform, eradicating the worship of a rival king's deity from the land—but perhaps inscriptions or figurines of that deity or temples dedicated to that deity in the countryside tell a different story, leading us to consider the rhetorical purpose for what the king claimed and to ask about the value of his claims.

What sources, methods, and materials do we have for understanding the history of the Levant? Broadly speaking, our evidence falls into two categories that come up repeatedly in this book: texts and archaeology.

TEXTS

Low literacy rates in the ancient Levant meant that only skilled scribes produced readable texts with ease. In some cases, common people could have read and written texts, but such things required training not available to the majority of premodern populations. Written sources can come from a *native* perspective, that is, from people representing themselves and their communities, or from an *outside* perspective, that is, one group writing about others. Which of these perspectives—the native or the outsider—proves more valuable to historians reconstructing an ancient society? Both are used, but you might imagine that native sources could have the advantage of at least explaining events from a participant's own experience, as opposed to the distorting effects of outsiders looking in. Yet native sources are in no way to be taken at face value; everything has to be studied carefully for what it is, for its motivations and internal logic. We can't take any shortcuts to history or truth when studying texts.

Here is a problem that will confront us repeatedly in our study: Israel's neighbors produced few surviving native texts about themselves. Consider the Philistines, for example. Scholars of this group are not even fully confident about what language they spoke, and we currently have discovered no lengthy narratives from a Philistine perspective about anything. The Bible, on the other hand, narrates many chapters of experience with the Philistines, telling us about their arrogance, their military and social failures, their false religion, and the submission of their deity, Dagan, to the god of the Israelites. Is this how Philistines would have described themselves? What would a more balanced portrait look like? Then again, from a certain theological perspective (e.g., a religious perspective from within some stream of Christianity or Judaism), one might ask, rhetorically, "Who cares what the Philistines would have said about themselves?" Fair enough. However, even if someone from a religious community wants to engage in a discussion about history, that person will have to do so with the realization that other historians may not share their devotion to a particular religious text as an authoritative guide to interpreting history. The conversation gets awkward fast. If one wants to talk about history in the scholarly sense, in the rational Enlightenment tradition, one will have to play by the rules of that game—rules based on evidence and argumentation.

ARCHAEOLOGY

Early archaeological excavations in the eighteenth and nineteenth centuries probably at times resembled an Indiana Jones movie, with armies of workers digging with shovels and pickax at promising sites looking for treasure, which they would then loot. As archaeology matured as a discipline throughout the twentieth century and into the present time, archaeologists developed a sophisticated set of methods and theory to guide their research that created a more controlled, scientific discipline. Today, scientific methods such as DNA testing, soil microbiology, satellite imaging, and a number of other methods help archaeologists develop a robust set of possibilities about the past. At its core, archaeology is all about layers of occupation and artifacts in the ground—that is, stratigraphy. With some exceptions for cases when ancient people reused parts of buildings from previous periods of occupation at a particular site, older things usually lie farther down in the ground, and newer things on top. And since different kinds of people in different places used various kinds of tools, objects, building styles, and writing media, archaeologists can attempt to correlate layers of occupation to one another regionally and to discern when and by whom the various layers were occupied.

Subjective interpretation is still needed. Ancient pottery does not speak for itself, nor do the walls of ruined temples. The job of the archaeologist is to put this material reality into a larger conversation with geography, regional patterns, and other data. As we will see in the chapters to come, archaeology has a complicated story to tell about the past for all the regions and people in question—a story sometimes at odds with the biblical textual portrait, sometimes cohering with that portrait, but always nuancing and complicating it.

When Was the Bible Written?

Speaking of knowing things about the past and situating our study in some clear historical context: one of the most difficult problems anyone who studies the Bible academically encounters has to do with providing a historical setting for the authorship of a given part of the Bible. This could become important in specific cases as we attempt to use the Bible for historical information about a group's neighbors, or anything else, for that matter.

Let's say, for example, that an author composed the story of David and the Philistine Goliath (1 Sam 17) in the middle of the sixth century BCE, based on assumptions that author had about the way Philistines wore armor or fought in battles at that time—but within the world of the text itself, the setting of the story suggests a rough date in the eleventh or tenth century BCE (when David and Saul supposedly lived). Our knowledge of what the Philistines were actually like, then, insofar as the Bible could provide accurate historical data, hangs in the balance depending on the dating of the text. We might learn through the Bible in this hypothetical case something about what the Philistines were like in the mid-sixth century BCE, but we would have to do investigative work to know that the information we're getting is in fact relevant to the sixth century and not the tenth century BCE (or some other century entirely). Moreover, even if a biblical author wrote about an event at a time contemporary to that event, we have no guarantee about whether that information is historically accurate. It may be accurate in some other way, but history, specifically, requires its own tools and investigative structure.

Like scholars in a lot of other academic disciplines, beginning especially in the eighteenth and nineteenth centuries CE, biblical scholars began to question traditional ideas about nearly everything. The most famous case dealt with authorship of the Torah; traditionally attributed to Moses, readers soon began to find places in the text where it seemed that definitely someone other than Moses did the writing. Other traditional authors, such as the prophet Isaiah, also came under suspicion. If roughly the second half of the book of Isaiah seems directly relevant to the period of the Persian Empire in the sixth century BCE, while the first portion of the book seems directly relevant to the late eighth century BCE Assyrian context, then it stands to reason that the text was in fact written in two distinct historical periods, at least, and then edited together later, all under the heading of "Isaiah."

Knowing the historical context of the book or its references in any given location would depend heavily on making a correct judgment about the time of authorship for that particular place in the text. In a biblical book, we may find a piece of information written, say, around the year 750 BCE and then handed down for centuries, placed right in the middle of a longer narrative that was composed in its final form, say, around the year 400 BCE. The text may be a composite. Some books, such as Jeremiah, make a lot of sense when considered within the exact historical context that the book itself provides (the early sixth century BCE), while other books, such as Deuteronomy, can make a lot more sense historically if we read it not in its putative narrative setting (i.e., in the time of Moses, maybe around 1200 BCE?) but rather in the seventh century BCE, as some scholars do for complicated reasons. Other books have yielded hugely deviating estimates for the time of authorship or editing into their final book form, such as Job. Others are mostly thought to be a composite of texts dating to eras as far apart as five or six hundred years, such as Genesis or Exodus. Indeed, the classic theories about distinct literary sources in books like Genesis and Exodus posit that the earliest layers of the text may date to around 1000 or 900 BCE, while the latest portions may date to the 500s or 400s BCE.[5]

We cannot untangle problems like this and solve them for the present study merely by asserting one particular dating scheme, or by simply reverting to traditional assumptions about authorship. I am not denying that some religious communities place high value on particular authors writing their texts—they clearly do. But even from most religious perspectives, *a text does not automatically achieve the label history simply because it appears within the Bible.* Things need to be taken on a case-by-case basis, and in this book I make broad suggestions about dating that could form the basis for further work. In the end, of course, we should find ourselves concerned with more than just mere history—most readers of the Bible who want to know more about Israel's neighbors probably also will want to know more in general about these other people's religious practices and how the Bible's authors interpreted the experiences of Israel vis-à-vis others around them. Along with

---

5. For information about issues like this, beginning readers can consult an introductory textbook such as Michael D. Coogan, *A Brief Introduction to the Old Testament: The Hebrew Bible in Its Context*, 3rd ed. (Oxford: Oxford University Press, 2015).

a concern for history, then, in this book we always have an eye out for a wide range of issues.

The Problem of the Other

Now that we are getting into the details of what it might mean to consider the Bible as a source for historical knowledge, we reach a potentially harder issue. In contemporary discourse, one often encounters the social problems that come with creating a strong and distorted image of the other—that is, some person or group that one comes to define as fundamentally different, most often in a negative way, from one's own self. In fact, identifying people who are similar to us as within our sphere of protection and sympathy as opposed to those outside that sphere as strange or wrong or defiled may be one of our most fundamental human social proclivities. Sometimes, this process of othering may be more harmless—like shaking your head in disgust at fans of a musical group you detest. However, to create these boundaries, we may resort to a number of tactics—all of them questionable in terms of their fairness and truth value. We may, for example, create racial categories or enhance our perception of other differences in order to help us commit some act of violence or theft against others. And in fact, whether those who read the Bible in deep commitment to its spiritual values like it or not, interpreters have used the Bible as a source of direct inspiration in these violent projects. For example, the books of Deuteronomy and Joshua tell a story in which God commands Israel to completely eradicate the Canaanite inhabitants of the land of Israel, all so that the incoming Israelites can inhabit their rightful land. Even if one believed that there was a real God who commanded this in the past, and one believes it was a just command for those people at that time, one may still question whether such a plan should be replicated in the contemporary world. What if, for example, a new group of people (say, European settlers) began to inhabit a land (like America), and the settlers saw themselves as a "new Israel" and then cast the native inhabitants of that new land (First Nation / Native Americans) as equivalent to the biblical Canaanites? Should they, too, not be killed and driven off the land? In fact, the Bible's depiction of the others surrounding it or within it— in this case, the Canaanites—was used in exactly this way during the eighteenth, nineteenth, and even twentieth centuries by Americans of European descent to justify their military and political program against native people. If the Bible, still considered by many to be a bedrock of instruction for hundreds of millions, if not billions, of people, could cast its nearest neighbors in the role of defiled villains who must be constrained or destroyed, why should those who follow in the biblical tradition today refrain from doing so?

Like the larger problem of history within which it resides, identity and the role of the other is complicated. Biblical authors sometimes decried various practices, such as worshiping deities like Baal and Asherah, as foreign practices, invented by the other nations surrounding them. But if archaeologists have found evidence that these deities were worshiped *regularly within Israel itself*, which they have, then wouldn't it be fair to say that these were Israelite religions as well? To be sure, the Bible itself routinely blames Israel for these very types of infractions. In various places, biblical authors assert that the practice of child sacrifice to a deity to achieve some desired end was a Moabite, Ammonite, Phoenician, or Canaanite activity generally—though in fact Israel is also accused of the practice within the Bible (e.g., 2 Kgs 21:6; compare with Gen 22). Did Israel import this activity from its neighbors? Possibly. However, at one point the prophet Ezekiel suggests that Israel's own God had commanded child sacrifice (Ezek 20:25–26), and at least one particular passage in the book of Exodus, presented as God's command from Mount Sinai to Israel, suggests that children could legitimately be sacrificed or "offered" in some way (Exod 22:29–30). So what is happening here? What is the practice of the other, and who is the other?

Consider yet one further level of complication to this problem of othering: within the biblical storyline, Israel even manages to become an other and a neighbor to itself. First Kings 12 narrates the process by which the northern part of the country, called "Israel," as opposed to the tribe of "Judah" in the south, breaks away and becomes its own nation with its own kings (perhaps around 920 BCE). The following texts then treat that northern kingdom as a rogue, foreign group that had defied God's commands for unity of worship in Jerusalem (i.e., in Judah, in the south). When the Assyrians destroyed this northern part of the country, Israel, around 720 BCE, they allegedly imported foreigners into the space to resettle it, creating a population of those who had lived there previously mixed with those brought in from elsewhere (2 Kgs 17:24–25). To make a long story short, by the time of Jesus in the New Testament (first century CE) many of the Jews held a negative view of this group of supposedly mixed-race people in the north around the city of Samaria, the Samaritans, and saw them as religiously other to the Jews and Judaism practiced at the temple in Jerusalem. This sense of the Samaritans' otherness comes up in John 4, when Jesus confronts a Samaritan woman, and in one of his most famous parables, that of the Good Samaritan (Lk 10:25–37), Jesus asks his audience to consider their own views about racial otherness in light of what it might mean to "love your neighbor as yourself" (Lev 19:18).

In some cases, textual materials such as monumental inscriptions from empires like the Assyrians, Babylonians, and Egyptians provide data on Israel's neighbors, and wherever possible we consider this evidence. But we simply cannot ignore the Bible as a historical source, and in some cases the Bible is the primary source of information for at least certain aspects of the identity of Israel's neighbors. Thus, a problem that we run into repeatedly in this book has to do with the Bible-centric view we almost inevitably come to have regarding the identity of the nations surrounding the Bible. The series in which this book appears is called "Essentials of Biblical Studies," and the title of this book is *Ancient Israel's Neighbors*. The Bible and Israel act as the organizing principle from the start; such labels do not even make any attempt to hide the fact that Israel and the Bible it produced set the terms for discussion. Readers of this book should ask themselves: Would you be interested in reading about the ancient Edomites if they had no relation whatsoever to the Bible? What about the Phoenicians? The Ammonites? Perhaps you would, in an ideal world of learning—but it is extremely likely that one's interest in these groups comes directly from a desire to understand the context of Israel's Bible. Acknowledging these facts can help us approach the material in this book in a mature, reflective manner—not pretending that we can eliminate our biases, but rather acknowledging our motivations, whatever they are, and proceeding with honesty and energy to learn.

2

The Canaanites

THE STUDY OF THE CANAANITES involves problems of definition and identity that are in some ways more difficult than any of the other groups we'll be thinking about in this book. In fact, many books of this type, which treat the various nations surrounding Israel, skip the Canaanites completely, perhaps because they are so difficult to categorize and also because they do not occupy a clear geographical territory outside of Israel during any one period. In my view, however, the Canaanites become one of the most intriguing examples of the neighboring group as other in the Bible, and because the narrator of the book of Genesis repeatedly calls the land Israel's ancestors occupy "Canaan," I begin with them. It is not too much of a stretch to say that the Canaanites are Israel's first neighbor, their most primordial neighbor, setting a pattern of tensions and interaction that prove instructive for thinking about other neighboring groups.

We find that the archaeological record of the Canaanites in the period before "Israel" arrives on the scene is difficult on many fronts, and the problem doesn't end when Israel arrives either, since the Canaanites seem to coexist alongside Israel in an ambiguous manner. The Hebrew Bible considers the Canaanites and groups associated with them—Amorites, Hittites, Jebusites, Hivites, Perizzites, and Girgashites—constituting what tradition calls the "seven nations of Canaan," as distinct people who are to be variously resisted or destroyed. The phrase "land of Canaan" occurs many times in a seemingly neutral geographical sense throughout the Torah (Genesis–Deuteronomy) and Joshua, but only rarely

Ancient Israel's Neighbors. Brian R. Doak, Oxford University Press (2020). © Oxford University Press.
DOI: 10.1093/oso/9780190690595.001.0001

outside of these six books, whereas the phrase "land of Israel" is the standard description that appears dozens of times in books like Samuel, Kings, and Ezekiel (but never in the Torah or Joshua). Thus, on biblical terms, "Canaan" designates a region or the people who live in that region before Israel arrives on the scene.

THE ARCHAEOLOGY OF CANAAN AND THE CANAANITES

When we use the word "Canaan," what territory or ethnicity are we designating? And during which periods? The first reference to this term occurs around 1750 BCE, from a document produced in the ancient city of Mari (in contemporary Syria), and seems to describe people who live in a region that would much later be identified with biblical Israel. Throughout the rest of the second millennium, and particularly in a set of documents called the "Amarna Letters" from the 1300s BCE, "Canaan" comes up repeatedly to designate a roughly defined strip of land up the Levantine coast northeast of Egypt during the time when Egypt exercised provincial control of parts of Asia.[1] Instructively, one of these Amarna letters, sent by a king positioned north of Canaan (in a kingdom called Mitanni) named Tushratta to one of his messengers, functioned as a kind of ancient passport for that messenger to use as he traveled south through Canaan down to Egypt:[2]

1. I follow Nadav Na'aman, "The Canaanites and Their Land," and "Four Notes on the Size of Late Bronze Canaan," both reprinted in his book *Canaan in the Second Millennium B.C.E.*, Collected Essays, vol. 2 (Winona Lake, IN: Eisenbrauns, 2005), 110–133, and 134–144, respectively.
2. Translation from Na'aman, "Canaanites and Their Land," quoted from William L. Moran, *The Amarna Letters* (Baltimore: Johns Hopkins University Press), 1992; Na'aman, "Canaanites and Their Land," 114.

> To the kings of Canaan, servants of my brother: Thus [says] the king. I herewith send Akiya my messenger, to speed posthaste to the king of Egypt, my brother. No one is to hold him. Provide him with safe entry into Egypt and hand (him) over to the fortress commander of Egypt. Let him go immediately, and as far as his presents are concerned, he is to owe nothing.

Now, the reference here "to the kings of Canaan" and the situation of the letter make it sound as though the author and presumed readers of this document considered many of the places through which a person would travel down through the land to be "Canaan," and the rulers of these places would be the "kings of Canaan." These "Canaanites," then, were subjects of the Egyptian pharaoh living in a particular space: between the Mediterranean Sea to the west and the Jordan River to the east, as far north as the northern border of contemporary Lebanon, and certainly as far south as Gaza and then congruous with the ancient border of Egypt itself (see Fig. 2.1).

Scholars will continue to debate the exact boundary of Canaan. How far up the coast did it reach—all the way to Anatolia (contemporary Turkey)? Were certain exact cities "Canaanite," based on the people who lived in them, but then others, even nearby, were not? Or was "Canaanite" an extremely broad, relative term, used with little consistency to designate various kinds of people all over the region who would never have called themselves "Canaanite"?[3] Much of the attention surrounding Canaanite identity fixates on the period of the Late Bronze Age, around 1500–1200 BCE, since this is the era leading up to the establishment of Israel in the land of Canaan. Since Israel settled in and around the land formerly occupied by the Canaanites, and could not be easily distinguished from

---

3. Niels P. Lemche, *The Canaanites and Their Land: The Tradition of the Canaanites* (Sheffield: Sheffield Academic Press, 1991).

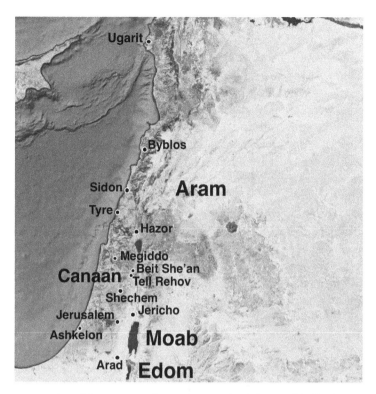

FIG. 2.1 Map of Canaan; Map data ©2019 Google, with text added by the author.

Canaanites, we immediately confront difficult issues involving identity, history, and ideology.

Avraham Faust, an archaeologist who has devoted extensive attention to the question of figuring out how we can define the ethnic boundaries of groups living in the Levant at the dawn of Israel's existence in the land, appropriately advises caution when trying to identify ancient ethnic differences in the archaeological record. Faust puts the issue this way: "The ethnic boundaries of a group are not defined by the sum of cultural traits but by the idiosyncratic use of specific material and behavior symbols as compared with other groups."[4] In other words, we can't define a group based only on simple lists of practices or objects associated with that group—rather, people define themselves in complex ways in relationship to *other people*. So the question becomes very complex, hinging on a nuanced analysis of all kinds of potential factors.

Who, then, are the Canaanites—not to mention Perizzites, Hivites, or any other more ambiguous group? Most scholars agree that these groups are not distinct racial or ethnic categories, and they are certainly not nations. For example, another archaeologist who has tackled this thorny problem of ethnicity and the origins of early Israel with reference to prior "Canaanite" populations in the land, Ann Killebrew, sees the Canaanites not in terms of any one particular set of traits, common ancestry, or practice but rather considers them as a "mixed" population, whose similarities and identity Egypt helped to create during centuries of Egyptian imperial control over the region in the second half of the second millennium BCE.[5] We might think of these Canaanites broadly as the people who shared a significantly overlapping linguistic, religious, and material culture. Domestic pottery—that is, ancient cookware and storage vessels—among these Canaanite sites was largely shared throughout the region, and remained consistent in terms of types and features for many hundreds of years in the second millennium BCE.

However, in other areas that archaeologists see as definitive for marking the identity of a particular group, such as burial practices and cultic remains (temples, small structures, places where offerings were made, etc.), we find not homogeneity but

---

4. Avraham Faust, *Israel's Ethnogenesis: Settlement, Interaction, Expansion and Resistance* (London: Equinox, 2006), 15.

5. Ann E. Killebrew, *Biblical Peoples and Ethnicity: An Archaeological Study of Egyptians, Canaanites, Philistines, and Early Israel, 1300–1100 B.C.E.* (Atlanta: Society of Biblical Literature, 2005), 249.

rather variety and difference among sites.[6] In Killebrew's analysis, Egyptian control of Canaan during the second millennium BCE—especially during the fourteenth century—forced a specific amount of social and economic similarity in the region. At the end of the Bronze Age (around the 1200s–1100s BCE), during a time of great upheaval and change throughout the Mediterranean world generally, Egypt lost control of Canaan. As a result, smaller groups had an opportunity to distinguish themselves from one another—indeed, during this period, perhaps as part of this differentiation among various "Canaanite" groups, we get our first glimpse of the group that emerged as "Israel" in the twelfth century and onward.[7]

Where, exactly, were the major Canaanite populations located, and what types of religion did these populations practice? Excavations at sites like Hazor and Megiddo in the north, Ashkelon along the southern coast, and Jerusalem in the hill country reveal much about the people who lived there. Sites like Hazor, Megiddo, and Shechem all feature well-preserved and large rectangular temple structures from the Canaanite period in the middle of the second millennium BCE; such buildings indicated powerful centers of religion and economy, perhaps exercising control along a "city-state" model over surrounding territories (Hazor, in particular, seems to have functioned in this way over a cluster of sites in the northern region of Canaan, and Megiddo was very powerful as well).[8] These large urban structures could have united

6. Killebrew, *Biblical*, 105–110, 138. For more on burial customs, see Elizabeth Bloch-Smith, *Judahite Burial Practices and Beliefs about the Dead* (Sheffield: Sheffield Academic Press, 1992).

7. Killebrew, *Biblical*, 138. See also Donald B. Redford, *Egypt, Canaan, and Israel in Ancient Times* (Princeton, NJ: Princeton University Press, 1992).

8. Beth Alpert Nakhai, *Archaeology and the Religions of Canaan and Israel* (Boston: American Schools of Oriental Research, 2001), 92–108, and Jonathan N. Tubb, *Canaanites* (Norman: University of Oklahoma Press, 1998), 67–68.

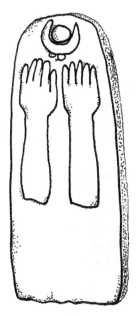

FIG. 2.2 "Standing stone" from Hazor; 1300s–1200s BCE; after drawing in Othmar Keel and Christoph Uehlinger, *Gods, Goddesses, and Images of God in Ancient Israel*, trans. Thomas H. Trapp (Minneapolis: Fortress Press, 1998), 52 illus. 46.

surrounding rural populations for major religious events, though small shrines in rural areas could have also functioned as pilgrimage sites for city-dwellers. Though people could travel, religion and social practices probably remained family focused and decidedly local for most people.[9] Another very common religious structure at Canaanite sites is the so-called *massebah*, or standing stone (see Fig. 2.2). Typically, these objects stood in courtyards or religious structures and must have functioned in some ritual—perhaps they indicated places where deities appeared, or they

9. Nakhai, *Archaeology*, 110–111.

stood as memorials for the dead, or served different functions according to local custom.

Although specialists debate about whether or to what extent the Ugaritic language or culture was truly "Canaanite," most agree that a set of written tablets discovered at the Late Bronze Age site of Ugarit, a coastal city in contemporary Syria, contains evidence of something like a Canaanite religious and literary culture. These writings, first unearthed in 1929, tell us about practices such as animal sacrifice, rituals involving priests, and various other things people said and did with relation to their deities.[10] Most famously from Ugarit, a cycle of stories featured a deity named Ba'al (pronounced in the Hebrew Bible with two syllables accent on the first, *bah*-ahl), alongside goddesses such as Asherah and Anat as well as an older deity named El ("El" is a generic word for "god" in ancient Semitic languages). Readers of the Bible will notice that these deities, and others like them, are mentioned as "false gods" or "idols" that the Canaanites worshiped, and indeed, the evidence we have from Canaan in the second millennium broadly suggests that Canaanites worshipped a range of deities associated with basic human concerns—fertility (crops and children), protection from sickness, victory in war, romantic success, political stability, and so on. The religious system was certainly polytheistic—involving many deities—and featured both male and female deities, though in certain times or places a single deity may have been worshiped primarily above others.

In other areas of history, culture, technology, and politics, our evidence is scattered but reveals hints of Canaanite activity.[11] The Middle Bronze period (2000–1550 BCE) saw increasingly sophisticated military fortifications around major sites, such as large

---

10. Dennis Pardee, *Ritual and Cult at Ugarit* (Atlanta: Society of Biblical Literature, 2002), and Simon B. Parker (ed.), *Ugaritic Narrative Poetry* (Atlanta: Scholars Press, 1997).
11. For the following, Amihai Mazar, *Archaeology of the Land of the Bible, 10,000–586 B.C.E.* (New York: Doubleday, 1992), 174–294.

ramparts and elaborate gate systems, though Late Bronze period (c. 1500–1200 BCE) Canaanite cities for the most part lacked these fortifications. Egyptian control over the region grew more intense in the aftermath of the expulsion of a group of Semitic people the Egyptians called "Hyksos" (foreign rulers) from Egypt, followed by frequent Egyptian incursions into Canaan. Other people groups living in Canaan during the Late Bronze period, such as the "Habiru," belonged to no particular territory but rather functioned as military bands, raiding and threatening the established city-states. Ancient Egyptians also mentioned a group generically called "Shasu," fully or partly nomadic people who lived on the edges of Canaan. Canaan was truly a mixed population of different kinds of people living in different ways.

In terms of art and culture, we have traditions of Canaanite metalworking in the form of jewelry, weapons, and tools, as well as ivory carvings (see the "Megiddo Ivory," Fig. 2.3) and seal impressions, but no monumental art or royal inscriptions that would indicate a particularly wealthy "nation" in the land. A language called Akkadian was used for trade and diplomacy in second millennium Canaan, and major cities employed scribes to compose documents (such as the previously mentioned Amarna letters). It is also very likely that Semitic-speaking Canaanites living in Egypt invented the first alphabet sometime early in the second millennium BCE (the so-called Proto-Sinaitic

FIG. 2.3 Ivory plaque from Megiddo with image of king and procession; c. 1200s BCE; after drawing in Othmar Keel and Christoph Uehlinger, *Gods, Goddesses, and Images of God in Ancient Israel*, trans. Thomas H. Trapp (Minneapolis: Fortress Press, 1998), 63 illus. 65.

or Proto-Canaanite alphabet)—creating a simplified writing system pared down from and partly based upon more complicated, older writing systems that used hundreds of symbols. This new alphabet used only around two dozen letters, each representing a single sound and making it possible, eventually, for even average people to write (Fig. 2.4). One of the great scholars of ancient Israel in the twentieth century, Frank Moore Cross, praised the Canaanite invention of the alphabet as "a stunning innovation . . . one of the great intellectual achievements of the ancient world." The ease of writing brought about by an alphabet—as opposed to more complicated pictographic or cuneiform systems—created, in Cross's opinion, "the first opportunity for the democratization of culture," ushering in "a new epoch of cultural history."[12]

In order to use the terms "Canaan" and "Canaanite," we must work with a possibly false assumption about the difference between the Canaanites and Israelites or other groups. When, exactly, do we stop talking about "Canaanites" in the land and begin talking about "Israelites"? If the Canaanites occupied Canaan before Israel arrived, should we assume that they disappeared after that point? What happens to the Canaanites in the archaeological record? At this point, I have to admit that we're in over our heads: the problem of Israelite identity in the early Iron Age (around 1200–900 BCE) has been one of the more vexing problems in all of archaeological research relating to the Bible. We cannot solve it here in a few paragraphs. However, we can highlight some issues to open the door to the problem.

Beginning in the 1960s, scholars proposed a twist in the biblical storyline about the Canaanites. In particular, two prominent voices in the field of biblical studies, George Mendenhall

12. Frank Moore Cross, "Early Alphabetic Scripts," in *Symposia Celebrating the Seventy-Fifth Anniversary of the Founding of the American Schools of Oriental Research*, ed. Frank Moore Cross (Cambridge: American Schools of Oriental Research, 1979), 97–111, here 110–111.

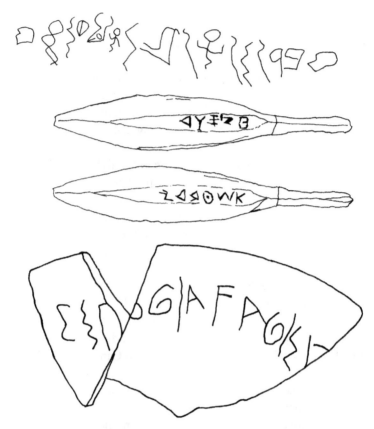

FIG. 2.4 Three examples of early "Canaanite"-style writing, from top to bottom: (1) Wadi el-Hôl early alphabetic inscription; early second millennium BCE; after photo in John Coleman Darnell, F. W. Dobbs-Allsopp, Marilyn J. Lundberg, P. Kyle McCarter, and Bruce Zuckerman, with the assistance of Colleen Manassa, *Two Early Alphabetic Inscriptions from the Wadi el-Hôl: New Evidence for the Origin of the Alphabet from the Western Desert of Egypt* (Boston: American Schools of Oriental Research, 2005), Pl. III. (2) Inscription on a bronze arrowhead (front and back); c. eleventh century BCE; after drawing in Frank M. Cross, "The Arrow of Suwar, Retainer of 'Abday," in *Leaves from an Epigrapher's Notebook: Collected Papers in Hebrew and West Semitic Palaeography and Epigraphy* (Winona Lake, IN: Eisenbrauns, 2003), 195–202, here 196, Fig. 29.2. (3) Inscription on a bowl from Qubūr Walaydah; c. 1200 BCE; after drawing in Frank M. Cross, "Newly Found Inscriptions in Old Canaanite and Early Phoenician Scripts," in *Leaves from an Epigrapher's Notebook: Collected Papers in Hebrew and West Semitic Palaeography and Epigraphy* (Winona Lake, IN: Eisenbrauns, 2003), 213–230, here 214, Fig. 32.1.

and Norman Gottwald, made a proposal about the identity of early Israel: they argued that the earliest Israelites were actually Canaanites.[13] They came not from outside the land, and not primarily (or at all) as runaway slaves from Egypt, but rather from some revolutionary process internal to Canaan itself after the system of Egyptian control collapsed in the Levant in the thirteenth–twelfth centuries BCE. Those who came to call themselves "Israelites" did so not because they didn't look and act like Canaanites, but rather because of some crucial manner in which *they perceived themselves different* from Canaanites. Gottwald thought the Israelite differentiation was about material factors (along a Marxist sociological model), while Mendenhall argued that theological ideas caused the rift. Either way, the core argument remained the same: the "Israelites" did not come from outside the land and defeat the "Canaanites"—rather, the Israelites were former Canaanites who separated themselves from their own Canaanite origin.

In the realm of religion, we know from the Ugaritic texts mentioned previously that Israel inherited notions of divinity from its surroundings. Biblical psalmists adopted epithets frequently applied to Baal in Ugaritic myth, such as "cloud-rider" (see Ps 68:4), and descriptions of a creature called "Leviathan" in the Bible at points closely mimic language used for a creature with a cognate name, Lotan, in the Ugaritic texts (see Isa 27:1 compared to the Ugaritic Baal Epic).[14] The prestige of a specifically northern mountain by the sea where deities live, such as Mount Zaphon in Syria—where the pantheon presided in the Ugaritic texts—seems to be the basis of the imagery in Psalm 48, and Psalm 29 may have a similar origin in an earlier Canaanite hymn.

---

13. Norman K. Gottwald, *The Tribes of Yahweh: A Sociology of the Religion of Liberated Israel, 1250–1050 B.C.E.* (Maryknoll, NY: Orbis Books, 1979); George E. Mendenhall, "The Hebrew Conquest of Palestine," *Biblical Archaeologist* 25.3 (1962): 66–87.

14. Parker (ed.), *Ugaritic Narrative Poetry*, at location KTU 1.5.i.1–4.

How has this idea about Israel's origins vis-à-vis the Canaanites been received? In mixed ways. For example, even while acknowledging deep similarities between language, style, and religious imagery between Israelite and Canaanite literature, William Foxwell Albright—the dominant American biblical scholar and archaeologist of the twentieth century—made his views clear in the title of one of his last major publications: *Yahweh and the Gods of Canaan: A Historical Analysis of Two Contrasting Faiths*.[15] Whatever these two groups shared, for Albright, was not enough to overcome the fact that Israel and Canaan ultimately *contrasted* with one another. Others, however, pointed to continuity. In a pioneering early study of the early Israelite hill country settlements at the beginning of the Iron Age (around the 1200s–1100s BCE), the Israeli archaeologist Israel Finkelstein claims that the word "Israelite" in the early periods should be "no more than a *terminus technicus* [i.e., a technical shorthand] for 'hill country people in a process of settling down.'" In Finkelstein's analysis, Israelites mostly settled in previously unsettled sites of the central hill country, thus not really displacing the Canaanites; in the northern part of the country, Canaanites lived alongside Israelites for centuries.[16] Some have pointed specifically to striking similarity in pottery between pre-Israelite Canaan and post-Canaanite Israel to suggest continuity between the "Canaanite" and "Israelite" populations,[17] while others, such as the archaeologist Elizabeth Bloch-Smith, see subtle distinctions marking off Israelites from Canaanites not related to pottery but rather focusing on refusal to eat pork, circumcision,

15. William F. Albright, *Yahweh and the Gods of Canaan: A Historical Analysis of Two Contrasting Faiths* (Garden City, NY: Doubleday, 1968), and also Albright's *From the Stone Age to Christianity* (Baltimore: Johns Hopkins University Press, 1940), esp. 281.

16. Israel Finkelstein, *The Archaeology of the Israelite Settlement* (Jerusalem: Israel Exploration Society, 1988), 28–29.

17. William G. Dever, *Who Were the Early Israelites and Where Did They Come From?* (Grand Rapids: Eerdmans, 2003), 91–128.

self-perception about their military or political power, and even beard length.[18] The debate is far from resolved. Most archaeologists working in the field today, however, agree that there is little evidence for a sweeping Israelite military "conquest" of the land at the beginning of the Iron Age. Although some sites, such as Hazor and Megiddo, have destruction layers dating roughly to this time, others show no sign of disruption at all, and some major sites mentioned in the Bible, such as Jericho and Ai, were likely not even inhabited in a significant way during the period. Archaeology thus raises the question, with urgency: What were the biblical authors up to in their presentation of the Canaanites?

CANAAN AND THE CANAANITES IN THE HEBREW BIBLE

The Bible's depiction of the Canaanites has generated difficult ethical problems for contemporary readers. What's more, archaeological, historical, and sociological reflection on the historical identity of Israelites versus Canaanites created one of the biggest bombshells in the history of biblical scholarship in the twentieth century with the theory that the earliest Israelites were actually Canaanites. All of this means that smart readers will need to be armed with many questions and a sharp eye for detail when considering the way the Bible treats the category of the Canaanites. In what follows, I review the way various authors in the Hebrew Bible write about the Canaanites and gesture toward the difficulties inherent in the very definition of the term.

First, the etymology of the Hebrew word "Canaan" (*kĕnā'an*, pronounced ke-*na*-an; note the related Hebrew term *kĕnā'ănî*

---

18. Elizabeth Bloch-Smith, "Israelite Ethnicity in Iron I: Archaeology Preserves What Is Remembered and What Is Forgotten in Israel's History," *Journal of Biblical Literature* 122.3 (2003): 401–425.

"Canaanite"): the Hebrew root that seems to be at the core of this word, *kānaʿ*, means "bow down, subdue, be low, depressed." Are the Canaanites "the ones bowed down or depressed"? Probably not; the term could be geographical, marking those who lived in a "low" area (valleys and plains), or those who live where the sun "goes down," that is, a western area. Alternatively, some have connected this term to a similar-sounding word for a special kind of purple dye (e.g., for clothing), for which ancient traders in the region were known for providing. None of this is very clear, and we cannot understand very much about how the Bible presents the Canaanites by appeal to the word itself.

The original biblical Canaanite, a man named Canaan, appears in Genesis 9—the sons of Noah who go into the ark, Shem, Ham, and Japheth, all have children after the flood and spread out upon the earth. One of the sons of Ham is a man named Canaan (Gen 9:18). Noah curses Canaan, somewhat inexplicably, when Canaan's father Ham sees Noah drunk and naked, and in the curse Canaan is twice relegated to serving as a slave to both Shem and Japheth (Gen 9:25–27). In the so-called Table of Nations in Genesis 10 (see also 1 Chr 1)—which may originate from source material quite different from that in Genesis 9—Canaan is positioned alongside three other sons of Ham: Cush, Egypt, and Put. Canaan would seem to be the outlier here, as Cush, Egypt, and Put are all biblical terms for people living in the northeast part of Africa. In Genesis 10, Cush fathers Nimrod, the first Babylonian (Gen 10:8–10), and Egypt bears a host of groups including the Philistines (Gen 10:14). Canaan becomes the ancestor of Sidon (a major Phoenician city), as well as Heth (related to the Hittites?), the Jebusites, Amorites, Girgashites, Hivites, Arkites, Sinites, Arvadites, Zemarites, and Hamathites, eventually extending their territory across much of the land that Israel would later attempt to occupy (Gen 10:15–19).

As a geographical title, "Canaan" itself appears nearly one hundred times in the Bible, and the adjective "Canaanite" around seventy-five times. However, "Canaanites" are not alone as inhabitants of Canaan. In several lists, biblical authors mention alongside the Canaanites several other groups—comprising the "seven nations of Canaan" (some of which are descendants of the ancestor Canaan). Deuteronomy gives the exact list in what became the traditional form of this list of nations, repeated elsewhere in the Bible but also occurring piecemeal or in combination with other groups in different places: "When the LORD your God brings you into the land that you are about to enter and occupy, and he clears away many nations before you—the Hittites, the Girgashites, the Amorites, the Canaanites, the Perizzites, the Hivites, and the Jebusites, seven nations mightier and more numerous than you" (Deut 7:1; see also Josh 3:10; 24:11; Neh 9:8).

For many of these Canaanite subgroups, we simply have no good data about who they were. The Girgashites, Perrizites, and Hivites, for example, were not obviously known people groups in any place or time period. While I doubt that the biblical authors invented the names of these subgroups completely, they should not be considered "nations." The "Hittites" mentioned in these lists are not the Hittites of the empire by that name from Anatolia in the middle of the second millennium BCE but rather a more disparate group (or several different groups) that existed regionally to the southeast of the Hittite center in the Levant for hundreds of years after the fall of the formal Hittite Empire around 1200 BCE. The term "Jebus" in the Bible describes the city of Jerusalem before King David arrived (e.g., Josh 15:8; 1 Chr 11:4), and so presumably the "Jebsusites" could describe those who lived in Jebus before David's arrival. The Amorites, like the Canaanites, have a firmer footing in history, usually being equated with the Amurru, a Semitic-speaking people that inhabited land in western Mesopotamia (including the Levant and Israel). The famous king Hammurabi of Babylon (of "Hammurabi's Laws") was Amorite, as were others in ruling ancient Near Eastern dynasties throughout the second millennium BCE.[19]

---

19. Bill T. Arnold, *Who Were the Babylonians?* (Atlanta: Society of Biblical Literature, 2004), 35–60.

Even though references to these groups vary throughout the Bible, the Canaanites are a stock part of the lists and often appear as the first of the subnations listed. The sheer number of references to the "land of Canaan" marks the Canaanites as the group that must have loomed largest in the biblical imagination, though the Amorites, too, feature prominently—especially in descriptions of people who live in the northern Transjordan region (that is, east of the Jordan River).[20] My own speculation: the Bible's use of these smaller and lesser-known groups alongside the better-known groups functions as a literary device—the authors attempt total geographical and population coverage by listing not only the "Canaanites" and "Amorites" but also any more obscure label possible, all by way of saying: *when we mention these groups, we're talking about all the people and groups that live in the region Israel must occupy.* The Canaanites, Hittites, Girgashites, Hivites, and so on are a biblical umbrella term for "all those non-Israelite people living in the land," all the people not like "us."

In all of this book's chapters in which we look at the "biblical representation" of one of Israel's neighboring lands, we'll have to select instructive or particularly fascinating passages as examples for analysis. The material is too voluminous and rich to treat in full. For the subject at hand, let's begin by taking a closer look at Deuteronomy 7 in order to understand a common way that biblical authors talked about the Canaanites and their relationship to Israel:

When the Lord your God brings you into the land that you are about to enter and occupy, and he clears away many nations

---

20. Daniel E. Fleming, "The Amorites," in *The World around the Old Testament: The People and Places in the Ancient Near East*, ed. Bill T. Arnold and Brent A. Strawn (Grand Rapids: Baker Academic, 2016), 1–30.

before you—the Hittites, the Girgashites, the Amorites, the Canaanites, the Perizzites, the Hivites, and the Jebusites, seven nations mightier and more numerous than you—and when the LORD your God gives them over to you and you defeat them, then you must utterly destroy them. Make no covenant with them and show them no mercy. Do not intermarry with them, giving your daughters to their sons or taking their daughters for your sons, for that would turn away your children from following me, to serve other gods. . . . this is how you must deal with them: break down their altars, smash their pillars, hew down their sacred poles, and burn their idols with fire.

For you are a people holy to the LORD your God; the LORD your God has chosen you out of all the peoples on earth to be his people, his treasured possession. It was not because you were more numerous than any other people that the LORD set his heart on you and chose you—for you were the fewest of all peoples. It was because the LORD loved you and kept the oath that he swore to your ancestors, that the LORD has brought you out with a mighty hand, and redeemed you from the house of slavery, from the hand of Pharaoh king of Egypt. (Deut 7:1-8, abridged)

This passage contains many references that are instructive for thinking about how biblical authors portrayed the Canaanites and groups associated with them living in the land on the eve of Israel's arrival. This is indeed Deuteronomy's literary context: the people, recently escaped from Egypt, wait on the east side of the Jordan River for their entry into the promised land. First, notice the use of the number seven, "seven nations mightier and more numerous than you." In biblical terms, seven indicates a totality—as in the seven-day week established in Genesis 1 at creation (for other symbolically significant uses of seven in the Bible, see, e.g., Gen 7:2-4; Exod 12:15; Lev 8:33-35; Josh 6:4-15). Notice also the fact that the narrator casts these nations as "mightier and more numerous" than Israel. Israel is the tiny newcomer to the region, belittled numerically in the sight of a mightily populated Canaan. This is potentially jarring, since the total population of Canaan on the eve of Israel's purported entry there cannot have been more than two hundred thousand individuals (perhaps even much smaller),[21] while the Bible repeatedly claims that Israel's males alone numbered six hundred thousand or more at the time (Exod 12:37; 38:26; Num 1:46; 2:32; 11:21; the translation of the number here for "thousand" in Hebrew remains disputed by some).

This numerical advantage for the nations of Canaan finds a match in the physical size of some inhabitants. In Numbers 13:25–33, a passage where the various peoples of Canaan are also listed, Israelite spies who go into the land ahead of time to have a look report back to Moses and the camp:

> They brought to the Israelites an unfavorable report of the land that they had spied out, saying, "The land that we have gone through as spies is a land that devours its inhabitants; and all the people that we saw in it are of great size. There we saw the Nephilim (the Anakites come from the Nephilim); and to ourselves we seemed like grasshoppers, and so we seemed to them." (Num 13:32–33)

Here the narrator makes a correlation between the bizarre scene in Genesis 6:1–4, in which divine beings intermarry with human women and have hybrid children, and the inhabitants of Canaan, who tower over the Israelites in a fearsome land that "devours its inhabitants." Thus, we see that a mythical or legendary coloring applies to the Canaanites—they are giants, and possibly all descended from a primeval semidivine race.[22]

---

21. E.g., John Bright, *A History of Israel*, 4th ed., with an introduction and appendix by William P. Brown (Louisville, KY: Westminster John Knox, 2000), 119 n. 28.

22. Brian R. Doak, *The Last of the Rephaim: Conquest and Cataclysm in the Heroic Ages of Ancient Israel* (Boston: Ilex Foundation; Washington, DC: Center for Hellenic Studies, 2012).

Back to the Deuteronomy 7 passage: we further notice that the Israelites receive a very specific military charge—to not only defeat them, but to "utterly destroy them" (Deut 7:2). They must receive no mercy, no plea deals. The Hebrew verb here for "utterly destroy" is *haram*, a technical term used frequently in the Bible meaning "to put out of normal use, to ban, to proscribe." The idea of a king's harem, a group of wives set aside only for the king, comes from the same Semitic root. A more elaborate set of rules for how to conduct warfare in this *haram* style appears in Deuteronomy 20, and then we see the Israelites attempt to carry out the *haram* on the native Canaanite population throughout the early chapters of the book of Joshua (most famously at Jericho and Ai). The ruling principle of *haram* war in these texts is indeed complete annihilation, of everything that breathes (men, women, children, old and young, and even animals), and the destruction of all property, precious goods, or anything that could be taken as a prize. Other nearby nations, such as the Moabites, also claimed to practice this type of warfare. Deuteronomy 20 situates the *haram* within a context of several ways that Israel might treat the Canaanites; towns that are not at the heart of the land Israel should inhabit can take a "peace deal" entailing total submission to Israel, and, failing that, Israel may kill only the males in those towns and take the women, children, and other things as war prizes (Deut 20:10–15). For those living in "the towns of these peoples that the LORD your God is giving you as an inheritance," however, Israel "must not let anything that breathes remain alive . . . so that they may not teach you to do all the abhorrent things that they do for their gods, and you thus sin against the LORD your God" (Deut 20:16–18, abridged).

Thus we arrive at the most persistent biblical theme regarding the Canaanites: their "abhorrent" religion. Repeatedly, and in many different passages, biblical authors have nothing good to say about the gods and goddesses of Canaan. Deuteronomy 12 puts the issue starkly:

When the LORD your God has cut off before you the nations whom you are about to enter to dispossess them, when you have

dispossessed them and live in their land, take care that you are not
snared into imitating them, after they have been destroyed before
you. . . . Every abhorrent thing that the LORD hates they have done
for their gods. They would even burn their sons and their daughters in the fire to their gods. (Deut 12:29–32, abridged)

What the Canaanites do, according to the narrator here, is *every abhorrent thing that the Lord hates*. A very polarizing statement. This
would include making physical images of their deities (see Exod 20:4–
6), worshiping at their sites of worship or using any of the objects or
items they use for worship—often characterized by worship under
or around certain kinds of trees, on hills or elevated platforms, and
using various kinds of altars, stone pillars (*massebah*), and "sacred
poles" (*asherah*; also the name of a female deity; see Deut 12:2–3).
Moreover, the practices include child sacrifice. Scholars have written
quite a bit on this topic. Was child sacrifice actually practiced? By
whom, and under what circumstances? Was child sacrifice ever a
part of Israelite religion? Since biblical authors often associate child
sacrifice practices with a deity named Molech, who is at one point
closely associated with the Ammonites (1 Kgs 11), and there is a narration of an actual child sacrifice by a Moabite king (2 Kgs 3), and
still other nonbiblical sources notoriously described the Phoenicians
as child sacrificers, I treat the topic in more detail in later chapters in
this book covering these specific groups. Admittedly, there is quite
a bit of overlap between what biblical authors consider, generically,
as "Canaanite" and what is Ammonite or Moabite or Phoenician,
and there is no clear biblical delineation about who, exactly or primarily, carried out such practices.[23] For now, suffice it to say that
we do have some evidence that child sacrifice was a living concept

23. In the Bible, see Genesis 22:1–19; Exodus 13:11–16; 22:29–30; 34:19–
20; Leviticus 18:21; 20:2–5; 27:28–9; Deuteronomy 12:31; 18:10;
Judges 11:29–40; 2 Kings 3:26–27; 16:3; 17:17; 21:6; 23:10; Isaiah
30:27–33; 57:5–6; Jeremiah 7:30–32; 19:5–6; 32:35; for analysis, see

in Israel's context—though whether Canaanites or any other group participated in the concept (or actually sacrificed children) as a distinctly "Canaanite" practice remains unclear.

The text from Deuteronomy 12 raises a further conundrum: if the LORD God is truly cutting off these native Canaanites completely, and if Israel is to conduct the totalizing *haram* on them, how will there be any Canaanites or abominable Canaanite religious practices left to imitate? The Bible itself gives a series of responses to this question. In short, within the book of Joshua, during the course of which Israel purports to carry out the total annihilation of the land's native inhabitants, what we actually find are multiple traditions of conquest.[24] Joshua 12 and 18, as well as 21:41–43, suggest complete victory; Joshua 18:1 plainly states, "The land lay subdued before them." However, Joshua 13 speaks of quite a lot of land and people *remaining* to be conquered, and that conquest does not occur in the book of Joshua; Joshua 17:12–13 slips in a brief notice concerning Canaanites who continued living in the land. Something seems incomplete. Even great victories, such as the one at Jericho in Joshua 7, are marred by the moral failure of the Israelites, as they are then prevented by God from winning further victories. The fate of the city of Hebron, at the heart of the land Israel was to inherit, sparked divergent traditions within Joshua

Heath D. Dewrell, *Child Sacrifice in Ancient Israel* (Winona Lake, IN: Eisenbrauns, 2017); Francesca Stavrakopoulou, *King Manasseh and Child Sacrifice: Biblical Distortions of Historical Realities* (Berlin: de Gruyter, 2004); Jon D. Levenson, *The Death and Resurrection of the Beloved Son: The Transformation of Child Sacrifice in Judaism and Christianity* (New Haven, CT: Yale University Press, 1993).

24. Nili Wazana, "'Everything Was Fulfilled' versus 'The Land That Yet Remains': Contrasting Conceptions of the Fulfillment of the Promise in the Book of Joshua," in *The Gift of the Land and the Fate of the Canaanites in Jewish Thought*, ed. Katell Berthelot, Joseph E. David, and Marc Hirshman (Oxford: Oxford University Press, 2014), 13–35.

and between Joshua and Judges; see Joshua 10:36–39 versus Joshua 14:13–15 versus Joshua 21:9–19 versus Judges 1:20.

Indeed, the book of Judges further complicates this: the first three chapters of that book openly admit that several cities that the book of Joshua claimed fell to Israel were in fact *not* taken—compare, in particular, the list in Joshua 12 versus Judges 1:27–29. Judges 1–3 offer a theological rationale for the failed conquest of Canaan, with three potentially competing reasons for the failure: (1) Israel sinned, so God decided to leave the natives there (Judg 1:3); (2) God leaves some Canaanites there as a test, to see if Israel will behave correctly in the face of temptations (Judg 2:20–23); (3) God leaves some left-over groups in the land so that new generations of Israelites will have to fight them, thus teaching the people fighting skills (Judg 3:1–4). Moreover, archaeology paints a picture of the transition between the Late Bronze Age and the early Iron Age—the era during which Israel first started settling in the land (between 1200 and 1000 BCE)—that is not primarily marked by every major city burned to the ground, but rather fits and starts of continuity with previous habitation, some destruction layers (most distinctly at the large site of Hazor), and some settlement in previously unoccupied regions in the rugged hill country. The story of Israel's elimination of the Canaanites, then, is by no means simple, and by no means comes without sometimes shockingly violent punishment for Israel. When Israelites inter-marry with non-Israelites (called "Moabites" and "Midianites" in Num 25) on their way into the land, God orders Israelite leaders to kill their own people, by the tens of thousands.

Even though we could argue that all biblical references to the Canaanites are "symbolic" of that which is other, different, detest-able, and so on, at points, biblical authors engage the categories of the Canaanite that seem to be particularly detached from what-ever historical reference we might be able to take from the bib-lical text. For example, in Ezekiel 16, the prophet offers a bizarre allegory about a baby abandoned at birth to die, with the baby's origins described this way: "Your origin and your birth were in the land of the Canaanites; your father was an Amorite, and your mother a Hittite" (Ezek 16:3). Though some might want to use this as evidence that a biblical author recognized the fact that Israelites were actually Canaanites, more likely the prophet is using words like "Canaanite," "Hittite," and "Amorite" symbolically—the baby in this allegory, which is a symbol for sinful Israel, has a tainted spiritual history, just like Israel thought these other groups had.

In Ezra 9:1 and Nehemiah 9:8, two texts likely written late in Israel's story (as told in the Hebrew Bible; perhaps in the mid–late fifth century BCE), narrators use labels like "Canaanite," "Hittite," "Perizzite," "Jebusite," "Amorite," and "Girgashite" to describe either groups with which Israelites (or, in this period, "Jews") are not to intermarry or, by allusion to Deuteronomy, to describe the land these groups had occupied that Israel must now again reoccupy after return from exile. By the fifth century BCE, however, labels like "Canaanite," and certainly "Jebusite," "Perizzite," and "Girgashite," had no real ethnic or national currency. Rather, they are ciphers for older scriptural traditions and for the status of various people in the land that Israel opposed. For Ezra and Nehemiah, it is *as though* the enemies in the land in their time are like the biblical memory of early Israel's Canaanite foes.

In sum, then, what does the Bible tell us about the Canaanites—specifically about their history, their art, their culture, and their humanity? Not very much, besides scattered references to famines occurring in the land of Canaan driving refugees down to Egypt (a known phenomenon from outside the Bible during the periods in question; see Gen 12:10; 26:1; 42:5) or other incidental details. What we read in the Bible—concerning the Canaanites and everything else, for that matter—is not disinterested "history" for documenting "what happened in the past" but rather a loaded, motivated, passionate *analysis* of the past, present, and future by way of theologically persuasive cultural memory. The Bible's Canaanites are primarily a symbol of the religious practices Israel should avoid, and the eradication of physical people and property Israel is to accomplish (but fails to accomplish) through the *haram* parallels the task of spiritually eradicating Canaanite religion from their midst.

WHAT HAPPENED TO THE CANAANITES?

What became of the Canaanites after the era of the Hebrew Bible, that is to say, roughly in the Hellenistic period (300s–100s BCE), then under the Roman Empire, and beyond? Very few references appear in the so-called intertestamental corpus, a set of Jewish writings in Greek from the Hellenistic period. One notable example comes in the Greek additions to Daniel ("Susanna"), where the hero Daniel proclaims, of a wicked character, "You [are] offspring of Canaan and not of Judah" (Sus 56), drawing on the simple dichotomy, explored above in Ezekiel 16 between Israel (Judah) and Canaan as spiritual types. In the Christian New Testament, most of which was likely written in the first century CE, we find only one explicit reference to a Canaanite or Canaan, in Matthew 15. A "Canaanite" woman begs Jesus to heal her daughter; the narrator tells us she had just come from the districts of Tyre and Sidon, prominent Phoenician cities. In the parallel account in Mark 7:24–30, the narrator labels her "Syro-Phoenician," perhaps indicating that for the author of Matthew, at least, the term "Canaanite" was synonymous with the non-Jewish population that lived along the northern coast. To be sure, various authors living in the Hellenistic and Roman periods used whatever contemporary political or geographical labels were available to them to name the inhabitants of a space; groups that may have previously been called "Canaanites" living in "Canaan" became, in the works of these authors, Syrians living in "Syria Palaistine," Itureans, Nabateans, Judaeans, and so on.[25]

---

25. Katell Berthelot, "Where May Canaanites Be Found? Canaanites, Phoenicians, and Others in Jewish Texts from the Hellenistic and Roman Period," in *The Gift of the Land and the Fate of the Canaanites in Jewish Thought*, ed. Katell Berthelot, Joseph E. David, and Marc Hirshman (Oxford: Oxford University Press, 2014), 253–274.

A survey of Jewish rabbinic literature, produced over the first three or four centuries of the Common Era, shows that these early Jewish voices—steeped as they were in the idiom of the Torah—mentioned the Canaanites frequently, acknowledging that they did indeed live in the land and persist alongside the Israelites despite biblical injunctions to eradicate them.[26] In one fascinating passage in the Mishnah, an important early Jewish text, the speakers discuss what Jews should do when they find old objects in the ground or buried in a wall—objects they assumed could have been objects belonging to ancient "Amorite" inhabitants of the land (at *m. Bab Metzia* 2.4, 8c, 25b–26a). Presuming the objects are some kind of usable tool, the rabbinic ruling held that Jews could keep the objects, and the sources acknowledge a continuing Canaanite presence in the land in continuing reality (even if tentative or temporary). Moreover, the Canaanites did not disappear from the idiom of Jews living on into the medieval period (c. 400s–1400s CE).[27] When Jews had servants or even slaves of non-Jewish ancestry, they commonly referred to these individuals as "Canaanites." Consider the statement from the Jewish intellectual Rashi (Solomon ben Isaac), who lived from 1040 to 1105 CE:

> All idolaters are like Canaanites when sold into slavery. Indeed, all slaves are called "Canaan" because it is written (Gen 9:25): "[Cursed be Canaan!] The lowest of slaves [will he be to his brothers]."

26. Eyal Ben-Eliyahu, "The Rabbinic Perception of the Presence of the Canaanites in the Land of Israel," in *The Gift of the Land and the Fate of the Canaanites in Jewish Thought*, ed. Katell Berthelot, Joseph E. David, and Marc Hirshman (Oxford: Oxford University Press, 2014), 275–284.

27. Evyatar Marienberg, "'Canaanites' in Medieval Jewish Households," in *The Gift of the Land and the Fate of the Canaanites in Jewish Thought*, ed. Katell Berthelot, Joseph E. David, and Marc Hirshman (Oxford: Oxford University Press, 2014), 285–296, esp. 288–289 for the quotes from Rashi and the *Mekhilta de-Rabbi Ishmael*.

Other sources claimed that the Canaanites took exile in Africa after the Israelites drove them out of the land, and in the *Mekhilta de-Rabbi Ishmael*, a collection of interpretations of the book of Exodus, the author attempts to explain why the land is called "Canaan" and not "Israel" already in the Torah:

> "After the LORD brings you into the land of the Canaanites" [Exod 13:11]: Canaan merited that the land would be called after him. What did the Canaanite do [to merit this]? When the Canaanite heard that Israel was coming to the land, [the Canaanite] evacuated it. God told the Canaanite, "You evacuated [the land] because of my sons; I will therefore call it after you, and will give you a land as beautiful as yours." And which one [was that]? Africa.

The neutral (or positive) valence of the term "Canaan" as a geographical description of the promised land lived on long after the Bible and its use in Judaism. "Canaan" could function as a cipher for the "promised land," the place where Israel—or anyone following in Israel's spiritual path, such as Christians—would want to go. Puritans in the sixteenth and seventeenth centuries used the phrase "language of Canaan" to describe the language that all of the redeemed would speak in the kingdom of God.[28] In the American folk and gospel music tradition, for example, the song "I'm on My Way to Canaan's Land" was famously performed by Mahalia Jackson and the bluegrass duo Flatt and Scruggs, and appears in a rousing rendition in the Academy Award–nominated 1960 adaption of the Sinclair Lewis book by the same title published in 1927, *Elmer Gantry*.

As the Canaanites were the putatively "native" inhabitants of the land before Israel arrived, and, as we saw above, in fact persisted

---

28. Mason I. Lowance Jr., *The Language of Canaan: Metaphor and Symbol in New England from the Puritans to the Transcendentalists* (Cambridge, MA: Harvard University Press, 1980), vii.

alongside (or *as*) Israel during the biblical period writ broadly, then it stands to reason that the general inheritors of "Canaanite culture" would be anyone who lived on in the land in any number of capacities and tribal or familial configurations for centuries or millennia after the biblical period. However, it is not so much the genealogical idea of who is technically a "Canaanite" as it is the symbolic equations one might make by way of the interpretive technique of *typology*—a nation, person, place, or institution in the *present* is equated on symbolic or moral levels to something in the *past*.

Thus, early Puritan settlers in the United States could see themselves as the "new Israel," which then raises the question: Who are the Canaanites in this scenario? The frequent appeal to the extermination of Canaanites in the Bible during periods of early American expansion into the west, such as for genocides and massacres of Native American populations and in rhetoric concerning Israel within the contemporary Middle East, indicates that the polemical rubric of "Canaanite" has not lost its violent hold on the contemporary imagination. One author, writing from the perspective of advocacy for Native American communities, suggests that the Canaanites should actually be "at the center of Christian theological reflection and political action," in order to ensure that silenced voices be heard and to ensure that readers are forced to reckon with ethical difficulties in the text.[29] Just as American settlers could appeal to the rhetoric of the expulsion of the Canaanite as justification for driving out First Nation / Native American populations, so too, around the creation of the contemporary state of Israel in 1948, there were a series of battles with and expulsions of Palestinian villagers from their homes to make space for the new Israeli settlers that could be considered along the pattern of the Israelite "conquest" of the land in the Bible.

---

29. Robert Allen Warrior, "Canaanites, Cowboys, and Indians: Deliverance, Conquest, and Liberation Theology Today," *Christianity and Crisis* 49.12 (1989): 261–265, here 264.

As the ethical problems of the Bible's violent heritage have increasingly become a problem for contemporary readers, the biblical treatment of the Canaanites in terms of the *herem* has prompted a flood of Christian apologetic writing (i.e., ways of defending the faith against criticisms).[30] These strategies for explaining the Bible's attitude toward the Canaanites span quite a range: (a) seeing the genocide as an act of "mercy," since the Canaanite children would go straight to heaven at their death and would not have the horrible experience of growing up in a community that would not or could not direct their worship toward the one true God (Lee Strobel, in *The Case for Faith*); (b) putting the *herem* within the context of ancient warfare practices and thus relativizing the strangeness of the practice; (c) arguing that the biblical "conquest" never happened historically at all; (d) seeing "internal critiques" of the Israelite conquest within the Bible itself and attempting to read narratives from the perspective of the Canaanites (Eric Seibert, in *The Violence of Scripture*, for strategies [b], [c], and [d]); (e) invoking Jesus's example of nonviolence as a standard by which to judge or correct the Hebrew Bible (many works, but recently, Gregory Boyd in *Cross Vision*).

---

30. For example: Lee Strobel, *The Case for Faith: A Journalist Investigates the Toughest Objections to Christianity* (Grand Rapids: Zondervan, 2000), 159–202; Eric A. Seibert, *The Violence of Scripture: Overcoming the Old Testament's Troubling Legacy* (Minneapolis: Fortress, 2012), 95–114; Gregory A. Boyd, *Cross Vision: How the Crucifixion of Jesus Makes Sense of Old Testament Violence* (Minneapolis: Fortress, 2017).

3

The Arameans

BECAUSE OF THEIR STRATEGIC PROXIMITY to major
Mesopotamian empires like the Assyrians and Babylonians—
closer than any of the other groups considered in this book—the
Arameans occupied an important political role in their ancient
Near Eastern world. We thus have more information on the
Arameans, from a variety of perspectives, than we do for many of
the other smaller groups surrounding Israel. However, we must be
clear at the outset: the Arameans were never, in fact, a single nation
or group, but rather Aram was a region with local centers of power
spread throughout contemporary Syria, Jordan, and Lebanon, at
major cities such as Damascus and Hamath. Recalling our discussion in chapter 1 of this book about the complications associated
with terms like "nation" and "state," archaeological investigation of
the region of Aram reveals a series of shifting borders, alliances,
and leaders. Further complicating the issue is the fact that the
Aramean language (Aramaic) was widespread in the ancient Near
Eastern world, becoming the language of diplomacy and trade for
the long-lasting and influential Persian Empire (c. 539–333 BCE)
and well beyond, even centuries into the Common Era in some
regions. Having said that, we find the biblical authors engaging in
more generalized notions of the Arameans as a distinct nation or
ethnic group without consideration of these complexities. In one
pivotal text, Israel considers itself to be genealogically (or spiritually? or socially?) connected with Aram in very deep ways. Within
the Bible, Aram and the Arameans occupy an ideological place
alongside Israel similar in some ways to the Edomites, in that the

Ancient Israel's Neighbors. Brian R. Doak, Oxford University Press (2020). © Oxford University Press.
DOI: 10.1093/oso/9780190690595.001.0001

relationship, though adversarial at times, blurs the boundary between discrete groups and merges into familial identity.

THE ARCHAEOLOGY OF ARAM AND THE ARAMEANS

The territory encompassing ancient Aram overlaps largely with the modern political boundaries of the state of Syria and far northwestern Iraq, and then extends west toward Lebanon and north along the Mediterranean coast into Turkey (Fig. 3.1). Political

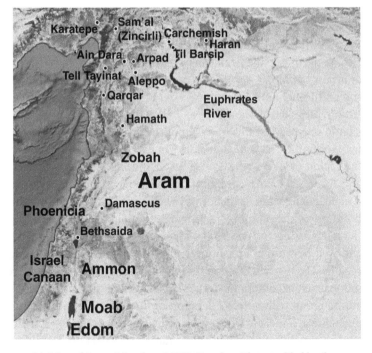

FIG. 3.1 Map of Aram; Map data ©2019 Google, with text added by the author.

borders and alliances between cities shifted frequently in the ancient world, as they often do today, and the political history of the Middle East certainly teaches us about the sometimes arbitrary and explosive nature of labels and territories. Aram's most prominent geographical feature, the Euphrates River, cuts from west to east across the territory, with tributaries branching out to the north and creating a series of valleys, marshes, and wooded areas. Nearer the coast, in the east, lies the Orontes River valley, which also supported a series of important settlements. Other portions of the territory, especially in the west, feature dry steppeland and plateaus, more suited to nomadic lifestyles and animal herding. On the whole, the territory is large and complex, featuring many different landscapes, agricultural zones, and geographical features, ranging from lush vegetation in low valleys around water sources to larger expanses of arid deserts and mountains.[1] In one prominent theory on the meaning of the term "Aram" itself, a scholar suggests the etymology has something to do with wild bulls, possibly a reference, in part, to the swampy geography of the Middle Euphrates region where such animals might wallow. Others, however, insist that the etymology of "Aram" is simply unknown, given our present state of knowledge.[2]

On the whole, evidence suggests that the term "Aram" was applied, in different time periods, to whatever city or ruler in the region was most dominant—in the tenth century BCE, that was Zobah; in the ninth–eighth centuries, Damascus; and in the eighth century, Arpad.[3] We first learn of the name "Aram" in an undisputed way through the encounters between the Arameans and an

1. K. Lawson Younger, *A Political History of the Arameans: From Their Origins to the End of Their Polities* (SBL Press: Atlanta, 2016), esp. 1–23; Edward Lipiński, *The Aramaeans: Their Ancient History, Culture, Religion* (Leuven: Peeters, 2000).
2. See, respectively, Lipiński, *Aramaeans*, 51–54, and Younger, *Political*, 38–40.
3. Younger, *Political*, 549.

Assyrian king named Tiglath-pilesar I, who lived c. 1114–1076 BCE. As the empire expanded westward, Assyrians saw conquest all the way to the Mediterranean Sea as a goal, and thus marching through lands occupied by various Aramean groups, taking plunder, and conducting military exploits there became a stock part of what it meant to run an empire in the ancient Near Eastern world. The people within Aram, as one might imagine, did not take kindly to being plundered—they often resisted, militarily and otherwise, thus creating a history of conflict that came to a head in the ninth and eighth centuries BCE. At this time, Assyrian incursions dealt major blows to Aramean independence; in nearly the same year that Israel's "northern kingdom" was finally destroyed, Sargon II destroyed the major Aramean city of Hamath in 722 BCE.

Various ancient sources refer to the residents of Aram as "the *ahlamu* Arameans," with "Aram" being a geographical designation and *ahlamu* being an Akkadian term that refers to shepherding or nomadic groups.[4] The use of this term need not imply that all Arameans were nomads or shepherds, however. Many of the new settlements in the territory of Aram during what archaeologists call the "Iron I" period, c. 1200–900 BCE, were small, rural, agriculturally oriented, and probably had a social structure similar to what many scholars assume was true in early Israel and other regional entities. When the Assyrians wrote about Arameans generally, they considered them to be desert-fringe (steppe-land) dwelling people.[5] Groups of family members lived near one another, and the social structure was probably focused on the identity of a primary

---

4. Helene Sader, "The Formation and Decline of the Aramaean States in Iron Age Syria," in *State Formation and State Decline in the Near and Middle East*, ed. Rainer Kessler, Walter Sommerfeld, and Leslie Tramontini (Wiesbaden: Harrassowitz, 2016), 61–76, here 64.

5. William M. Schniedewind, "The Rise of the Aramean States," in *Mesopotamia and the Bible: Comparative Explorations*, ed. Mark W. Chavalas and K. Lawson Younger Jr. (London: T&T Clark, 2003), 276–87, here 277.

male figure in the family ("patriarchal") and possibly even traced its roots to some local tribal ancestor, after which the group was named (e.g., Bit Adini, Bit-Agusi, Bit-Gabbari, Bit-Hazaili; the Semitic word "Bit" means "House of," followed by the name of a founding figure).[6] Most scholars who study the Arameans speak of their origins in terms of "tribes" and tribal leaders who took advantage of political instability in the region during certain time periods to expand their territory. Certain "capitals" or "royal cities" emerged, such as Sam'al/Zincirli, Arpad, Qarqar, Hazrak, and Damascus. These cities had kings, and inscriptions suggest that the kingship was hereditary, passed on from father to son. Smaller fortified cities surrounded the capitals, and borders around "districts" can be discerned in some cases but in most instances were rather fluid.[7] Moreover, some areas in the northern region near modern-day Turkey that had previously been under the control of the old Hittite Empire (c. 1600–1200 BCE) reappeared during the period of "Aramean" occupation in the Iron Age with neo-Hittite and Luwian identities (marked, for example, by the non-Semitic Indo-European languages we see attested in these areas), where Aramean and the Hittite or Luwian cultures blended in ways not always easy to disentangle. Identity in the region was complex and not static. When discussing the ancient world, we need to get comfortable with ambiguity and recognize that extraordinarily careful scholarship—such as that produced by specialists on the groups in question[8]—reveals a tremendous amount of nuance and yet provides only tentative reconstructions.

Of the many references to Aram in ancient Near Eastern sources (outside the Bible) that document major encounters

---

6. Sader, "Formation," 64–66.
7. Sader, "Formation," 70.
8. Younger, *Political*; Lipiński, *Aramaeans*; P. M. Michèle Daviau, John William Wevers, and Michael Weigl (eds.), *The World of the Arameans*, 3 vols. (Sheffield: Sheffield Academic Press, 2001); Herbert Niehr (ed.), *The Aramaeans in Ancient Syria* (Leiden: Brill, 2014).

between Aram and other major powers in the region, we are only able to trace the outlines of a few of the most notable instances.[9] Due to the lack of native Aramean sources, much of what we know comes from the Assyrians, an empire to the east that recorded ongoing encounters with the Arameans and others. Already in the twelfth century BCE, the Assyrian kings Tiglath-pilesar I and his son, Ashur-bel-kala, campaigned against groups living west of the northern portions of the Euphrates river and boasted of victories against the various Aramean groups living there. Though the Assyrians mostly recorded success in these ventures, at times the Aramean groups prevailed or at least held their ground. In fact, during the 900s and into the 800s BCE, the rising power of certain Aramean cities, marked by increasing centralization of local authority, set the stage for later conflicts with the Assyrian Empire.

Let's consider the case of the city Bit Adini, an important strategic region in the middle Euphrates with its capital at Til Barsib, ruled by a man named Ahuni beginning around the 870s BCE. The Assyrians were obsessed with conquering the territory, and they succeeded by the year 853 BCE, when Til Barsib was renamed "Shalmanesar's Harbor" after the Assyrian king, Shalmanesar III, who captured it.[10] These types of conflicts came to a head at the battle of Qarqar in the year 853 BCE. This battle became famous because of the large number of troops involved on both sides— Shalmanesar III's Assyrian army attacked a coalition of Aramean kings, including most prominently Hadad-ezer of Damascus and Irhuleni of Hamath, joined by Ahab of Israel. Though Shalmanesar III boasted in a long inscription (called the "Kurkh stele") of a decisive win over the coalition, the fact that Assyrian troops had to

9. Hélène Sader, "History," in *The Aramaeans in Ancient Syria*, ed. Herbert Niehr (Leiden: Brill, 2014), 11–36; Younger, *Political*; Lipiński, *Aramaeans*; Gotthard G. G. Reinhold, *The Rise and Fall of the Aramaeans in the Ancient Near East, from Their First Appearance until 732 BCE* (Frankfurt: Peter Lang, 2016), 33–71.

10. Sader, "History," 29–30.

continue to engage both Hadad-ezer and Irhuleni for a decade following their "defeat" proves that the battle offered no clear victory
to either side (if anything, it was a victory for the Aramean coalition). The end of the Aramean polities as powerful and independent groups came in the eighth century BCE, when victories by
the Assyrians between c. 740–720 BCE by Tiglath-pilesar III and
Sargon II subdued the region and annexed it into the Assyrian
Empire.

We learn of Aramean religion through excavated objects and
temples as well as through Aramaic literary sources—inscriptions
that they created, as well as names they had ("onomastica")
containing elements that tell us about the religious world of those
who gave the names.[11] Several first-millennium Aramean cities
have names (e.g., Sikkan, Nusaybin) that, in their Semitic etymology, refer to the religious practice of using a "standing stone"—
an upright, worked stone monument—for some religious purpose,
such as marking the presence of a deity or venerating the dead.
As far as we know, Aramean religion did not feature any one particular deity that could be called "the Aramean god(dess)" in the
same way that we might identify Yahweh as Israel's national deity,
or Chemosh for Moab, Qos for the Edomites, and so on. This
is no doubt due to the fact, as we have already noted, that there
was no single, coherent people group that called themselves "the
Arameans." Even so, in the surviving monuments and inscriptions
that we do have, some version of a weather-and-warrior god, such
as Hadad, seems most prominent (see Fig. 3.2).

Regionally, several deities appear prominently in inscriptions
and names—for example, "high gods" such as Il/El and Attar, various storm-god or warrior-god figures such as Hadad and Baal,
and a host of other figures, such as Shamash (associated with the
sun) and Resheph (associated with war and other calamities).
Excavations at the sites of Tell Tayinat and 'Ain Dara uncovered

11. Lipiński, *Aramaeans*, 599–640.

FIG. 3.2 Stele of a weather/storm god figure; Aleppo; ninth century BCE; after photo in Edward Lipiński, *The Aramaeans: Their Ancient History, Culture, Religion* (Leuven: Peeters, 2000), 635.

the remains of grand temple structures from the Iron Age—both often compared with the Israelite temple structure Solomon is said to have built. The 'Ain Dara temple features a set of giant footprints carved into stone, as if a giant deity (?) were striding into the temple space, and a series of intricate carved animal sculptures decorate the structure.[12]

One of the more direct and fascinating glimpses we have into a native Aramean religious view in a text comes through the so-called Fakheriye inscription, a bilingual text written on a statue

12. For 'Ain Dara, see Elizabeth C. Stone, Paul E. Zimansky, et al., *The Iron Age Settlement at 'Ain Dara, Syria: Survey and Surroundings* (Oxford: J. and E. Hedges, 1999).

dating to 850–800 BCE. Written in both Aramaic and Akkadian, the inscription's significance comes from its rare length and also for confirming Hadad's role as the key deity in the Khabur River area, where Sikani (Fakheriye) is located:[13]

(1) The statue of Haddayis'i, which he has set up before Hadad of Sikani, (2) regulator of the waters of heaven and earth, who rains down abundance, who gives pasture and (3) watering-places to all lands, who gives rest and vessels of food (4) to all the gods, his brothers, regulator of all rivers, who enriches (5) all lands, the merciful god to whom it is good to pray, who dwells (6) [in] Sikani. To the great god, his lord, Haddayis'i, King of Guzana, son (7) of Sasnuri, King of Guzana, set up and gave (the statue) to him, so that his soul may live, and his days be long, and (8) to increase his years, and so that his house may flourish, and his descendants may flourish, and (9) his people may flourish, and to remove illness from him, and for making his prayer heard, and for (10) accepting the words of his mouth. Now (11) whoever afterward, when it is in disrepair, re-erects it, may he put my name on it, but whoever erases my name from it (12) and puts his name, may Hadad, the hero, be his adversary. The statue of Haddayis'i, (13) King of Guzana and of Sikani and of Azran. For continuing his throne, (14) and for the length of his life and so that his word might be (15) pleasing to gods and to people, this image he made better than before. In the presence of Hadad (16), who dwells in Sikani, the lord of the Khabur, he has set up his statue. Whoever removes my name from the furnishings (17) of the house of Hadad, my lord: May my lord Hadad not accept his food and water (18) from his hand. May my lady Šuwala not accept food and water from his hand. When he (19) sows, may he

13. Translation from Herbert Niehr, "Religion," in *The Aramaeans in Ancient Syria*, ed. Herbert Niehr (Leiden: Brill, 2014), 127–203, here 130–131.

not reap, and when he sows a thousand (measures) of barley, may he take (only) a fraction from it. (20) Should one hundred ewes suckle a lamb, may it not be satisfied. Should one hundred cows suckle (21) a calf, may it not be satisfied. Should one hundred women suckle a child, may it not be satisfied. (22) Should one hundred women bake bread in an oven, may they not fill it. May his men glean barley from a refuse pit to eat. (23) May plague, the rod of Nergal, not be cut off from his land.

Here we notice common features of ancient Near Eastern religions, specifically the close relationship the text posits between king and deity, the concern for posterity, and the set of "blessings and curses" in the last several lines that are a stock part of covenant (treaty) traditions. Šuwala (in line 18) is likely a goddess of the underworld.

Those looking to delve further into native Aramaic inscriptions revealing aspects of religious and royal ideology should consult the following (all from the eighth century BCE): the Sefire inscriptions, recording a treaty and various magical rites; the Karatepe (or Azitiwada) inscription, a bilingual (Phoenician and Luwian) text on stone slabs recounting the exploits of a king; the Bar-rakib inscription, a loyalty oath from a king of Sam'al to an Assyrian ruler; the stele of Panumuwa I, a king of Sam'al, for his burial chamber; and the Katumuwa stele, an intriguing and still cryptic text discovered in 2008 that records a funerary ritual and hope for the afterlife.[14]

Turning to other written traditions, in the *Ahiqar* text we have what may well be a native Aramean wisdom tradition. In the earliest form we currently possess, the *Ahiqar* manuscript comes from the Jewish settlement of Elephantine in Egypt (fifth century

14. William W. Hallo and K. Lawson Younger, Jr. (eds.), *The Context of Scripture*, vol. 2: *Monumental Inscriptions from the Biblical World* (Leiden: Brill, 2002). I discuss the Tel Dan stele later in this chapter, in the consideration of the Arameans in the Bible.

BCE). Written in Aramaic, *Ahiqar* was among the most popular literary works circulated in the Mediterranean world during the middle of the first millennium BCE. *Ahiqar* assumes a polytheistic world populated by various deities, and dispenses wisdom to its readers after a folktale. In the folktale, Ahiqar, a high official in the court of the Assyrian kings Sennacherib and Esharhaddon, retires and installs a nephew-adopted-as-son in his place to serve the king. The nephew slanders Ahiqar to the king, however, forcing Ahiqar into hiding. Depending on the version of the story, another official sent to kill Ahiqar hides him instead, and Ahiqar reveals himself to the king in a moment of dire need and takes retribution upon his evil nephew. The text then proceeds into a long series of wisdom sayings, many of which would be familiar to readers of the Hebrew Bible: "Spare not your son from the rod"; "Above all else, guard your mouth; and as for what you have heard, be discreet! For a word is a bird, and he who releases it is a fool"; "Let the angry man gorge himself on bread, and the wrathful get drunk on wine."[15]

Our understanding of Aramean art is hampered by problems of cultural identification—was there a truly native "Aramean" aesthetic tradition? Can we distinguish Aramean art and architecture from the Luwian and broader Hittite traditions in the region, not to mention the dominant Assyrian influence? Aramean artisans participated in a broadly shared "international orientalizing" style,[16] producing monumental stone art and reliefs at locations like Sam'al, Carchemish, and Hamath, often featuring animals associated with deities. Upright-standing stone monuments depicted leaders, accompanied by inscriptions—such as the massive (nearly three-meter) image of Hadad on the stele of the king Panamuwa

---

15. J. M. Lindenberger, "Ahiqar," in *The Old Testament Pseudepigrapha*, vol. 2, ed. James A. Charlesworth (Peabody: Hendrickson, 1983), 480–507.

16. Dominik Bonatz, "Art," in *The Aramaeans in Ancient Syria*, ed. Herbert Niehr (Leiden: Brill, 2014), 205–253, here 253.

uncovered at Gercin, just northeast of Sam'al. This particular stele depicting Hadad shows us the integral link most Arameans probably saw between their king and the deity; the inscription along with the image in this stele conflates Panamuwa and Hadad as co-recipients of offerings, demonstrating the ruler's elevated position after death.[17] Although we currently have scant evidence for some smaller-scale artistic traditions, such as seals and impressions, Aramean territory in northern Syria has now been recognized as an important center for ivory circulation (and perhaps, in some cases, production), bronze metalworking, and small, intricately carved stone vessels.

ARAM AND THE ARAMEANS IN THE HEBREW BIBLE

The so-called Table of Nations in Genesis 10 contains a genealogy providing the origins of people groups spreading out from Noah and his three sons after the flood. This genealogy lists an individual named "Aram" among the sons of Shem (Gen 10:22–23), who is distinct from the Canaanites and from other groups (in Gen 10:2–20). This is significant because, unlike all of the other neighbors we're exploring in this book, the Bible presents Aram in the Table of Nations as a much closer relative to Israel, within the same Shem-itic (i.e., "Semitic") line of descent. We know almost nothing of Aram's four sons listed in Genesis 10:23: Uz, Hul, Gether, and Mash. Only Uz appears elsewhere: (1) equated with the region of Edom (a very different region from Aram; Lam 4:21, and see also Job 1:1); (2) 1 Chronicles 1, which often repeats the Genesis genealogy word for word, lists Uz, Hul, Gether, and Meshech (not Mash) as descendants of Shem *alongside* Aram, not as Aram's descendants (1 Chr 1:17).

17. Bonatz, "Art," 226.

Further complicating the situation, in Genesis 22:21 we find an extended genealogy of Abraham that lists an individual named Aram, the son of Kemuel—which cannot be the same Aram as in Genesis 10—as Abraham's great-nephew, that is, the grandson of Abraham's brother Nahor and Nahor's wife Milcah. Perhaps connected in some way to the genealogies in Genesis and Chronicles listed above, Nahor's oldest son is named "Uz." In the Genesis 22 genealogy, Aram is the only grandchild listed of any of the eight sons of Nahor, indicating that the author wanted to provide a link between Abraham and Nahor, whose origin came through Haran, within what we later know to be Aramean geography. In fact, the first appearance of a notable Aramean city in the Bible, Haran (Gen 11), is closely associated with the founding father and mother of Israel's ancestral group, Abram (later "Abraham") and Sarai (later "Sarah"). The line of Noah's son Shem (Gen 10:21–31) gets picked up again after the story of the Tower of Babel (Gen 11:1–9) and resumes tracing the line down through several figures, including a certain Eber (which the biblical authors may have associated with the word "Hebrew"?). A few generations later, a man named Terah in this line fathers three sons: Abram, Nahor, and Haran. Genesis 24:10 states that the city of Aram-naharaim was Nahor's city— "Aram-naharaim" means "Aram of/between the Two Rivers," presumably a reference to a region between the Tigris and Euphrates Rivers in northwestern Mesopotamia. Various second millennium BCE texts from Egypt refer to a region called "Nakhrima," a region along the northern Euphrates River area.

To be sure, this northern Euphrates River region plays a very prominent role in the Bible's ancestral narratives, particularly in the drama surrounding the acquisition of a wife for Abraham's sons, Isaac and Jacob. In Genesis 25, Isaac marries Rebekah, "daughter of Bethuel the Aramean of Paddan-aram, sister of Laban the Aramean." This is the first time the designation "Aramean" (Hebrew *ărami*) appears, though it's not clear that the text offers any singular notion of what it means to be "Aramean." Paddan-aram probably refers to the region around Haran, the ancestral home of Abraham and Sarah.[18] Jacob, too, ends up in Paddan-aram in Genesis 28, where he becomes embroiled in the family politics of Laban the Aramean, Rebekah's uncle, and marries both Leah and Rachel from the extended Aramean family group there. These women (with the help of their maidservants) end up birthing the sons who will form the majority of the twelve tribes of Israel: Reuben, Simeon, Levi, Judah, Dan, Naphtali, Gad, Asher, Issachar, Zebulun, Dinah, Joseph, and Benjamin. (Three of the other children, Dinah, Levi, and Joseph, do not have tribes named after them, and then two other children, later born to Joseph in Egypt, Ephraim and Manasseh, become the other two tribes.) In sum, the book of Genesis presents the birth of Israel with a very clear Aramean component—the two groups are intertwined with one another in profound ways from the beginning.

Within Genesis, we learn little of distinctly Aramean practice or belief. Laban the Aramean apparently worships in a polytheistic system; as Jacob and his wives and children flee Laban's supervision, Rachel steals her father's "household gods" (Hebrew *těrāpîm*), perhaps small physical images of deities forbidden in the Hebrew Bible (e.g., Exod 20:2–6; note also the reference in Judg 10:6 to "the gods of Aram" that Israel illicitly worships). Having stolen the images, Rachel sits on them to hide them as her father searches her tent, then claims that she cannot get up so he can search beneath her because, she claims, "the way of women is upon me" (i.e., she is having her period; Gen 31:25–35). Most scholars see in this passage a crude joke: Rachel defiles Laban's false gods, in the assumptions of this ancient culture, by menstruating upon them. While Aramean religion is thus mocked in this episode, Israel's God speaks directly to Laban within the same story (Gen 31:24) without a hint of mockery—God seems not to require any "conversion" by Laban—and he and Jacob come to an agreement between

---

18. Note also the reference to Jacob going down to Aram in Hosea 12:12; if the book of Hosea has its roots in the eighth century BCE, as many suspect, then the tradition of Jacob's time there is at least that old.

them not to harm the other (Gen 31:43–55). Neither man appears to have the upper hand in terms of virtue, though the narrative continues following only Jacob as inheritor of the divine promises to the group that will later become Israel.

In the book of Numbers, a figure comparable to Laban in terms of his ambiguous status as both enemy and helper to Israel is a seer (diviner) named Balaam, who in Numbers 23:7 claims to have been called forth "from Aram" (see also Num 22:5, where Balaam hails from Pethor, "in the land of Amaw," a site possibly near the major Hittite and neo-Hittite city of Carchemish in the northern Euphrates region). A Moabite king, Balak, recruits Balaam to curse the traveling Israelites, and Balaam seems prepared to comply, until Israel's God asks him to bless Israel instead. Balaam complies. The identity of this seer as an Aramean received new energy when archaeologists in 1967 uncovered a fragmentary inscription at the site of Deir 'Alla, just east of the Jordan River about halfway between the Dead Sea and the Sea of Galilee.[19] Though its translation and interpretation at many points are still an open question, many scholars think the text is written in some dialect of Aramaic (though this is disputed) from the ninth or eighth century BCE, making it, potentially, our earliest literary text in Aramaic. The text narrates an account from a certain "Balaam, son of Beor" (compare with Balaam's identical name and title in the book of Numbers), a seer who finds himself in the presence of a divine council:[20]

> The account of [Balaam, son of Beo]r, who was a seer of the gods. The gods came to him in the night, and he saw a vision like an oracle of El. Then they said to [Balaa]m, son of Beor: "Thus he

---

19. This text was first published, in full, by J. Hoftijzer and G. van der Kooij (eds.), *Aramaic Texts from Deir 'Alla* (Leiden: Brill, 1976).
20. Translation of the Balaam inscription passage emended from JoAnn Hackett, *The Balaam Text from Deir 'Alla*, HSM 31 (Chico: Scholars Press, 1980).

will do/make [ ] hereafter (?), which [ ]." And Balaam arose the next day. . . . And his people came up to him [*and said to*] him, "Balaam, son of Beor, why are you fasting and crying?" And he said to them: "Sit down! I will tell you what the Shadda[yyin *have done*.] Now, come, see the works of the gods! The g[o]ds gathered together; the Shaddayin took their places at the assembly. And they said to Sh[ ]: "Sew up, bolt up the heavens in your cloud, ordaining darkness instead of eternal light! And put the dear [se]al on your bolt, and do not remove it forever! For the swift reproaches the griffin-vulture and the voice of vultures sings out. The *st*[*ork*] the young of the NHS-bird (?) and claws up young herons. The swallow tears at the dove and the sparrow. . . .

Most interpreters of this text think Balaam's vision involves some kind of cosmic upheaval that is to come. The existence of this inscription suggests the great antiquity of a Balaam tradition in the Transjordan region from at least the ninth century BCE, if not earlier. Moreover, the text serves as a fascinating bridge between ancient Aramaic literary and religious traditions and those that became part of the Hebrew Bible. Nevertheless, the region where the text was found could conceivably be the product of some Ammonite or even northern Israelite culture, depending on one's analysis of the history of the region.

The cross-identity between Israel and Aram not only as geographical neighbors but also family members in the biblical story finds fascinating expression in Deuteronomy 26. Here, the narrator (Moses) records a ritual, including a response the individual Israelite is to recite:

> You shall make this response before the LORD your God: "A wandering Aramean was my ancestor; he went down into Egypt and lived there as an alien, few in number, and there he became a great nation, mighty and populous. When the Egyptians treated us harshly and afflicted us, by imposing hard labor on us, we cried to the LORD, the God of our ancestors; the LORD heard our voice . . .

and he brought us into this place and gave us this land, a land flowing with milk and honey. So now I bring the first of the fruit of the ground that you, O LORD, have given me." (Deut 26:5–9, excerpts)

In this summary formulation of Israel's history in the Torah, the story begins with an affirmation of Israel's identity in and with Aram, gesturing toward Abram's and Jacob's sojourn at Haran and the marriage within the family group located there. Scholars have debated the precise meaning of the Hebrew words in Deuteronomy 26:5 most commonly translated "My father was a wondering Aramean," *ărami̇̄ ōḇēḏ ʾāḇi̇̄*.[21] The German scholar Gerhard von Rad famously speculated that this little statement in Deuteronomy formed part of an ancient Israelite "creed," a memorable statement of faith that all Israelites were to repeat as an article of identity.[22]

Beyond the Torah, Aram and the Arameans appear frequently, almost exclusively in situations of conflict and condemnation by the biblical authors. Generally speaking, Israel's interaction with Aram can be considered under three headings: David's conflict with the Arameans in 2 Samuel 8 and 10; ongoing drama with the Arameans, particularly Hazael, in 1 Kings 19–2 Kings 16; and prophetic condemnations in Isaiah, Jeremiah, Amos, and Zechariah.

Part of David's effort to secure his kingdom in 2 Samuel involves subduing neighbors like Aram. In 2 Samuel 8:1–12, David defeats a certain Hadadezer son of Rehob of Zobah, a region in Aram, prompting other Arameans from Damascus to join in the fight

21. Yigal Levin, "'My Father Was a Wandering Aramean': Biblical Views of the Ancestral Relationship between Israel and Aram," in *Wandering Arameans: Arameans outside Syria. Textual and Archaeological Perspectives*, ed. Angelika Berlejung, Aren M. Maeir, and Andreas Schüle (Wiesbaden: Harrassowitz, 2017), 39–52, esp. 39–40.
22. Gerhard von Rad, *The Problem of the Hexateuch and Other Essays*, trans. E. W. Trueman Dicken (New York: McGraw-Hill, 1966), "The Form-Critical Problem of the Hexateuch," 1–26, here 3–5.

(who are also subdued by David's army). In 2 Samuel 10, conflict again flares up when the Ammonites hire Arameans to help fight against David. Although 2 Samuel 8:3 states that David had "struck down" Hadadezer, Hadadezer appears again to fight against David, garnering a coalition of other Arameans. David defeats the whole lot once again, and 2 Samuel 10:19 implies that David exercised some sort of control over the region of Aram.

Beginning in 1 Kings 19, and stretching many chapters all the way through at least 2 Kings 16, an elaborate series of conflicts between Israel and Aram unfolds. The drama begins when the prophet Elijah is, through a unique divine command, instructed to anoint a foreigner as king over a foreign nation (the actions of biblical characters typically do not extend beyond the borders of Israel in this manner, especially in Samuel–Kings), specifically, a man named Hazael as king over (all?) Aram (1 Kgs 19:15). Soon after, the currently reigning king of Aram, Ben-hadad, lays siege to the northern part of the country, ruled by King Ahab. With the encouragement of a prophet, Ahab routes Ben-hadad's army and ends up making a treaty with Ben-hadad (1 Kgs 20:34). Further prospect of war with Aram entices Ahab out to battle at Ramoth-gilead, where he dies by the arrow of an Aramean archer (1 Kgs 22). Aram reenters the picture in 2 Kings 5, where the prophet Elisha heals the commander of the Aramean army, Naaman, of a skin disease, and then the Aramean army suffers another defeat at the hands of Israel in 2 Kings 6–7.

Finally, in 2 Kings 8, after consultation with the prophet Elisha, Hazael becomes king by assassinating Ben-hadad (not, it seems, by the mere "anointing" of the prophet Elisha, as indicated in 1 Kgs 19:15). Beginning in 2 Kings 10:32, Hazael weaves in and out of the narrative, all the while acting as a divine agent of punishment against Israel. First, he trims off portions of Israel's territory for himself and threatens to take Jerusalem (2 Kgs 12:17–18), inflicting further multiple defeats on Israel (13:1–3). When Hazael dies, his son Ben-hadad succeeds him (13:24–25). Hazael's prominence in these narratives took on new significance when fragments of a royal stele were uncovered at Tell Dan in 1993 and 1994. In this inscription, the speaker—whom most presume to be Hazael, based on the estimated date of the text (c. 840–800 BCE)—makes, in part, the following claims:[23]

> . . . and my father lay down, he went to his [ancestors]. And the king of I[s]rael entered previously in my father's land, [and] Hadad made me king, and Hadad went in front of me, [and] I departed from the seven . . . of my kingdom, and I slew [seve]nty kin[gs], who harnessed th[ousands of cha]riots and thousands of horsemen. [I killed Jeho]ram son [of Ahab] king of Israel, and [I] killed [Ahaz]iahu son of [Jehoram kin]g of the House of David, and I set [their towns into ruins and turned] their land into [desolation]. . . .

Though this text received the most attention for its reference to the "House of David," possibly the earliest such nonbiblical reference to David that we currently possess, Hazael's claim to have (directly?) killed Jehoram/Joram and Ahaziah also raises eyebrows since the biblical narrative attributes these killings to Jehu (2 Kgs 9–10). The end of Israel's interaction with Aram then occurs in 2 Kings 16, when a coalition of Israelites and Arameans attempts (unsuccessfully) to confront the Assyrian monarch Tiglath-pilesar III. These events, also narrated in Isaiah 7, occurred in the 730s bce; the Arameans attempted, along with the northern Israelite king Pekah, to depose the Judean king Ahaz. Ahaz appeals to Tiglath-pilesar III and pays heavy tribute to Assyria—and ends up copying an altar design that he sees in Damascus and then using that altar for worship, an act about which the narrator is curiously silent (2 Kgs 16:10–16).

---

23. Translation adopted from Avraham Biran and Joseph Naveh, "The Tel Dan Inscription: A New Fragment," *Israel Exploration Journal* 45.1 (1995): 1–18.

Several of the prophets mention the Arameans, seemingly all in contexts of disapproval and judgment (e.g., Isa 17:1–3; Jer 49:23–27; Amos 1:3–5; Zech 9:1–4). Most famously, Isaiah enters into the conflict between Rezin of Aram and Pekah of Israel, as the two attempted to depose the southern Judean king Ahaz (whom Isaiah supports). Isaiah's involvement in chapter 7 culminates in the pronouncement about the coming birth of a child from the "young woman" (Hebrew 'almāh; understood as a "virgin" in the Christian tradition); "before the child knows how to refuse the evil and choose the good," Isaiah proclaims, "the land before whose two kings you are in dread will be deserted" (7:16). Moreover, the prophet Amos mentions the origins of the Arameans in Amos 9:7:

> Are you not like the Ethiopians to me, O people of Israel? says the LORD. Did I not bring Israel up from the land of Egypt, and the Philistines from Caphtor and the Arameans from Kir?

This passage is fascinating since it invokes a tradition of Aramean migration from this location, Kir (Hebrew qîr), though the location of Kir remains elusive.[24]

WHAT HAPPENED TO THE ARAMEANS?

Long after the loss of any clear political identity marked "Aramean," the Aramaic language thrived in a wide variety of contexts. One of the primary scholars of the history of Aramaic, Holger Gzella, describes the situation of the language's spread in terms of "bewildering diversity."[25] Given the fact that Aramaic

---

24. Younger, *Political*, 41–42.
25. Holger Gzella, "New Light on Linguistic Diversity in Pre-Achaemenid Aramaic: Wandering Arameans or Language Spread?" in *Wandering Arameans: Arameans outside Syria. Textual and Archaeological*

was "the great idiom of the Near East" throughout not only the Mesopotamian Empires of the first millennium BCE but also well into the Common Era, through the beginning of Islam, some have even called Aramaic "a language that holds the key to a good deal of the world's intellectual history" and asserted that "the history of Aramaic represents the purest triumph of the human spirit as embodied in language . . . over the crude display of material power."[26] Aramaic first spread as an international language of trade and commerce during the Assyrian and Babylonian Empires, took on an official role during the influential and long-lasting Persian Empire (note that the biblical book of Ezra [4:8–6:18; 7:12–26] purports to quote Aramaic documents from the Persian Empire), lived on in Palestine during the Roman period and was employed by the Nabataeans and at Palmyra, and then was spoken among Jews, Mandeans, and Christians (using Syriac, an Aramaic dialect) for centuries.

As of the time of the writing of this book, a large amount of damage has been done to various sites of great cultural importance in Syria during the ongoing civil war there, including (but not limited to) sites important to the Aramean/Aramaic heritage in the region—including Emesa (Homs) and Palmyra. Still, refugee populations continue to live in many places throughout the world. The *Chaldean Voice Radio Program*, airing weekly online and based in a small town in Michigan, continues to broadcast for local Chaldean Assyrian and Syriac listeners who are inheritors of the Aramaic tradition through their identity with the Chaldean Catholic Church (with its headquarters in Iraq, but with

Perspectives, ed. Angelika Berlejung, Aren M. Maeir, and Andreas Schüle (Wiesbaden: Harrassowitz, 2017), 19–37, here 34.

26. Quotes from the Aramaic scholar Franz Rosenthal, quoted in Holger Gzella, *A Cultural History of Aramaic: From the Beginnings to the Advent of Islam* (Leiden: Brill, 2015), 1.

populations across the Middle East and in diaspora around the world).[27]

Following Assyrian incursions and deportations that occurred during the ninth–seventh centuries BCE, populations from Aram migrated throughout the ancient Near Eastern world, to places like Egypt and far into the heart of Mesopotamia. Tracing these migrations and their consequences proves to be not straightforward,[28] and, as previously mentioned with the regard to the Ahiqar text, Aramaic traditions made their way all over the Mediterranean world and functioned as popular literature for hundreds of years. Although its background may overlap with the biblical period, a text known as Amherst Papyrus 63 preserves many different kinds of traditions in Aramaic from the end of the Iron Age and can serve as one further example of the way Arameans continued to think, worship, and act outside and beyond the biblical tradition.[29] The papyrus comes from Egypt and dates to around the fourth or third century BCE, and preserves perhaps around thirty-five to forty distinct literary compositions. Though ambiguity shrouds the text, one theory is that the text's community originally hailed from an ambiguous place named Rash and then settled alongside the Jewish residents of a colony at Elephantine in Egypt (where Jews living there around the time of the biblical Ezra and Nehemiah produced their own corpus of Aramaic texts[30]). These Rashans had

27. http://chaldeanvoice.com.
28. Angelika Berlejung, Andreas Schüle, and Aren M. Maeir (eds.), *Wandering Aramaeans: Aramaeans outside Syria. Textual and Archaeological Perspectives* (Wiesbaden: Harrassowitz, 2017).
29. Karel van der Toorn, *Papyrus Amherst 63* (Münster: Ugarit-Verlag, 2018), 3–39; Richard C. Steiner, "Papyrus Amherst 63: A New Source for the Language, Literature, Religion, and History of the Arameans," in *Studia Aramaica: New Sources and New Approaches*, ed. Markham J. Geller, Jonas C. Greenfield, and Michael P. Weitzman (Oxford: Oxford University Press, 1995), 199–207.
30. Bezalel Porten, *The Elephantine Papyri in English: Three Millennia of Cross-Cultural Continuity and Change* (Leiden: Brill, 1996).

been deported or migrated during the time of Assyrian rule, lived in Israel for a time (perhaps at Bethel), and then ended up, with many other exiles of the Babylonian onslaught of the early sixth century BCE, moving farther south, to Egypt. Amherst Papyrus 63 contains prayers to a chief deity named Mar ("lord") as well as to many other deities, and describes the destruction of the homeland, Rash. Included also are prayers for rain, a description of severe drought at Bethel, and a poem that has many parallels with the biblical Psalm 20—suggesting that either the composers of the Amherst papyrus poem knew Psalm 20 and composed their own Aramaic version, or that some older, traditional song underlies both compositions.

4

The Ammonites

CAST AS THE INCESTUOUS ANCESTORS of Lot (Abraham's nephew) and his daughters in Genesis 19, the Ammonites figure in moments of gritty intrigue at many points in the biblical narratives, fighting against Israel, making alliances with the Aramaeans, and enticing Israel with their forbidden deities. Unlike some other groups whose identity the Bible presents in terms of "familial" relationship with Israel, such as the Canaanites, Edomites, and Arameans, the Ammonites appear only as political and religious enemies. Although the identity of several of the groups we're examining in this book cannot be so easily pinned down to a specific name or clear geographic region, Ammonites seem to have occupied a small and delimited territory, and the pinnacle of their existence as "Ammonites" by name seems to have occurred during a relatively short time frame, between the eighth and sixth centuries BCE. Excavation at some key sites of Ammonite occupation gives us more data than might be expected on Ammonite language, religion, and culture. Scholars debate the extent to which the Ammonites of the Bible correspond to real historical figures; the Bible mentions several Ammonite kings by name (e.g., Baalis, Nahash, Hanun), though it is not always possible to correlate these leaders with known figures from other sources. Moreover, the biblical portrayal of Ammonite religion in a negative manner raises questions about the way our assumptions about religion in the ancient Near East have been colored by the biblical narrators.

Ancient Israel's Neighbors. Brian R. Doak, Oxford University Press (2020). © Oxford University Press.
DOI: 10.1093/oso/9780190690595.001.0001

FIG. 4.1 Map of Ammon; Map data ©2019 Google, with text added by the author.

THE ARCHAEOLOGY OF AMMON AND THE AMMONITES

The region of the Ammonites lies east of the Jordan River, in the so-called Transjordan region, around 20 miles/30 km northeast of the Dead Sea and limited in the north around the region of the Jabbok River (Fig. 4.1). In the current political geography, the heart of Ammon is situated within the country of Jordan, particularly centered around that country's capital, Amman—the name still preserved after thousands of years (Amman = Ammon, which most now agree is the biblical "Rabbath-Ammon").

The landscape just to the east of the Jordan River features rugged mountains, leveling off into a plateau in the east where most who were identified as Ammonites in antiquity probably lived. Given the lack of other defining features in this landscape, rivers may have played a key role as boundaries, and archaeologists continue to debate the exact extent of the territory.[1] Those living in this desert-fringe area could not rely on plentiful agricultural bounty, so animal herding was a primary occupation.[2]

Traces of early settlers in this region have been found at the Neolithic period site of 'Ain Ghazal, located near an airport in contemporary Amman, Jordan, where a sizable Neolithic population lived around nine thousand years ago. People no doubt lived in the region over many centuries, many of whom were likely mobile (nomadic or seminomadic) and left little trace in the material record. Before the Assyrian period in the eighth and seventh centuries BCE, we do not know what factors made it possible for the Ammonites to establish their small kingdom in the way that they did. Generally speaking, the collapse of the Late Bronze Age political system beginning in the thirteenth century BCE sparked a regional change during which established city-states fell apart or were transformed and new entities arose.[3] The settlement of the Philistines during the same time period along the coastal plain may have created a domino

1. E.g., P. M. Michèle Daviau, "Moab's Northern Border: Khirbet al-Mudayna on the Wadi ath-Thamad," *Biblical Archaeologist* 60.4 (1997): 222–228.
2. Yohanan Aharoni, *The Land of the Bible: A Historical Geography*, rev. and enlarged ed., trans. Anson F. Rainey (Philadelphia: Westminster Press, 1979), 36–39.
3. Randall W. Younker, "The Emergence of the Ammonites," in *Ancient Ammon*, ed. Burton MacDonald and Randall W. Younker (Leiden: Brill, 1999), 189–218.

effect—as an invading, organized group with strong rulers, the Philistines inadvertently forced other small groups settling around the same time (such as Israel, Ammon, Edom, and Moab) to get their acts together, so to speak, and organize into more formal political structures. Pressures for habitable land, refugees from other conflicts, and economic factors of various kinds no doubt played some role as well in the formation of polities like Ammon.[4]

The clearest archaeological evidence for the region comes from between the eighth and sixth centuries BCE, when first the Assyrians and then the Babylonians dominated the area.[5] Although the exact origin of the Ammonites (by that name) is unknown, we find them as a fully functioning polity by the time of Assyrian incursions into Israel during the 730s and 720s BCE—culminating in the destruction of the northern part of Israel around 720 BCE. Unlike Israel and Judah, Ammon did not resist the Assyrians. Instead, from Assyrian records we learn of an Ammonite king named Sanipu who sent tribute payment to the Assyrian king Tiglath-pilesar III in order to avoid conflict, and then in 701 BCE, when the Assyrians threatened the southern part of Israel (Judah), a certain "Pada'el the king of the sons of Ammon" fought alongside Sennacherib against Judah. The Assyrians claim that subsequent Ammonite kings helped their

4. Paul-Eugène Dion, "The Ammonites: A Historical Sketch," in *Excavations at Tall Jawa, Jordan*, vol. 1: *The Iron Age Town* (Leiden: Brill, 2003), 481–513, here 493–494.

5. Ephraim Stern, *Archaeology of the Land of the Bible*, vol. 2: *The Assyrian, Babylonian, and Persian Periods, 732–332 BCE* (New York: Doubleday, 2001), 236–258; Dion, "Ammonites"; and Mariusz Burdajewicz, "Rabbath-Ammon," in *The New Encyclopedia of Archaeological Excavations in the Holy Land*, ed. Ephraim Stern (Jerusalem: Israel Exploration Society and Carta, 1993), 1243–1249. For two recent books on the Ammonites, see Craig W. Tyson, *The Ammonites: Elites, Empires, and Sociopolitical Change (1000–500 BCE)* (London: Bloomsbury, 2014), and Burton MacDonald and Randall W. Younker (eds.), *Ancient Ammon* (Leiden: Brill, 1999).

empire through military aid and building projects. The mutual aid between Ammon and the Assyrians apparently resulted in a time of safety and wealth for the small kingdom of the Ammonites, and thus, given Ammon's small size and relative anonymity as a major actor on the ancient world scene, in the archaeological record we have an unusually large amount of Ammonite inscriptions, artwork, and other material culture.

Archaeologists have conducted detailed work at a number of putatively Ammonite sites—including Tell el-Mazar, Tell Jawa, Tell Jalul, Tell es-Sa'idiyeh, and Tell al-'Umayri, among others. Although in the previous chapter on the Arameans we treated an inscription concerning Balaam, because its language is probably Aramaic, the site where this Balaam inscription was found, Tell Deir 'Alla, is assumed by many to be an Ammonite site. For our purposes here, we focus on the Rabbath-Ammon area as a case study—it was the capital of Ammon, and excavations there have uncovered a range of fascinating materials (tombs, iconography, a palace, and inscriptions).

Archaeologists uncovered a large building in the southern part of the city of Rabbath-Ammon, which dates to the seventh century BCE (though possibly built on a structure that existed long beforehand). Interpreted by many as a "palace," the structure had a sizable courtyard (10 × 15 m) and a floor plastered in a particularly refined way (30 cm thick), suggesting something of the building's importance and the wealth of those who created and used it. The building contained several rooms, including one with a lavatory featuring a limestone seat. In many respects the building resembles Assyrian palaces at locations like Nimrud and Khorsabad, and the Assyrian influence in the region at the time likely prompted the similarity of style. Excavators believe the structure had an upper story, and many notable items found at the site probably fell down from that upper story and were buried when the building was destroyed: pottery, glass jewelry and beads, ivory pieces, and a clay mask. Archeologists also discovered in the building a fascinating set of sculpted limestone heads of the deity Hathor—the images are "double-facing," front

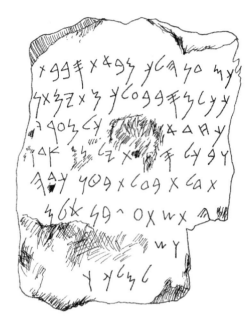

FIG. 4.2 Ammon Citadel Inscription; ninth century BCE; after photo from http://www.inscriptifact.com/aboutus/index.shtml (retrieved March 9, 2019).

and back on two sides, perhaps suggesting that they were to be situated in the windows of the palace.[6]

At the center of Amman lies the "citadel," a hill with fortification walls, rampart, and a sizable cistern for water cut underground. The site functioned through many periods, dating from at least the Middle Bronze II (c. 1700 BCE) through the Hellenistic and Roman periods in various iterations. One particularly notable find from this citadel is an inscription—one of the longest in antiquity in any northwest Semitic language from this region (Fig. 4.2).[7]

6. For the palace, see Stern, *Archaeology*, 245, and Burdajewicz, "Rabbath-Ammon," 1248.
7. Siegfried H. Horn, "The Amman Citadel Inscription," 1–12, and Frank Moore Cross, "Epigraphic Notes on the Amman Citadel Inscription,"

Though fragmentary and difficult to translate, enough of the words remain to discern that it probably had a dedicatory function for a building and began with a line that read something like, "This is the Temple that [name of king or sponsor] built for you, O Milkom . . ." (Milkom was a major Ammonite deity—perhaps even their chief deity). What remains of the inscription reads, in the interpretation of its original publisher, as follows:[8]

> [Mi]lkom has built for you entrances round about
> . . . according to all that surrounds you from *Tymtn* . . .
> . . . what had been destroyed I . . . throughout the west . . .
> . . . and on every threshold . . . of the legitimate wall . . .
> . . . door, at the inner door he dug . . .
> . . . fear was among the men of the portico . . .
> . . . [undecipherable line] . . .
> . . . for you . . .

The inscription dates to the ninth century BCE and was likely part of a much larger inscription, perhaps with an accompanying statue or other objects.

Another example of native Ammonite literature comes on an inscribed bronze bottle, uncovered in 1972 at Tall Siran, a site on the campus of the modern-day University of Jordan in the northern part of the city of Amman. Though the bottle is small and the translation debated, the object is completely intact and the letters of text are very clear:[9]

13–19, both in *Bulletin of the American Schools of Oriental Research* 193 (1969).

8. Horn, "Amman."

9. Walter E. Aufrecht, "Ammonite Texts and Language," in *Ancient Ammon*, ed. Burton MacDonald and Randall W. Younker (Leiden: Brill, 1999), 163–188, here 164.

May the produce (or: deeds) of 'Amminadab king of the
Ammonite, the son of Hassil'il king of the Ammonites, the son of
'Amminadab king of the Ammonites—the vineyard and the gar-
dens and the hollow and the cistern—cause rejoicing and glad-
ness for many days to come and in years far off.

Inside the bottle, archaeologists found fragments of some un-
identified (disintegrated) object, as well as some bits of wheat.[10]
This text may have originated as a commemorative inscription for
the dedication of a royal structure or garden, or as a votive (offering) in some kind of religious context. The text's concern for
King 'Amminadab's success in terms of agricultural bounty and the
overall happiness of the community seems simple enough—these
are things that all leaders, in all places and at all times, wish for
their communities. The term used for "Ammonites," *bn 'mn*, literally "sons of Ammon," indicates a group that thought of itself
in tribal or familial terms, not unlike other similarly organized
groups in the region (such as the Israelites, i.e., "the sons of Israel,"
as described in the Hebrew Bible). Historians find great interest
in the kings named here in the inscription—a source like this
is clearly native to the historical period in which it was written,
around 600 BCE, so the text has little motivation to distort any
names or facts, few though they may be, given the brevity of the
invocation. The grandfather of the present king 'Amminadab of
the inscription, also named 'Amminadab, likely correlates to a certain "'Amminadab king of the House of Ammon" mentioned in an
Assyrian inscription; this king, according to the Assyrian record,
assisted Assyria with troops for a battle against Egypt fought by
King Assurbanipal around the year 667 BCE.[11]

There has been some debate about whether the Ammonites
possessed a "national script" (form of writing) and language, or

---

10. Tyson, *Ammonites*, 83–84.
11. Tyson, *Ammonites*, 84.

whether their texts were written in a more generic, regional script that is essentially indistinguishable from Aramaic—a problem we are not be able to solve here. Those who argue for a distinct Ammonite writing system believe that the Ammonite script coincided with the Aramaic system until about the middle of the eighth century BCE, at which point it broke off to form its own independent style. The question of whether Ammonite inscriptions are written in a dialect that should be classified within the broader "Canaanite" language family or whether Ammonite is truly a distinct language on its own cannot be resolved given the present state of evidence.[12]

Ammonite political affairs were intricately bound up with the affairs of empire during the eighth through sixth centuries BCE, as the Assyrians and then the Babylonians dominated the region. One scholar has recently argued that the Ammonites developed an "elite culture" during this time period, a process that came as the result of their interaction with imperial powers.[13] As a vassal (something of a servant state) of the Assyrian Empire, for example, Ammonites were allowed to rule over their own internal politics and arrange their society independently after first paying tribute—in the form of materials and oaths—and then renewing that tribute at regular intervals. The Babylonians employed a similar system. Prior to the eighth century, archaeologists find little evidence of international trade or any great level of societal complexity and wealth. Given new needs based on Assyrian control, however, we find a distinct pattern of settlement intensification, and a boom in certain types of local agriculture. Perhaps the stability of the empire allowed these changes, and a growing upper class within Ammon had access to wealth and power that allowed them to erect monuments, create inscriptions, and develop architecture

---

12. Aufrecht, "Ammonite Texts and Language," 167–71.
13. Craig W. Tyson, "Peripheral Elite as Imperial Collaborators," *Journal of Anthropological Research* 70.4 (2014): 481–509, as well as Tyson, *Ammonites*, 146–232.

in specific ways that were not possible in prior eras. Iconography grew more sophisticated and begins to show evidence of influence from Mesopotamia, Egypt, and Phoenicia. Luxury goods appear with more frequency, and elite Ammonites likely became quite good at negotiating their relationship between the Assyrians and Babylonians, on the one hand, and their fellow Ammonites, on the other, in ways that brought greater wealth to the region and bolstered their own status in the process.

In the realm of religion and culture, relatively speaking, we are fortunate to have a reasonable amount of evidence for materials that can be more or less confidently assigned the label "Ammonite." However, in the realm of religion, we usually cannot be certain about which features were distinctly Ammonite, as opposed to features that almost all groups in the region largely shared. We have no distinct, clear expression of any kind of state-sponsored practice in Ammon.[14] The Siran bottle inscription and the fragmentary citadel inscription may reflect some aspects of a royal practice of building dedication; coupled with the reference to Milkom, perhaps a chief deity of the Ammonites, these texts could point to something distinctly "Ammonite," but then again building and royal dedications with reference to a deity are very common throughout the ancient Near Eastern world. Some argue that the Ammonites worshiped as their highest deity a god named Il/El, a Semitic term that can be a generic noun for "God" but also a proper name (as it may be in the Deir Alla inscription of Balaam, as cited in the chapter in this book on the Arameans). At any rate, of the recorded proper names ("onomastica") that we have for Ammonites, the name element *'il* appears very commonly, suggesting that this deity played some key role.[15]

14. Walter E. Aufrecht, "The Religion of the Ammonites," in *Ancient Ammon*, ed. Burton MacDonald and Randall W. Younker (Leiden: Brill, 1999), 152–162, here 155–156.
15. Aufrecht, "Religion," 156–160.

Regarding burial customs, which can tell us a lot about a society and its beliefs, Ammonite graves from the seventh and sixth centuries BCE closely resemble the range of burials we find throughout the region more generally, including in Israel.[16] Archaeologists have uncovered burials in natural and artificial caves, shaft tombs, structures built of mud-brick, pits lined with stones, and very simple pit graves. In a few notable cases, we also have burials in coffins—some "anthropoid" (decorated like a human on the outside), as well as some in bathtub-shaped boxes and some within jars (mostly of young children). Clay coffins became especially popular during the Assyrian period among presumably wealthier individuals, since this type of burial was also an Assyrian practice. Grave goods often accompanied the body, though it is difficult to know how the people who buried the dead thought these grave goods functioned—did they play a role for afterlife ideology, as in ancient Egypt? Were they emotional tokens, to help the living grieve their loss? Or did they play some religious role of a different kind? At Tall al-Mazar, near the Jordan River, excavators discovered the burial of an individual who may have been considered a warrior, based on the grave goods: seven arrowheads, possibly once part of a quiver, a glass bottle, a bronze fibula, several spear-points near the right knee (indicating they may have been attached facing downward, at the waist), and an iron knife. Such items probably indicate that the individual was dressed for burial in full military gear; an injury to the head on the skeleton that had healed before the individual's death could indicate a battle wound.[17]

Ammonite artistic production survives most prominently through iconography on seal impressions, stone figures, and

16. Khair Yassine, "Burial Customs and Practices in Ancient Ammon," in *Ancient Ammon*, ed. Burton MacDonald and Randall W. Younker (Leiden: Brill, 1999), 137–151, and Stern, *Archaeology*, 255–257.
17. Yassine, "Burial," 141–142.

monumental architecture. Ammonite seals—carved in hard stone or gem, and pressed onto clay—are usually of a high quality and display motifs clustered into two groups: a "Phoenician-Israelite" tradition and an "Assyrian-inspired" set.[18] Of the Phoenician-Israelite type, scenes include various kinds of mythical animals, such as sphinxes, as well as monkeys and Egyptian-themed iconography (Egyptian deities, floral motifs, etc.). The Assyrian group displays individuals praying in front of an altar and astral emblems (sun, moon, stars), a scene common in Assyrian art. The prominent archaeologist Ephraim Stern claims that Ammonite stone sculptures, particularly of male figures, "are executed in a characteristic and easily identifiable style, which differs from that of all other Levantine sculpture," and argues that this style is the result of a "local school" of Ammonite artisans.[19] These statues, in the male form, wear a stylized crown or headdress, which may indicate the divine status of the character in the image; females are much rarer, and don a wig that may have origins in Egyptian representation (see Fig. 4.3). Of smaller clay figurines, whether male, female, or animal, all extant examples have been painted in black and white tones.[20]

AMMON AND THE AMMONITES IN THE HEBREW BIBLE

Unlike many of the other neighbors we're examining in this book, the Ammonites receive no mention in the early genealogy of Genesis 10—though oblique references to the "Canaanites" at locations like Sodom, Gomorrah, Lasha, and elsewhere do at least

18. Stern, *Archaeology*, 243–244.
19. Stern, *Archaeology*, 249.
20. Stern, *Archaeology*, 254.

FIG. 4.3 Stone statues of male and female figures; Iron Age Ammon; after photos in Ephraim Stern, *Archaeology of the Land of the Bible*, vol. 2: *The Assyrian, Babylonian, and Persian Periods, 732–332 BCE* (New York: Doubleday, 2001), 250, I.103.

gesture to territory east of the Dead Sea (though too far south to be considered Ammonite in any clear way). However, biblical narrators do give a separate story of origins for the Ammonites. In the biblical imagination broadly, origins equate with destiny; for neighbors who were experienced as severe enemies, such as Ammon, those origins are bound to be degraded—and in the present case, quite horrible indeed.

Genesis 19:30–38 tells the story of the fate of Lot, Abraham's nephew. Lot and his family had settled at the infamous sites of Sodom and Gomorrah, which were subsequently destroyed by fire—Lot's wife never made it out, for she looked back at the burning cities and turned into a pillar of salt (Gen 19:26). Now bereft of his wife and afraid to settle in the city of Zoar, which he had been granted as a place of asylum from the destruction, Lot takes refuge in a cave with his two daughters. The daughters soon realize that their own fate in life is rather grim, and seeing that they may not have another opportunity to bear children, they make their father drunk and rape him while he is unconscious on subsequent nights. Notably, Lot had unsuccessfully offered up these same two daughters to a mob gathered outside of his house in Sodom, presumably to be raped or killed (Gen 19:8). The encounter in the cave results in both daughters getting pregnant. The first gives birth to a son named Moab, who becomes the ancestor of the Moabites, while the second gives birth to a son named Ben-Ammi (Gen 19:38). This latter son, the narrator tells us, is the ancestor of the Ammonites (the name Ben-Ammi in Hebrew presumably means "Son of My People" or something to that effect). The narrator does not peek out from behind the scenes of the story to offer explicit comment on the scene—perhaps no such judgment is needed, because the story obviously casts the Ammonites in a bad light, the product of a deeply dysfunctional family and a drunken, incestuous drug-rape scene.

The Ammonites do not feature any further in the stories of the ancestors in Genesis. However, they appear in many geographical notices, stories of conflict in the wilderness before Israel settles the land of Israel, and in a few incidental details of various kinds. Numbers 21 describes the approach of the Israelites to the region east of the Dead Sea, where they confront a "King Sihon of the Amorites" who ruled over Heshbon (probably modern Hisban), possibly a city near or within the borders of ancient Ammon (at least in later periods; the story at hand would purportedly have taken place hundreds of years before we know of Ammon formally as a political entity, and the border between Ammon and Moab is not always clear).[21] The narrator of this story recounts how Israel

---

21. Larry G. Herr, "The Ammonites in the Late Iron Age and Persian Period," in *Ancient Ammon*, ed. Burton MacDonald and Randall W. Younker (Leiden: Brill, 1999), 219–237, here 220–221.

defeated Sihon and his people, and routed them up to—but not past—the border of the Ammonites at the Jabbok River, because, the narrator states, "the boundary of the Ammonites was strong." The Numbers 21 text includes a poem about the founding of Heshbon and the way that Sihon had defeated the Moabites farther south (vv. 27–30). The relationship between Sihon's "Amorites" and the "Ammonites" is unclear (but see Deut 2:16–25, where the narrator clearly sees Sihon/Heshbon and the Ammonites as distinct); the Amorites were a known group in the ancient Near Eastern world, but they have no clear historical overlap with the Ammonites of the eighth–sixth centuries BCE, at least.

The book of Deuteronomy is almost entirely framed as the final speech of Moses, the leader of the wilderness group out of Egypt, to the people of Israel. In the early chapters of Deuteronomy, Moses recounts the battles his group had faced while approaching their promised land, including some hitherto unknown reasons why Israel had not engaged the Ammonites or tried to take their land (Deut 2:16–22):

> Just as soon as all the warriors had died off from among the people, the LORD spoke to me, saying, "Today you are going to cross the boundary of Moab at Ar. When you approach the frontier of the Ammonites, do not harass them or engage them in battle, for I will not give the land of the Ammonites to you as a possession, because I have given it to the descendants of Lot." (It also is usually reckoned as a land of Rephaim. Rephaim formerly inhabited it, though the Ammonites call them Zamzummim, a strong and numerous people, as tall as the Anakim. But the LORD destroyed them from before the Ammonites so that they could dispossess them and settle in their place. He did the same for the descendants of Esau, who live in Seir, by destroying the Horim before them so that they could dispossess them and settle in their place even to this day . . .)

In the world of this text, God had given various small nations surrounding Israel their own land, including the Edomites, descendants of Esau in Seir, and also the Ammonites, who had apparently displaced a group of giants. The biblical term for these giants is "Rephaim," though here the author notes that the Ammonites have their own name for the group, "Zamzummim." What all of this tells us about the Ammonites is unclear. Deuteronomy 3 adds more information, telling us that Israel had indeed taken much of the land to the north, south, and west of Ammon, and that Og the king of Bashan was the only remaining member of the group of giant "Rephaim" mentioned in Deuteronomy 2:20–21. In Deuteronomy 3:11, we read this incidental detail:

> Now only King Og of Bashan was left of the remnant of the Rephaim. In fact his bed, an iron bed, can still be seen in Rabbah of the Ammonites. By the common cubit it is nine cubits long and four cubits wide.

How the biblical author came by this information is unknown, and scholars have debated the historical value of the references to the Ammonites in these texts and the relative date of their authorship.[22] If it is the case, as previously discussed, that the Ammonites were relatively unknown in any clearly datable historical source before the eighth century BCE, and reached the zenith of their notability only between the eighth and sixth centuries BCE, then it would stand to reason that the biblical descriptions of them in Genesis, Numbers, and Deuteronomy—not to mention the other references to the Ammonites in the Bible—also have their origins in this period. Of course, the groups of people who did settle in the region of Ammon after the breakdown of the Late Bronze Age city-state system may not have called themselves "Ammonites" by that name, but they still could have functioned as a political unit and thus they could be spoken of under titles that only appeared later.

22. E.g., Tyson, *Ammonites*, 131–132.

Having said that, we must ask about the degree to which the Hebrew Bible itself counts as a "source." It is, of course, a historically ancient source, and a valuable one at that; the questions regard its historical accuracy. If a biblical author living in the seventh century BCE wrote about events purported to occur six hundred years prior, we would have to engage with some hard questions. Did the author rely on sources? Oral memory? Could authors have "read back" realities contemporary to their own time into much earlier periods? Assyrian sources must be engaged on this same level—they distorted their own sources for all sorts of ideological reasons, and no serious historian would take everything ancient Assyrian kings said at face value. However, in the case of the Assyrian records, because of the nature of the texts—cuneiform writing on baked clay tablets, often uncovered in royal cities as part of an archive—we at least have the reasonable assurance that the source stands in close historical relationship to the events it describes. What motivation would an Assyrian scribe have for inventing details about the Ammonites and their tribute payments? In the case of Lot's daughter bearing the descendant of the Ammonites after a drunken rape scene in a cave in a time period possibly up to one thousand years earlier than we could reasonably think a biblical author wrote the story down, we would be hard-pressed by the basic rules of history to understand how a biblical author would possess this information with an acceptable degree of accuracy.

The Ammonites play an enemy role toward Israel during the period of the Judges, and this antagonistic relationship continues on into the monarchy, as the Ammonites oppress Israel during the reigns of Saul and David and ensnare Solomon with their illicit religion. The first sign of trouble appears in Judges 10, where we are told Israel worships

> the gods of the Ammonites. . . . Thus they abandoned the
> LORD. . . . So the anger of the LORD was kindled against Israel, and
> he sold them into the hand of the Philistines and into the hand
> of the Ammonites, and they crushed and oppressed the Israelites

that year. The Ammonites also crossed the Jordan to fight against [Israel] . . . so that Israel was greatly distressed. (Judg 10:6–9, excerpts)

The nature of this "oppression" is not clear; probably the narrator intends for us to think that the Ammonites not only dominated Israel militarily but also that the "gods of the Ammonites" ensnared Israel into false religious practice. The religious problem seems cyclical in Judges; at first, the Israelites do "evil" with regard to Ammonite deities, after which point the LORD "sold them" over into the oppression of the Philistines and Ammonites. The animosity toward Ammonite religion and prohibition against associating with the Ammonites makes itself known perhaps nowhere more bluntly than in the declaration of Deuteronomy 23:3–4:

No Ammonite or Moabite shall be admitted to the assembly of the LORD. Even to the tenth generation, none of their descendants shall be admitted to the assembly of the LORD, because they did not meet you with food and water on your journey out of Egypt.

The ensuing drama in Judges leads to the rise of a character named Jephthah (Judg 11–12), a story further evoking the themes from Numbers and Deuteronomy regarding the engagement with Ammon during the time of wilderness wandering. The elders of the Gileadite community—a territory east of the Jordan, bordering on Ammon—approach Jephthah in his capacity as a warrior and implore him to help them defeat the Ammonites, after which they pledge to make Jephthah their political leader. Jephthah immediately turns to parlay with the Ammonite king, asking about the origins of their conflict; the response gives us the purported speech of an unnamed native Ammonite ruler (Judg 11:13): "The king of the Ammonites answered the messengers of Jephthah, 'Because Israel, on coming from Egypt, took away my land from the Arnon to the Jabbok and to the Jordan; now therefore restore it peaceably.'" Jephthah responds with a very long speech, invoking the history of

Israel's travels and claiming that Israel's God had given Israel whatever land they took. Jephthah asks the Ammonites, "Should you not possess what your god Chemosh gives you to possess?" (Judg 11:24). The question presumes that Chemosh is the head deity of the Ammonites, though from other sources (including the Hebrew Bible), most scholars presume Chemosh to be more closely associated with the Moabites (e.g., Num 21:29; 1 Kgs 11:7; Jer 48:46), with no particular pride of place among the Ammonites. Whatever the case, Jephthah makes an infamous vow to the Lord: if he will gain victory over the Ammonites, then he will sacrifice the first thing that comes out of the door of his house when he returns— which ends up being his own daughter (Judg 11:29–40).

The Ammonites return to oppress Israel during the reign of Israel's first king, Saul. After the prophet Samuel anointed Saul king, a king of the Ammonites named Nahash—known to us only from this biblical story—appears on the scene with no introduction (1 Sam 10:27–11:2):

> Now Nahash, king of the Ammonites, had been grievously oppressing the Gadites and the Reubenites. He would gouge out the right eye of each of them and would not grant Israel a deliverer. No one was left of the Israelites across the Jordan whose right eye Nahash, king of the Ammonites, had not gouged out. But there were seven thousand men who had escaped from the Ammonites and had entered Jabesh-gilead. About a month later, Nahash the Ammonite went up and besieged Jabesh-gilead; and all the men of Jabesh said to Nahash, "Make a treaty with us, and we will serve you." But Nahash the Ammonite said to them, "On this condition I will make a treaty with you, namely that I gouge out everyone's right eye, and thus put disgrace upon all Israel."

The first half of this passage, incidentally, was not definitely known to scholars as part of the biblical account until the discovery of the so-called Dead Sea Scrolls, particularly a scroll called 4QSam[a], wherein the longer version of the biblical text (quoted in full above)

appears. From this probably more original version of the story preserved in the scroll, we learn that Nahash's acts of eye-gouging had
been going on before his siege of Jabesh-gilead, and the terms of
the treaty he offered were in line with his previous mutilations of
Israel. The story resolves when Saul grows enraged and decisively
defeats the Ammonites (1 Sam 11:11). The prophet Samuel invokes
the Nahash incident in one of his farewell speeches to the people,
chiding them for demanding a king like Saul based on their fear of
military oppression by groups like the Ammonites (1 Sam 12:12).

Further intrigue involving the Ammonites occurs in 2 Samuel
10, during the reign of David. Nahash—who had apparently been
alive up until this point? or another Nahash?—dies, and his son,
Hanun, succeeds him. Resolved to have a peaceful relationship
with Hanun and the Ammonites, as apparently he had enjoyed
(unlike Saul) with the father, Nahash, David sends an envoy to
Ammon. The Ammonites react suspiciously, dishonoring David's
men and eventually hiring the Arameans to join them to fight
against Israel. David's men rout both armies. In 2 Samuel 12,
David's army further routs the Ammonites, taking the city of
Rabbah of the Ammonites (Amman). David entered the city and
"took the crown of [the deity] Milcom from his head; the weight
of it was a talent of gold, and in it was a precious stone; and it
was placed on David's head" (2 Sam 12:30). Moreover, David
plundered "all the cities of the Ammonites," making its people
slaves.

Though the Ammonites do not oppose David's son Solomon,
their religion appears again as a snare to the worship of Israel's
God. Among the many foreign women Solomon loved and married were Ammonites (1 Kgs 11:1); perhaps because of their influence, the text tells us, Solomon followed "Milcom the abomination
of the Ammonites" and had a religious structure of some sort built
for "Molech the abomination of the Ammonites" (1 Kgs 11:6–7).
The names Milcom and Molech are built on the same Semitic root,
mlk, meaning "king, rule," and it is possible that the names are
variants of one another. Leviticus 20 mentions "Molech" several

times, seemingly as a deity to which someone might sacrifice their own child (see also 2 Kgs 23:10; Jer 32:35).

Various prophets speak out oracles of doom against the Ammonites, such as Amos:

> Thus says the LORD: For three transgressions of the Ammonites, and for four, I will not revoke the punishment; because they have ripped open pregnant women in Gilead in order to enlarge their territory. So I will kindle a fire against the wall of Rabbah, fire that shall devour its strongholds, with shouting on the day of battle, with a storm on the day of the whirlwind; then their king shall go into exile, he and his officials together, says the LORD. (Amos 1:13–15)

Whether Ammon's king suffered such a fate in history is unknown (see also Zeph 2:8–9, as well as Ezek 21 and 25 and Jer 49, predicting doom for Ammon). Though it is often assumed that the existence of the Ammonites ended around the same time as Israel's existence ended, during the early sixth century BCE through the incursion of the Babylonians, evidence may show that in fact the Ammonites continued on for some centuries.[23] After the destruction of the Temple in 586 BCE, the books of Jeremiah and Nehemiah record various episodes of intrigue involving the Ammonites. Jeremiah 40–41 recounts a story in which a certain Baalis, king of Ammon, sends a man named Ishmael to assassinate the Babylonian-appointed governor of the land in Israel, Gedaliah.[24] The books of Chronicles, which often run parallel to the books of Kings but which, most presume, were written decades or even centuries later, also provide supplemental material that mention the Ammonites paying tribute to Israelite kings

---

23. Herr, "Ammonites."
24. We may have confirmation of the existence of Baalis through an Ammonite inscription; Herr, "Ammonites," 230.

(e.g., 2 Chr 26:8; 27:5). In Nehemiah, a man named "Tobiah the Ammonite" becomes enraged that the Jews have been sent home to Jerusalem to rebuild the walls of their city, and tries (unsuccessfully) to prevent the restoration project from going forward. Given the fact that the Ammonites were known, from other sources, to be collaborators and allies with imperial powers like Assyria and Babylonia, it is not out of historical character to see biblical authors reflecting negatively on Ammonites and their political involvement in the region.

WHAT HAPPENED TO THE AMMONITES?

How long after the sixth century BCE would inhabitants of key sites in Ammon consider themselves "Ammonite"? Little is known about the formal demise of the Ammonite polity. In the end, perhaps the most compelling surviving testament to the power of the Ammonites remains in the name of Jordan's largest city, the contemporary capital of the nation: Amman.

Based mostly on biblical evidence (e.g., prophetic oracles of doom), scholars had for decades presumed that Ammon eventually rebelled against the Babylonian Empire and suffered destruction, resulting in their conversion into a "province" of that empire and under the subsequent Persian Empire (c. 539–333 BCE). Newer research, however, may suggest that in fact Ammon continued on with relatively little disruption, flourishing well into the fourth century BCE. Evidence from pottery and inscriptions that date to the late sixth century BCE (i.e., after the Babylonian destruction in the region) suggests that at least some scribes continued to write in the Ammonite script and language and perhaps some elements of the Ammonite community continued on at key sites unabated.[25] Other evidence suggests

---

25. Herr, "Ammonites," 227–228. See also Craig W. Tyson, "Josephus, *Antiquities* 10.18–182, Jeremiah, and Nebuchadnezzar," *Journal of Hebrew Scriptures* 13.7 (2013): 1–16.

Ammon was indeed a self-standing province in the Persian administrative system, and a seal impression may even give us the name of one of its officers, someone named "Shuba." The Ammonite language continued to appear in inscriptions from the Persian period, and pottery traditions in the region do not show a significant disruption at key sites like 'Umayri and Hisban.[26]

How long beyond the Persian period (e.g., after 333 BCE) we can continue to speak of anything that is distinctly Ammonite is unclear, though authors in later periods still referred to inhabitants of the region generally by traditional titles (such as "Ammonite"), and authors in much later periods could write of Ammonites in literature meant to reflect life as it was lived in earlier periods of Ammonite flourishing (eighth–sixth centuries BCE). In the books of Ezra and Nehemiah (middle or late fifth century BCE?), for example, the term "Ammonites" occurs alongside other indicators for Israel's neighbors in situations where the characters want to radically separate themselves from their neighbors on ethnic, linguistic, and religious levels. Ezra, for example, states that the

> people of Israel, the priests, and the Levites have not separated themselves from the peoples of the lands with their abominations, from the Canaanites, the Hittites, the Perizzites, the Jebusites, the Ammonites, the Moabites, the Egyptians, and the Amorites. (Ezra 9:1)

Nehemiah 13:1 records a memory (presumably) from the book of Deuteronomy that Israelites were not to allow Ammonites or Moabites into the "assembly of God," and in Nehemiah 13:23–24 the narrator laments the intermarriage he sees between Jews and women of Ashdod and Ammon. He goes on to decry the fact that Jews could not speak their own language, but rather "spoke the languages of various peoples."

---

26. Herr, "Ammonites," 233–234.

In the book of Judith (second century BCE?), a piece of historical fiction reflecting on a much earlier period involving Assyrian and Babylonian characters, a mercenary named Achior the Ammonite gives a long speech recounting the history of Israel, and ultimately ends up as an ally of Israel against the foreign powers. Achior is an exception, however, as the majority of the Ammonite army joins in the attack against Israel (Jud 7:17–18). In 1–2 Maccabees, also from the same time period, the narrator mentions battles against the Ammonites and people fleeing to "the land of the Ammonites." On the whole, these references suggest that a word like "Ammon" could be used to evoke notions of foreignness and otherness in the face of cultural pressures, perhaps at a time when "Ammonite" was not a living cultural reality.

5

The Moabites

THE BIBLICAL MOABITES ORIGINATE IN a less-than-noble
story in the book of Genesis, going on to become an enemy of
Israel throughout the monarchy and receiving sporadic prophetic
condemnation. However, in one sense, we might say that the
Moabites play one of the most nuanced roles of any of Israel's close
neighbors. The reason? The heroine of the book of Ruth has all
of its action centered upon the person and identity of a woman,
Ruth, who happens to be identified as "Moabite." No other biblical book besides Job focuses on a foreigner to Israel in this way,
and we have no other single account in the Bible of this length (or
anything close to it) outside of Ruth about a character from one
of the neighbor groups treated in this review of Israel's neighbors.
Unfortunately, for historical concerns and purposes of religious or
social comparison, the book of Ruth really does not tell us anything about the Moabites as such. Even so, the fact that Ruth the
Moabite becomes the great-great-grandmother of King David tells
us that biblical authors were able to see some of their neighbors in
familial terms, as an integral part of Israel's own story.

Much of the scholarly attention on the Moabites not filtered
through the Bible focuses on the Mesha Stele, a long inscription
commissioned by a Moabite king in the middle of the ninth century BCE. Since it is the longest text of its type from this time period originating from one of the smaller polities in the Levant, the
Mesha Stele offers an invaluable opportunity to look at a native
text and the views of the king, Mesha, who produced it. The stele
gives us native insight into Moabite religious and royal ideology,

Ancient Israel's Neighbors. Brian R. Doak, Oxford University Press (2020). © Oxford University Press.
DOI: 10.1093/oso/9780190690595.001.0001

and at the same time provides a large percentage of what we know of the Moabite language and dialect. Thus, we devote ample space to discussing this text.

THE ARCHAEOLOGY OF MOAB AND THE MOABITES

The heart of Moabite territory lies directly to the east of the Dead Sea; although rivers like the Zered in the south could have provided natural markers for Moabite territory in some periods, borders could fluctuate dependent on a number of factors, and at maximum, Moabite territory may have extended as far north as Heshbon and up to the southern border of Ammon (Fig. 5.1). Indeed, this northern border was much more ambiguous for Moab, and it created opportunities for conflicts with neighbors in the region.

The region's terrain varies from extremely steep cliffs rising up from the Dead Sea and river ravines to rough wilderness areas and high plains or tableland, suited to animal herding and limited forms of agriculture (such as "dry farming").[1] In the northern part of the country we find sites like Medeba (contemporary Madaba) and Diban (contemporary Dhiban), the latter becoming the capital of Moab at a certain point (probably beginning with King Mesha and his successors). In the southern region, cities like Aroer and Kerek (biblical Kir-Moab or Kir-hareseth) were prominent.[2]

1. Bruce Routledge, *Moab in the Iron Age: Hegemony, Polity, Archaeology* (Philadelphia: University of Pennsylvania Press, 2004), 48–57; Piotr Bienkowski (ed.), *Early Edom and Moab: The Beginning of the Iron Age in Southern Jordan* (Sheffield: J. R. Collis Publications, 1992).
2. Yohanan Aharoni, *The Land of the Bible: A Historical Geography*, rev. and enlarged ed., trans. Anson F. Rainey (Philadelphia: Westminster Press, 1979), 39–40.

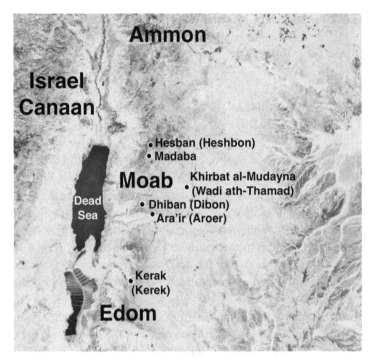

FIG. 5.1 Map of Moab; Map data ©2019 Google, with text added by the author.

Archaeological surveys throughout Moab for the early period of the Iron Age revealed only scant settlements and remains—it seems clear that between 1200 and 1000 BCE, Moab was not a notable entity in the region, though we do have an early reference to "Moab" by an Egyptian king, Ramses II (middle to late thirteenth century BCE), who recorded places where he enacted military campaigns.[3] Some northern sites that we might think to classify as

3. Routledge, *Moab*, 7; on the characterization of Iron I settlement in Moab, see Amihai Mazar, *Archaeology of the Land of the Bible, 10,000– 586 B.C.E.* (New York: Doubleday, 1992), 358–359.

Moabite, such as Jawa, Umayri, and Heshbon (Hisban), have been excavated, but the remains there could tie these locations more closely to Ammon than to Moab.[4] Though the archaeological picture overall is quite scarce, a few remains indicate that Moabites built a system of fortresses that could protect against desert invaders (nomadic groups). At Khirbat al-Mudayna (on the Wadi ath-Thamad), for example, on the eastern front of Moabite territory, a unique defensive fortress existed from around the eighth century BCE all the way into the Hellenistic period. Part of the fortress discovery from this Mudayna included a "proto-Aeolic capital," an architectural design flourish on pillars found throughout the region.[5]

When major empires like the Assyrians rolled into the region for conquest in the eighth–sixth centuries BCE, collecting plunder and allegiance, smaller entities like Moab had to make a decision: Would they rebel against the Assyrians, perhaps joining a coalition of other like-minded regional groups, or would they join the Assyrian cause and pay tribute? In the previous chapter, we discovered evidence that the neighboring Ammonites were very much joined with the Assyrians, providing military support and payment in return for the right to self-govern and Assyrian protection. As far as we can tell, the Moabites took up a similar strategy. Assyrian inscriptions mention the names of Moabite kings who paid tribute to the empire: Salamanu, Kammushu-Nadabi, Musuri, and Kamashkhalta. Other than their names and their role vis-à-vis the Assyrians—as reported by the Assyrians—we know very little

---

4. See the ongoing work of the Madaba Plains Project, https://www.madabaplains.org.

5. Ephraim Stern, *Archaeology of the Land of the Bible*, vol. 2: *The Assyrian, Babylonian, and Persian Periods, 732–332 BCE* (New York: Doubleday, 2001), 262–264. For updated details on the archaeology of the Mudayna ath-Thamad site, see Paulette M. Michèle Daviau and Margreet L. Steiner (eds.), *A Wayside Shrine in Northern Moab: Excavations in the Wadi ath-Thamad* (Oxford: Oxbow Books, 2017).

about these kings. As was also the case from Ammon, we know from excavations in Moab that many Assyrian-style buildings existed in the area, further suggesting Assyrian influence and cooperation.[6] Although so much remains that we do not yet know about Moabite territory and archaeology, we are fortunate in this case to have one of the most spectacular artifacts from any of Israel's neighbors (indeed, more spectacular in terms of an object of its type than anything from Israel, too). The so-called Mesha Stele or Moabite Stone (c. 840 BCE), discovered in 1868 squarely within ancient Moabite territory at Dhiban, is the longest single inscription from the Iron Age Levant. Indeed, it is the only such royal dedicatory inscription from a native king of its length, and it is unparalleled in its importance for understanding not only the Moabite king Mesha's political and religious views in the middle of the ninth century BCE in Moab, but also the Moabite language, the development of local writing scripts, and the development of prose narrative style in the region. The inscription reads as follows, in full:[7]

I am Mesha the son of Kemosh-yat[?] king of Moab, the Daibonite. My father reigned over Moab thirty years and I reigned after my father.

I built this altar platform for Kemosh in the citadel, an altar platform of salvation because he saved me from all the kings and because he gave me victory over all my adversaries.

Omri was king of Israel and he oppressed Moab many days because Kemosh was angry with his land. And his son replaced him and he also said, "I will oppress Moab." In my days he spoke

6. Stern, *Archaeology*, 259–260.
7. Adapted from Anson F. Rainey and R. Steven Notley, *The Sacred Bridge*, Carta's Atlas of the Biblical World (Jerusalem: Carta, 2006), 211–212. See also Routledge, *Moab*, 133–53, and Andrew Dearman (ed.), *Studies in the Mesha Inscription and Moab* (Atlanta: Scholars Press, 1989).

this way but I was victorious over him and his house and Israel suffered everlasting destruction.

But Omri conquered the land of Mehedeba and he dwelt there during his reign and half the reign of his son, forty years, but Kemosh returned it in my days. So I rebuilt Baal-maon and I made the reservoir in it and I built Kiriaten.

The man of Gad had dwelt in Atarot(h) from of old and the king of Israel built Atarot(h) for him. But I fought against the city and I took it and slew all the people, but the city became the property of Kemosh and of Moab and I confiscated from there its Davidic altar hearth [or: the altar-hearth of its beloved][8] and I dragged it before Kemosh in Kerioth, and I settled in it men of Sharon and men of Maharoth.

And Kemosh said to me, "Go! Seize Nebo against Israel," so I proceeded by night and I fought with it from the crack of dawn to midday and I took it and I slew all of it, seven thousand men and youths and women and maidens and slave girls because I had dedicated it to Ashtar-Kemosh. And I took the altar hearths of Yahweh and I dragged them before Kemosh.

And the king of Israel had built Yahaz and he dwelt in it while he was fighting with me, but Kemosh drove him out before me, so I took from Moab two hundred men, all of his best, and I brought them to Yahaz and I seized it in order to add it to Daibon.

I myself built for the citadel the "wall of the forests" and "the wall of the rampart" and I built its gates and I built its towers and I built a royal palace and I made the channels for the reservoir for water in the midst of the city. But there was no cistern in the middle of the city, in the citadel, so I said to all the people, "Make for yourselves each man a cistern in his house." And I hewed the shafts for the citadel with prisoners of Israel.

---

8. The phrase in question here, *'ryl dwdh*, has been the subject of debate. See Routledge, *Moab*, 237–238 n. 8, who favors the translation "the altar-hearth of its beloved [i.e., city-god]."

I built Aro'er and I made the highways in the Arnon. I built Beth-bamoth because it was in ruins. I built Bezer because it was a ruin. The men of Daibon were armed because all of Daibon was under orders and I ruled over one hundred towns which I had annexed to the land. And I built the temple of Madeba and the temple of Deblaten and the temple of Baal-maon and I carried there my herdsmen to tend the small cattle of the land.

And as for Hawronen, the House of David [?] dwelt in it while it fought with me and Kemosh said to me, "Go down, fight against Hawronen," so I went down and I fought with the city and I took it and Kemosh returned it in my days.

Then I went up from there to make . . . to do justice and I . . . [broken]

Of the many issues that we could discuss in this inscription, let us choose a few related to what it tells us about Moabite politics, religion, and narrative style.

This text provides us with our primary (and only extended) example of Moabite, a Semitic language—or dialect of a broader regional language—very similar to Hebrew but distinguished by its own script and a few grammatical features. Whether the Moabites truly had their own distinct language as opposed to a dialect is an open question. As the Russian linguist Max Weinreich famously put it, "A language is a dialect with an army and a navy." This would raise the question of whether the Moabites were truly a state. Did they have elements like borders, a standing army, a formal government, and a clear self-identity? Scholars have been divided about questions like these for smaller entities like Moab. On the one hand, there are clearly tribal elements at play, and an argument for decentralization, but on the other, evidence is present of increasingly formal categories and an administrative apparatus and self-expressions that might nudge us toward viewing Moab as something like a state or nation. One recent interpreter has made a strong case that in the Mesha Stele we find evidence that Moab was a "segmentary state," incorporating (rather than completely repressing) local or tribal identities beneath Mesha's political program of expansion and domination.[9]

The inscription's opening phrase, "I am Mesha," was a common type of beginning for a text in this genre, showing at once the speaker's self-awareness, his claim to significance, and the intentional engagement with the genre of royal inscription. The stele celebrates Mesha's military, political, and religious achievements—those of us who live in the democratic Western world may consider religion and politics to be categories that would ideally be separated, but clearly, for Mesha, these categories bleed into and fuel one another. Why was Israel able to oppress Moab for so long, according to the text? Because Kemosh, a major Moabite deity, was angry with the Moabites. And how was Mesha able to accomplish this turnaround of fortunes? As the inscription carefully narrates, by the direction and power of Kemosh (sometimes spelled "Chemosh," i.e., the chief deity of Moab). The battle Moab fights against Israel, according to the inscription, is clearly religious in nature—the Moabites seize "the altar hearths of Yahweh" and drag them "before Kemosh." The military victory, in this way of thinking, is also a battle of the gods, and the victor in battle shows their religious fidelity as a corollary to their tactical savvy. Modern readers will, of course, have a cynical take on language like this—but we should consider the possibility that Mesha really meant it and believed it, and saw himself in a fully functioning religious world populated with deities who could help him in the right circumstances.

On a political and historical level, the inscription narrates a step-by-step program of territorial expansion.[10] Mesha claims to have campaigned from his capital at Dibon (Dhiban), in the center of the territory, to the south, as far as Hawronen (Horonaim),

---

9. Bruce Routledge, "The Politics of Mesha: Segmented Identities and State Formation in Iron Age Moab," *Journal of the Economic and Social History of the Orient* 43.3 (2000): 221–256.

10. Rainey and Notley, *Sacred Bridge*, 203–204.

near the southeastern corner of the Dead Sea, all the way north to Ataroth, Jahaz, and several locations around Nebo at the far northeastern corner of the Dead Sea. Building projects abound after the conquest, including the construction of a citadel with gates and towers, and a reservoir in the city. Securing water for citizens is a basic civic need, but also resonated on deeply symbolic levels in the ancient Near Eastern imagination—flowing water had cosmic dimensions, showing a king as an ideal "garden keeper" of a pristine place where life could flourish.[11]

On a broader literary level, the Mesha text shows us how an author living in the region in the ninth century BCE put together an extended narrative that fused coherent ideologies of kingship, religion, geography, and propaganda. For those who study ancient Israel, this is no small feat, because scholars of the Hebrew Bible have long wondered (to no current consensus) how and when the Bible itself was first written, and under what conditions scribes could have produced the very complex political narratives we find in the books of Judges, Samuel, and Kings. Though the Mesha Stele is short compared with a biblical book, its dating to around 840 BCE is quite secure, and thus it shows us a sophisticated author using the space available on the artifact to tell a story. If a text like this existed, and was preserved by accident of its very durable medium (etched into stone), what other kinds of narrative prose might have been produced—and lost—on less durable media, like papyrus?

---

11. Lawrence E. Stager, "Jerusalem and the Garden of Eden," *Eretz-Israel* 26 (1999): 183–194, here 185–186. On the reservoir, see Jonathan Kaplan, "The Mesha Inscription and Iron Age II Water Systems," *Journal of Near Eastern Studies* 69 (2010): 23–29, and Bruce Routledge, "On Water Management in the Mesha Inscription and Moab," *Journal of Near Eastern Studies* 72.1 (2013): 51–64.

A few other inscriptions, all of them quite fragmentary and short, illuminate Moabite literary sensibilities.[12] Two other royal inscriptions, one at the base of a small statue from Kir-Moab and the other on a basalt cube, provide broken details mentioning the god Kemosh, taking prisoners, building projects, and a defeat of the Ammonites. An intricate stone incense altar, found among other religious objects near a city gate about 10 miles/16 km north of Dibon, reads as follows: "Incense altar which Elisama made, to add to the oracle house" (though the translation is debated). Clearly the craftsman took great pride in the object. A short legal text on papyrus—which many believe authentic but some suspect is a forgery—appeared on the antiquities market around 1990 and may have originated in the region of Moab and has been classified by some as Moabite due to the script on a seal that bound the document:

> Thus the gods spoke to Gera: To you belong the *marzeach* and the millstones and the house and Yis'a is alienated from them. And Malka is the depositary.

Though the content of this papyrus is quite pedestrian, the reference to a *marzeach* shows potential Moabite participation in a widely practiced religious ritual (the so-called marzeach), possibly akin to a Greek symposium or perhaps a funerary custom.

Aside from learning about Kemosh's prominent role as a deity through the Mesha inscription, what we otherwise know of Moabite religion is rather scattered. The name Kemosh appeared in many different formulations of personal names from the region, both for kings (Kemosh-yat, Kemoshshaltu, etc.) as well as others (Kemosh-el, Kemosh-zedek, etc.). In the case of warfare

---

12. Examples in Shmuel Ahituv, *Echoes from the Past: Hebrew and Cognate Inscriptions from the Biblical Period* (Jerusalem: Carta, 2008), 386–431.

against Nebo and Ataroth, the Mesha Stele mentions the concept of the *herem* ("ban, proscription"), that is, slaying all of the living beings in a city as an act of "holy war," to be dedicated to the deity. Such an act of warfare can also be found in the Hebrew Bible (Deut 20; Joshua), but the appearance of this same Semitic terminology in the Mesha Stele suggests Moabite participation in this ideology. The deity Kemosh continued to appear, in transformed ways, for centuries—as part of personal names and as a deity to be worshiped—on into the Hellenistic period.[13]

Presumably there were sacred spaces devoted to Kemosh and to the goddess Ashtar-Kemosh in Dibon itself (according to the Mesha Stele) and in surrounding areas, though for many years we had no clear evidence of a distinctly Moabite place of worship. However, archaeologists published material in 2010 suggesting an intricate religious site inside of a city wall at Khirbat al-Mudayna (ath-Thamad), northeast of Dibon in central Moab.[14] The area, measuring around 8 × 8 meters and accessed somewhat privately of an alleyway off sorts just inside the city gate, features architecture (such as a nice plastered bench) and objects (several intricate altars) that mark it off as sacred space. The space dates to the early eighth century BCE, and perhaps its most spectacular features are the finely carved stone altars (Fig. 5.2)—some with painting or other décor, and one inscribed for use at the "altar house" (*bet 'ot*).[15]

13. See Gerald L. Mattingly, "Moabite Religion and the Mesha Inscription," in *Studies in the Mesha Inscription and Moab*, ed. Andrew Dearman (Atlanta: Scholars Press, 1989), 211–238; Stern, *Archaeology*, 264–266; Collin Cornell, "What Happened to Kemosh?" *Zeitschrift für die alttestamentliche Wissenschaft* 128.2 (2016): 284–299.

14. P. M. Michèle Daviau and Margreet Steiner, "A Moabite Sanctuary at Khirbat al-Mudayna," *Bulletin of the American Schools of Oriental Research* 320 (2000): 1–21; P. M. Michèle Daviau and Paul-Eugène Dion, "Moab Comes to Life," *Biblical Archaeology Review* 28 (2002): 38–49, 63.

15. Others translate the inscription differently as: "[The] incense altar which Elishama made for YSP [a personal name], daughter of 'WT

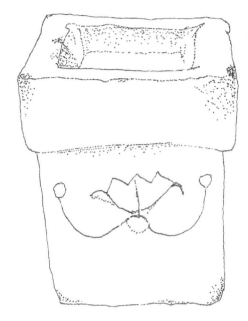

FIG. 5.2 Limestone altar from Khirbat al-Mudayna (ath-Thamad); eighth century BCE; after photo in P. M. Michèle Daviau and Paul-Eugène Dion, "Moab Comes to Life," *Biblical Archaeology Review* 28 (2002): 38–49, 63, here 43.

We have few examples of what could properly be called "Moabite art."[16] A stele depicting a warrior (the "Shihan Warrior Stele") with spear from Rujm al-'Abd may date to the twelfth century BCE or somewhat later (even as late as the eighth century), though the identity of the male figure depicted is unclear. Another stele, called the "Balu'a Stele," probably dates to a similar time period and depicts an ambiguous scene involving three figures

[another personal name]." See Ahituv, *Echoes*, 423–426, vs. Daviau and Steiner, "Moabite Sanctuary," 11.

16. Routledge, *Moab*, 178–182; Mattingly, "Moabite Religion," 222–225.

(Fig. 5.3). Though scholars continue to debate the meaning of the scene, it seems clear that they represent something of religious significance, perhaps with Kemosh standing at the center and his "consort," Ashtar-Kemosh, behind him to the right and a worshiper or priest or king (at left) approaching the couple.

Other small statues, seal impressions, and artifacts show us that Moabites produced images of various kinds, though we will have to await further excavations to get a clearer picture.

FIG. 5.3 At left, the Balu'a Stele," after photo at https://www.researchgate. net/figure/The-Balua-Stele-from-Jordan-Note-the-crescents-above-the-shoulders-of-the-central_fig5_303157891; at right, the basalt Shihan Warrior Stele from Rujm al-ʿAbd (twelfth–eighth century BCE?), after image online at https://www.louvre.fr/en/oeuvre-notices/stele-warrior-god (both retrieved on March 12, 2019).

MOAB AND THE MOABITES IN THE HEBREW BIBLE

Many of Israel's other geographical neighbors appear in the Bible's first book, Genesis, particularly in genealogies of Genesis 10, where a Table of Nations lists the peoples of the world descended from Noah's children as they spread across Asia and Africa. The Moabites receive no such explicit mention. However, ancestors or locations identified in the genealogy of Noah's cursed grandson Canaan in Genesis 10:15–20 mention the "families of the Canaanites" who "spread abroad," including those who settled "in the direction of Sodom, Gomorrah, Admah, and Zeboiim, as far as Lasha." Though the exact locations of these cities is in many cases unknown—or some of these locations may be purely legendary—in the biblical geographical imagination they would be located east of the Dead Sea, in territory that would more or less belong in the sphere of the Moabites.

Beyond this, the narrators of Genesis do provide us with an origin for the Moabites—one closely connected with the Ammonites. In Genesis 19:30–38, we learn of the adventure of Abraham's nephew, Lot, whose family ended up as refugees from the destruction of Sodom and Gomorrah—Lot's wife, famously, had turned into a pillar of salt for looking back at the burning cities (Gen 19:26). Lot is thus left alone with his two daughters, and refuses the asylum granted to him in the town of Zoar. Instead, the family settles in a cave, and the daughters quickly enact a plan to intoxicate their father and have sex with him—essentially a "drug rape" in today's terminology—so that they can bear children. Though contemporary readers might not be able to find reasons to justify this act by the daughters under any circumstance, there is perhaps for the biblical authors a type of turnabout in the sense that Lot had proposed these same daughters be offered up for rape to a mob back in Sodom (see Gen 19:8). The daughters enact their plan on two consecutive nights, and both become pregnant with sons, named Moab and Ben-Ammi (i.e., the Ammonites) (Gen 19:38).

"Ben-Ammi" presumably means "Son of My People," while "Moab" could be read, in Hebrew, to mean *m-* ("from") + *-av-* ("father") + *-i* ("my"), "From My Father." In other words, whatever the historical origin of the names, and whatever Ammonites and Moabites thought the names referred to, the biblical authors engaged in "folk etymology," drawing Ammon and Moab together in this shameful incident to make a blunt comment about their perception of the moral character of the people in the lineage of these families. In the spiritual imagination of Genesis, the origin of a people determines its destiny—and for Moab, that destiny will be, mostly, as an enemy of Israel.

Genesis 35 makes reference to an Edomite king defeating some entity named "Midian in the country of Moab," but beyond that in the Torah, the Moabites feature prominently in the stories of wilderness wandering in Numbers and Deuteronomy if for no other reason than simple geography. The Hebrews who escaped from Egypt must pass through the land of Moab on their way out of Egypt into the promised land of Israel/Palestine, as they journey northward on the eastern side of the Dead Sea region. How much of this territory should technically be considered Moabite during the putative time period of the exodus (c. 1250–1150 BCE?) is open to question—and sometimes biblical authors refer to characters or territories as "Moabite" in a rather general way (even though at times authors make very specific claims about Moabite territory, such as in Numbers 21:13, which cites the Arnon as "the boundary of Moab, between Moab and the Amorites"). Numbers 22–23 tells a story about a king of Moab, named Balak son of Zippor. Fearing that the wandering Hebrews would overrun his land, he hires a "seer" (a religious professional of some kind) to curse the Israelites named "Balaam son of Beor at Pethor, which is on the Euphrates, in the land of Amaw" (Num 22:1–6). Presumably, then, the biblical author sees Balaam living in the land typically allotted as Aramean, and Balaam was famous enough to draw attention for his skills. Rather than cursing the Israelites, however, Israel's God tells Balaam to bless the people, which he does, to the consternation of

Balak and the Moabites. The story then goes on to narrate Balaam's adventures, but since he's not really a Moabite, the role of Moab fades into the background—they are merely a group of people unsuccessfully trying to oppose Israel as they move through the land on the way to Israel/Palestine.

Later in the story, the Hebrews have sex with Moabite women (Num 25:1–16), and these sexual relationships are linked by the narrator, as they often are in the Bible, with religious apostasy: the people eat a sacrificial meal and worship "Baal of Peor," perhaps a local Moabite version of the Baal deity (a popular male god in the region). The incident reaches a severe climax (Num 25:6–9):

> Then an Israelite man brought into the camp a Midianite woman right before the eyes of Moses and the whole assembly of Israel while they were weeping at the entrance to the tent of meeting. When Phinehas son of Eleazar, the son of Aaron, the priest, saw this, he left the assembly, took a spear in his hand and followed the Israelite into the tent. He drove the spear into both of them, right through the Israelite man and into the woman's stomach. Then the plague against the Israelites was stopped; but those who died in the plague numbered 24,000.

The zeal of Phinehas later became a trope of faithfulness to the law, against mixing with the religions of other people and the perils of intermarriage (e.g., Ps 106:30; 1 Macc 2:26, 54; 4 Macc 18:12). The problem of worshiping "other gods," sometimes linked with intermarriage, comes up throughout the Hebrew Bible, and the Moabites are one of the early examples of this phenomenon.

The Moabite encounter with the exodus group continues to resound throughout the book of Deuteronomy—particularly because this exodus group, about to cross over into the land of Israel, stands perched on the east side of the Jordan River in the territory of Moab. At the end of Deuteronomy, the Hebrew leader Moses dies in Moab, and he is mysteriously buried there at an undisclosed location (Deut 34:5–6). In Deuteronomy 2, Moses recounts to the Israelites various things about Moab, specifically the Lord's commands not to harass or fight them along with some antiquarian notes about Moabite geography, history, and linguistics:

> When we had headed out along the route of the wilderness of Moab, the LORD said to me: "Do not harass Moab or engage them in battle, for I will not give you any of its land as a possession, since I have given Ar as a possession to the descendants of Lot." (The Emim—a large and numerous people, as tall as the Anakim—had formerly inhabited it. Like the Anakim, they are usually reckoned as Rephaim, though the Moabites call them Emim. . . .) (Deut 2:8–11)

A text like this raises fascinating questions about source material: How did the biblical author know that the Moabites called "Rephaim" by the name "Emim," and why would anyone care about this? Moreover, the passage evokes a notion of divine gift from Israel's God to the Moabites—the deity gives them their own land, at least Ar.

Lest one think that the Lord's attitude toward Moab is favorable, however, Deuteronomy 23:3–6 ensures by command that Moab can never be a friend of Israel:

> No Ammonite or Moabite shall be admitted to the assembly of the LORD. Even to the tenth generation, none of their descendants shall be admitted to the assembly of the LORD, because they did not meet you with food and water on your journey out of Egypt, and because they hired against you Balaam son of Beor, from Pethor of Mesopotamia, to curse you. . . . You shall never promote their welfare or their prosperity as long as you live.

The book of Judges continues themes of hostility between Israel and Moab. At this point in the Hebrew Bible's narrative, Israel has settled in their land but struggles to defeat their enemies. Among the first named enemies of Israel, a certain King Eglon of Moab oppresses Israel—he is not, however, presented as an autonomous agent but rather one who had been "strengthened" by the Lord in response to the evil activities of Israel (see Judg 3). The Moabites take land from Israel and oppress them for eighteen years, until a deliverer, Ehud, rises up and assassinates the king of Moab through a covert plot. After this deliverance, Israel rises up against Moab and defeats them in battle, purportedly killing ten thousand of their troops. Judges 10:6 mentions Israel worshiping "the gods of Moab," among other foreign gods, and thus abandoning the Lord. On the terms of the biblical authors, the primary deity of the Moabites is indeed Kemosh (Chemosh; see Num 21:29), the same deity mentioned in the Mesha Stele.

However, the book of Ruth (set "in the days of the Judges," but probably written much later) presents a potentially alternate view of the Moabites—one not predicated on total hostility but rather upon family adoption and genealogical identity. In this book, an Israelite couple named Elimelech and Naomi travel with their two sons to Moab to escape a famine. The sons marry Moabite women, named Ruth and Orpah, but all of the men in the family die—leaving Naomi alone with her two Moabite daughters-in-law. Naomi asks them to leave, and Orpah does, but Ruth insists on staying with Naomi and returning with her to the land of Israel, where the famine had subsided. Ruth's moving words in response to her mother-in-law emphasize the connection between deities and land in this context, as Ruth enacts a type of "conversion," stating, "Where you go, I will go. . . . Your people shall be my people, and your God my God" (Ruth 1:16). After the women return to Israel, Ruth meets an Israelite man, Boaz, and they marry and have a child, Obed. That child, the last few verses of the book tell us, becomes the father of Jesse, the father of David, who becomes the paradigmatic king of Israel (and by further extension in the New Testament, an ancestor of Jesus).

Thus, despite the Torah's negative view of the Moabites, the book of Ruth seems to celebrate the value of a Moabite woman. As one interpreter speaking from a postcolonial theoretical perspective puts it, "The author(s) of Ruth demonstrate that we can use history as a platform to correct the mistakes of past generations in our present moment for the sake of our progeny."[17] Some readers, however, may question whether Ruth remains truly "Moabite" in the book of Ruth. Does her "conversion" and the fact that she gives her child Obed immediately over to Naomi as nurse indicate that Ruth was no longer Moabite, and that the child somehow was (at least symbolically) no longer hers? Whatever the case, the book repeatedly refers to Ruth as "Ruth the Moabite," frequently emphasizing her identity as Moabite. This is astonishing, since it is particularly intermarriage and sex with Moabite women that Numbers 25 had treated with such harshness. Moreover, much later in the biblical story, in Nehemiah, the main actor—a Jewish leader named Nehemiah—recounts having to deal with the presence of Moabite people among the Jews who had returned to their land after exile:

> On that day they read from the book of Moses . . . and in it was found written that no Ammonite or Moabite should ever enter the assembly of God, because they did not meet the Israelites with bread and water, but hired Balaam against them to curse them . . . When the people heard the law, they separated from Israel all those of foreign descent . . . In those days also I saw Jews who had married women of Ashdod, Ammon, and Moab; and half of their children spoke the language of Ashdod, and they could not speak the language of Judah, but spoke the language of various peoples. And I contended with them and cursed them and beat some of them and pulled out their hair; and I made them take an oath in the name of God, saying, "You shall not give your daughters to their sons, or take their daughters for your sons or for yourselves." (Neh 13:1–3, 23–31, excerpts)

---

17. R. S. Wafula, *Biblical Representations of Moab: A Kenyan Postcolonial Reading* (New York: Peter Lang, 2014), 224.

Ezra 9:1 also mentions the problem of separation from many foreign groups, including the Moabites specifically, in a similar context. The memory of Balaam and the Moabites, the motif of intermarriage, and questions of the national language were thus very live issues for the early Jewish community in the fifth century BCE, when Ezra and Nehemiah were presumably written. Was the book of Ruth written contemporaneously with Ezra and Nehemiah, as an attempt to rehabilitate the status of Moabites within the community? Or if Ruth was written much earlier, did it preserve some sense of Moabite belonging that simply could not be erased, but which books like Ezra and Nehemiah tried to erase?[18]

In the books recording Israel's adventures during the period of the monarchy—1–2 Samuel, 1–2 Kings (with parallels in 1–2 Chronicles), and then many of the prophets—the Moabites do not play a major role, though they appear in gritty moments of political intrigue, religious apostasy, and battle. Saul fights Moabites and other neighboring groups (1 Sam 14:47), as do some of David's fighting men (2 Sam 23:20). First Kings 11 records Solomon's misadventure with foreign women; continuing the theme of intermarriage and religious failure with the Moabites from the book of Numbers, Solomon's love for Moabite women leads to idolatry as he worships "Chemosh the detestable god of Moab," among others (1 Kgs 11:7). This type of apostasy leads Israel's God to declare that he will split the country apart (1 Kgs 11:31–33). Thus we see a repeated theme regarding the religion(s) of Israel's neighbors: their ways are to be avoided at all costs, and failure on this front leads to divine punishment.

A point of overlap between the biblical story and what we know of Moab outside the Bible occurs in 2 Kings 3, when King

---

18. Samuel L. Adams, "The Book of Ruth as Social Commentary in Early Judaism," in *Figures Who Shape Scriptures, Scriptures That Shape Figures: Essays in Honour of Benjamin G. Wright III*, ed. Géza G. Xeravits and Greg Schmidt Goering (Berlin: de Gruyter, 2018), 127–139.

Mesha—presumably the same Mesha mentioned in the long Moabite inscription discussed earlier in the chapter—fights against Israel.

> Now King Mesha of Moab was a sheep breeder, who used to deliver to the king of Israel one hundred thousand lambs, and the wool of one hundred thousand rams. But when Ahab died, the king of Moab rebelled against the king of Israel. So King Jehoram marched out of Samaria at that time and mustered all Israel. (2 Kgs 3:4–6)

The text here presents Mesha as being under the political and military subjugation of Israel, then rebelling against that yoke when the powerful king Ahab dies. This comports with Mesha's story in his stele (even though Mesha claims he was victorious over Ahab during Ahab's life); recall that he states,

> Omri was king of Israel and he oppressed Moab many days because Kemosh was angry with his land. And his son [Ahab] replaced him and he also said, "I will oppress Moab." In my days he spoke this way but I was victorious over him and his house and Israel suffered everlasting destruction.

At any rate, in the biblical story the Moabites end up fighting a coalition of regional kings, including Israel's Jehoram and Judah's Jehoshaphat. Boosted by a prophet (Elisha) and some miraculous occurrences, Israel and Judah come to the brink of victory over Moab, when Mesha is said to have sacrificed his (unnamed) firstborn son and royal successor on the city wall at Kir-hareseth. The act apparently has such power that Israel was forced to withdraw.

In typical form, Israelite prophets launch invectives against Moab alongside other nations. Isaiah 15 is a good example, mentioning key Moabite cities and informing us that Moab will suffer destruction—while not really telling us anything else specifically about Moab. Jeremiah 48 relays a detailed condemnation of

Moab: Moab has deviously plotted against Israel, it has been proud and trusted in its military strongholds instead of obeying Israel's God, it has been at ease with its wealth while Israel suffered, indeed the Moabites have laughed at Israel through it all. Jeremiah's oracle ends, however, with a brief, ambiguous note of hope (vv. 46–47):

> Woe to you, O Moab! The people of Chemosh have perished, for your sons have been taken captive, and your daughters into captivity. Yet I will restore the fortunes of Moab in the latter days, says the LORD. Thus far is the judgment on Moab.

Ezekiel 25:8–11 repeats some of these judgments against Moab, and Amos 2:1–3 condemns Moab because "he burned to lime the bones of the king of Edom," an obscure reference to some act of aggression against another of Israel's neighbors, the Edomites.

WHAT HAPPENED TO THE MOABITES?

Moab seems to have ceased to exist sometime after the Babylonian campaigns in the region (sixth century BCE), though people continued to live the region and of course still do, in the contemporary nation of Jordan. Two aspects of the ongoing drama to define and understand Moab continue to appear in the biblical tradition after the Hebrew Bible: in the figure of Balaam and in the identity of Ruth. Balaam in particular continues on a complicated trajectory—first he is an agent of Israel's God in Numbers, but then later authors (Deut 23; Josh 13; 24) describe him as an outright enemy who tried to curse Israel. The New Testament follows this development, as Balaam is one who "loved the wages of doing wrong" (2 Pet 2), is known for "Balaam's error" (Jude 11), and is cited as the progenitor for idolatrous teaching (Rev 2). Ruth appears in Matthew's genealogy of Jesus, which serves as a reminder of the value of intermarriage with individuals from Israel's neighbors. On a more general level, the designation "Moabite" continued to function in roll calls of Israel's enemies on into early Judaism—for example, in the War Scroll, one of the Dead Sea Scrolls (c. second century BCE—first century CE), the Moabites are to participate alongside Edom, Ammon, Philistia, and others in an apocalyptic battle against Israel.

The Nabataeans, a desert group that flourished from the fourth century BCE to the first century CE, controlled trade routes in the region, and various Christian groups began to occupy parts of the territory once controlled by Moab after the first century CE. The site of Medeba (Arabic Madaba) in the northern part of ancient Moab houses a famous archaeological discovery—the Madaba Map, a floor mosaic created in the middle of the sixth century CE and rediscovered in 1896. The map was positioned in an important place within a Byzantine Christian church located at the site, and stands as the oldest map of its type in the world.[19] Muslims conquered the region in 636 CE. After centuries of rule under the Ottoman Empire, the modern boundaries of the nation of Jordan took shape after both world wars and a series of conflicts with the modern state of Israel during the 1940s–1970s.

The fact that Moab functioned, in the books of Numbers and Deuteronomy, as the final geographical staging ground for the Hebrews before they entered the promised land and became "Israel" has made the name "Moab" a symbolically meaningful designation for some groups who see themselves on the border of their own promised lands. The Moabit neighborhood in the Mitte district of Berlin, Germany, may have acquired its name from Huguenot refugees who settled there during the seventeenth or eighteenth century CE, and who saw the location in terms of a

---

19. Michelle Piccirillo, in *The New Encyclopedia of Archaeological Excavations in the Holy Land*, ed. Ephraim Stern (Jerusalem: Israel Exploration Society & Carta, 1993), 992–1001.

temporary residence, and the city of Moab, Utah, acquired its name by a similar process from Mormon settlers traversing the region.[20] One small but fascinating piece of Moabite identity—as the Bible reports it, at least—has made its way into the media culture of the twentieth and twenty-first centuries: the name Orpah, a Moabite woman from the book of Ruth. The cultural icon Oprah Winfrey was originally named "Orpah" (on her birth certificate), not Oprah, after the Moabite biblical character, but due to constant mispronunciation as "Oprah" and the fact that few understood the obscure biblical origins of the name, she took on the name Oprah.[21]

20. See entries in the *Dictionary of the Bible and Western Culture*, ed. Mary Ann Beavis and Michael J. Gilmour (Sheffield: Sheffield Academic Press, 2012).
21. Academy of Achievement interview with Oprah Winfrey, conducted February 21, 1991, www.achievement.org/autodoc/page/win0int-1.

6

The Edomites

THE GEOGRAPHICALLY SOUTHERNMOST ENTITY AMONG Israel's neighbors, the Edomites, appear in the Hebrew Bible in a fascinatingly close role to Israel—literally as Israel's twin brother. Edom appears in the Torah primarily in Genesis 25–26, but then also in Exodus 15, Numbers 20 and 24, and Deuteronomy 2 and 23. At times Esau/Edom is the bad guy, while other texts take a gentler tone, affirming the brotherly connection. In Deuteronomy God warns Israel not to harass or attempt to take any land in Edom, for God had given it to the Edomites. In Samuel–Kings, all of the major Israelite monarchs in the early period—Saul, David, and Solomon—engage in constant war with Edom. Preexilic prophets condemn Edom, and the exilic/postexilic tradition faults Edom for participating with Babylon in the destruction of the Temple (e.g., Ps 137; Obadiah; Ezek 25; 36). Most like its assessment of the Arameans, the biblical tradition thus acknowledges the familial bonds between Israel and Edom but at the same time blames Edom for various political infractions and disloyalty.

We know the names of some Edomite kings from Assyrian administrative texts in the eighth century BCE, a period of Assyrian domination generally over the region and during which Edom came under Assyria's orbit. The Edomites were similar to the Ammonites in that their fortunes improved during the period of Assyrian expansion, and Edom apparently managed to take disputed territory away from Judah in the southern Negev desert region. We do not have a plethora of Edomite written materials, and we have no royal inscriptions. However, a small number of native inscriptions attest

Ancient Israel's Neighbors. Brian R. Doak, Oxford University Press (2020). © Oxford University Press.
DOI: 10.1093/oso/9780190690595.001.0001

to the prominence of the deity Qos as the primary Edomite deity, and excavations at key sites such as Qitmit and En Hatzeva within the last few decades have revealed artifacts that help us begin to understand Edomite religion and iconography.

THE ARCHAEOLOGY OF EDOM AND THE EDOMITES

The ancient territory of Edom was situated to the southeast of the southern part of Israel, bordering on Israel only along the far southern desert boundary of the tribe of Judah. As with Moab and Ammon, the core of Edom lies within the contemporary political borders of the country of Jordan (though some sites associated with ancient Edom, such as Qitmit and Hazeva, are within contemporary Israel; see Fig. 6.1).

The region is particularly sparse, dry, and rugged. A line of mountains reaching heights of 5,600 feet/1700 meters runs south from the lower tip of the Dead Sea. Even though many of the shrub forests that once covered much of the western plateau areas are now gone, some still remain; pockets of cultivatable land could be found on these plateaus, and the thick shrub growth was perhaps the impetus for the etymology of a name for the region: "Mount Seir," that is, "the hairy mountain." As we will see in our discussion of the biblical story of Edom's most famous ancestor, Esau, the hairiness motif comes to play an important literary and theological role.

Of the three Transjordan groups—Ammon, Moab, and Edom—the region of Edom was the most sparsely settled, and its agricultural base the least able to support a major population.[1]

---

1. Øystein S. LaBianca and Randall W. Younker, "The Kingdoms of Ammon, Moab, and Edom: The Archaeology of Society in Late Bronze / Iron Age Transjordan (ca. 1400–500 BCE)," in *The Archaeology of Society in the Holy Land*, ed. Thomas E. Levy (London: Leicester University Press, 1995), 407.

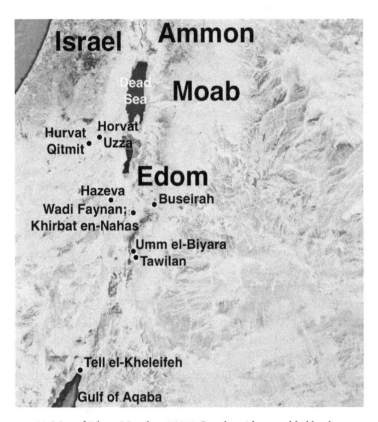

FIG. 6.1 Map of Edom; Map data ©2019 Google, with text added by the author.

This does not mean, however, that Edom was not a strong or sophisticated entity. The rugged landscape bordering on desert areas gave Edom a strategic military and trade advantage, as strongholds were easier to build and protect. Thus, the region's important copper mines and sparse oases were relatively easy to defend.[2] The social roots of the people who lived in Edom remain

2. Burton MacDonald, *The Southern Transjordan Edomite Plateau and the Dead Sea Rift Valley: The Bronze Age to the Islamic Period* (3800/

obscure, though most scholars trace the origins of the groups that developed in the Transjordan region to some kind of "tribal" arrangement. However informal their hierarchies may have been at points, Edom did develop a monarchy—Assyrian sources from the eighth century BCE mention the names of Edomite kings such as Qosmalku, Qosga, and Qosgabru. These were leaders strong enough to be considered "kings" (Edomite *mlk*) by the Assyrian empire, and they ruled over lands prosperous enough to offer taxes and supplies to the Assyrian Empire.[3] Along with the Ammonites, the Assyrians seem to have considered the Edomites to be local allies during the period of Assyrian imperial expansion in the seventh century BCE, and thus Edom flourished during this era while Israel and Judah suffered in various ways (e.g., the northern kingdom of Israel was destroyed by the Assyrians around 720 BCE, and the southern part of the country, Judah, was threatened between 730 and 700 BCE).

Indeed, the existence of Edom as a powerful regional entity seems coterminous with the rise of the Assyrians, though Egyptian references and other archaeological evidence from earlier times indicate scattered populations living in the area.[4] The major growth of Edom seems to have occurred particularly during the eighth and seventh centuries BCE, and the population in the region may have remained somewhat stable—even if the

3700 BC–AD 1917) (Oxford: Oxbow Books, 2015), chapter 1; Yohanan Aharoni, *The Land of the Bible: A Historical Geography*, rev. and enlarged ed., trans. Anson F. Rainey (Philadelphia: Westminster Press, 1979), 40–41; Ephraim Stern, *Archaeology of the Land of the Bible*, volume 2: *The Assyrian Babylonian, and Persian Periods, 732–332, BCE* (New York: Doubleday, 2001), 269; John R. Bartlett, *Edom and the Edomites* (Sheffield: JSOT Press, 1989), 33–54.

3. Stern, *Archaeology*, 268.
4. Edelman, "Edom," 9.

location of that population shifted—during the following periods of Babylonian and then Persian rule. Serious archaeology work in Edom began with Nelson Glueck's pioneering surveys in the Transjordan,[5] and subsequent work during the second half of the twentieth century and continuing on today at sites like Buseirah (probably Edom's capital), Tawilan, Tell el-Kheleifeh, Mezad Hazeva, the Wadi Faynan, and other locations have revealed tantalizing clues about the Edomites of the Iron Age.[6] More recent research at copper mines in Edom, such as those in the Faynan area, has showed that a large, nomadic population lived in the area to work in the mines. Specifically, the site of Khirbat en-Nahas was likely the largest copper smelting site in the region, and according to some assessments, the evidence from this region may indicate that these mines were used during a time period roughly overlapping with the Hebrew Bible's description of David and Solomon's activity vis-à-vis the Edomites.[7]

The Edomites used a writing system that is extremely similar to that used by other regional groups, such as the Moabites, Israelites, and Phoenicians. A leading scholar who analyzes the writing systems of groups in this region has recently suggested that a specifically Edomite script and literacy may have developed as early as the ninth century BCE.[8] Certain features of the letters may

5. Nelson Glueck, *The Other Side of the Jordan* (New Haven, CT: American Schools of Oriental Research, 1940).

6. Stern, *Archaeology*, 273–279; Piotr Bienkowski (ed.), *Early Edom and Moab: The Beginning of the Iron Age in Southern Jordan* (Sheffield: J. R. Collis Publications, 1992).

7. Thomas E. Levy, Mohammad Najjar, and Erez Ben-Yosef (eds.), *New Insights into the Iron Age Archaeology of Edom, Southern Jordan*, 2 vols. (Los Angeles: Cotsen Institute of Archaeology Press, 2014).

8. Christopher A. Rollston, "The Iron Age Edomite Script and Language: Methodological Strictures and Preliminary Statements," in *New Insights into the Iron Age Archaeology of Edom, Southern Jordan*, 2 vols., ed. Thomas E. Levy, Mohammad Najjar, and Erez Ben-Yosef (Los Angeles: Cotsen, 2014), 961–975,

signify a local variation on the writing script for both the Moabites and the Edomites.[9] The longest Edomite inscription we possess so far comes from ancient Horvat Uzza, a location east of what might traditionally be thought of as the "border" of Edom in the northeastern Negev desert of Israel but which nonetheless may have been occupied by Edomites in various periods (such as the sixth century BCE, when this inscription was likely written).[10] It is a short letter, and seems to concern a type of food used in a religious ritual for the Edomite deity Qos:

> Message of Lammelek, Speak to Bilbel: Is it well with you? Now I have blessed you to Qos. And now give the bread which is with Ahimmoh and Sha'ul shall offer it on the altar of Qos lest the bread become leavened.

The other more substantial inscription we have, also written in ink on a piece of potsherd, comes from Tell El-Kheleifeh, located at the northernmost tip of the Gulf of Elath (Aqaba). Dating to the seventh or sixth century BCE, this inscription is a list of personal names, many containing the element "Qos":

> Reuel
> Bad-Qos
> Shallum

---

9. Joseph Naveh, *Early History of the Alphabet: An Introduction to West Semitic Epigraphy and Palaeography*, 2nd rev. ed., reprinted (Jerusalem: Magnes Press, 1997), 101–105; David S. Vanderhooft, "The Edomite Dialect and Script: A Review of Evidence," in *You Shall Not Abhor an Edomite for He Is Your Brother: Edom and Seir in History and Tradition*, ed. Diana V. Edelman (Atlanta: Scholars Press, 1995), 137–157.

10. Translation of both of these inscriptions adapted from Shmuel Ahituv, *Echoes from the Past: Hebrew and Cognate Inscriptions from the Biblical Period* (Jerusalem: Carta, 2008), 351–356.

Qos-banah
Pega-Qos
Nedab-Qos
SKK
Rapu'
Pega-Qos
Qos-nadab

These are presumably the names of Edomites, but little is known about their identity otherwise or why this inscription was made.

Most scholars presume that the primary Edomite deity was named Qos (or Quas), based on the frequency with which that name appears in theophoric names (i.e., names bearing the name of a deity) of Edomites.[11] Already in the thirteenth century BCE, Egyptian lists recording the names of various groups of Shasu (Semitic-speaking nomadic people in the region that later became Edom) contain several names such as "Qos is my shepherd," "Qos is verily exalted," and "Qos is my friend." The etymology of the name Qos may be connected with the "bow," as in the weapon a major male deity might carry, though the bow can also be connected with animals and hunting. Edomite kings also frequently had the name Qos as part of their own names, and the inscription from Horvat Uza has the sender of a letter blessing the recipient in Qos's name. Probably beginning around the eighth century BCE, when the Edomites had a more formal political organization, the deity Qos was adopted as the divine sponsor of the polity. The use of Qos in personal names remained popular for king and commoner alike in the region for hundreds of years, persisting through the Hellenistic period and even into the Common Era—an inscription records the dedication of an object to Qos from the second or third century CE. Thus, it is reasonable to conclude that Qos was a

11. Ernst A. Knauf, "QÔS," in *Dictionary of Deities and Demons in the Bible*, ed. Karel van der Toorn, Bob Becking, and Pieter W. van der Horst, 2nd ed. (Leiden: Brill, 1999), 674–677.

popular regional deity for around fifteen hundred years. However, the meager evidence we have for Edomite religion should caution us against making far-reaching conclusions about the identity of Qos vis-à-vis the Edomites. We could fall victim to circular reasoning, where it is assumed that all Edomites worshiped Qos, and everywhere that we find a Qos name or Qos worship, then that place is labeled Edomite.[12]

Two archaeological discoveries shed light on what could be "Edomite" religion in spectacular (even if enigmatic) ways: at Hurvat Qitmit, an isolated site on a hill just south of the Israelite city of Arad in the Negev desert, and further south, also in the desert, at Hatzeva.[13] Though the site of Qitmit may appear on a map to be within the orbit of Israelite territory, some believe it was under Edomite control during the first half of the sixth century BCE, which is the era of the use of the shrine uncovered there. Qitmit had two buildings, and the style of the structures there differs from what we know of Israelite architecture during this time. Ash deposits with animal bones marked a site of sacrifice, and many cultic implements such as clay stands, animal figures, and anthropomorphic statues played some role in religious worship. Hollow clay vessels were shaped in the form of a bearded male—is this the deity Qos, or a human worshiper? Since some of these clay objects had inscriptions of dedication to Qos, we can

---

12. J. Andrew Dearman, "Edomite Religion. A Survey and an Examination of Some Recent Contributions," in *You Shall Not Abhor an Edomite for He Is Your Brother: Edom and Seir in History and Tradition*, ed. Diana V. Edelman (Atlanta: Scholars Press, 1995), 119–136, here 120–121.

13. Itzhaq Beit-Arieh, "The Edomite Shrine at Horvat Qitmit in the Judean Negev Preliminary Excavation Report," *Tel Aviv* 18 (1991): 93–116; Itzhaq Beit-Arieh and Pirhiya Beck, *Edomite Shrine: Discoveries from Qitmit in the Negev* (Jerusalem: Israel Museum, 1987); Othmar Keel and Christoph Uehlinger, *Gods, Goddesses, and Images of God in Ancient Israel*, trans. Thomas H. Trapp (Minneapolis: Fortress Press, 1998), 382–385; Stern, *Archaeology*, 280–288.

assume Qos was worshipped at the site, possibly along with an unknown female deity. A fascinating three-horned head of a figure with large eyes—perhaps a god or goddess—was also found at the site (see Fig. 6.2). Also at Qitmit, archaeologists found various animal images, including many of ostriches. As a desert animal, the ostrich could represent all that was untamed and strange in that landscape, and perhaps the deity Qos or some other element of worship at the site was connected with the ostrich.

At En Hatzeva, excavated in 1993, archaeologists found a long, narrow religious structure located outside of a military fort located at the same site, dating to the seventh or sixth century BCE. Over seventy objects lie crushed in a pit inside the religious structure,

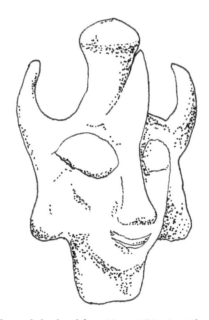

FIG. 6.2 Three-horned clay head from Hurvat Qitmit; sixth century BCE; after photo in Ephraim Stern, *Archaeology of the Land of the Bible*, vol. 2: *The Assyrian, Babylonian, and Persian Periods, 732–332 BCE* (New York: Doubleday, 2001), 283 fig. I.112.

including several stone altars and many other clay objects, some quite similar to those found at Qitmit. The objects may have been intentionally destroyed, to put them out of mundane use (*favissa*). Several intricate hollow objects in the shape of human beings stand out for their detail—with hands sticking out, differentiated locks of hair, and even some bits of reddish paint clinging to the figures.

As with Qitmit, the style of objects and architecture at En Hatzeva does not match those of Israel/Judah to the northeast, and it seems reasonable to associate the site with Edomites and their religion. Even if this assumption is correct, however, there remain significant unanswered questions about who worshiped at these

FIG. 6.3 Front and side view of a clay figure from Hatzeva; seventh–sixth century BCE; after photos in Ephraim Stern, *Archaeology of the Land of the Bible*, vol. 2: *The Assyrian, Babylonian, and Persian Periods, 732–332 BCE* (New York: Doubleday, 2001), 284–85, fig. I.114.

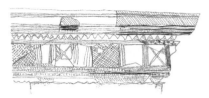

FIG. 6.4 Examples of Edomite pottery decoration from Kadesh Barnea; Iron Age; after drawings in Ephraim Stern, *Archaeology of the Land of the Bible*, vol. 2: *The Assyrian, Babylonian, and Persian Periods, 732–332 BCE* (New York: Doubleday, 2001), 291, fig. I.118.

sites, which deities were worshiped, and what identity the native worshipers would have ascribed to themselves.[14]

Although in archaeological circles it is often said that "pots do not equal people"—in other words, we should always be cautious about identifying an ancient people group based only on the pottery they used—it is also true that pottery usage was typically conservative in the ancient Levant, and many groups did have distinct styles. For the Edomites, a unique style of pottery has been found at many sites, divided into two groups: undecorated, and decorated (usually) with geometric patterns marked with black, red, brown, and white paint (Fig. 6.4).[15]

Scientific analysis of the clay from which selections of Edomite pots were made demonstrates that the clay was local, from the Negev desert, and thus we can assume this pottery was truly native to Edomite artisans.

14. Dearman, "Edomite Religion," 120–123.
15. Stern, *Archaeology*, 288–292.

EDOM AND THE EDOMITES IN THE
HEBREW BIBLE

Unlike some other neighbors of Israel, the genealogists who produced the Table of Nations in Genesis 10 made no reference to the Edomites. Rather, our introduction to Edom appears through the character of Esau—the twin brother of Jacob. How are "Esau" and "Edom" connected, for the biblical authors? Consider the following stories. First, we meet the baby Esau in the birth narrative of the twins:

> And the LORD said to [Rebekah], "Two nations are in your womb, and two peoples born of you shall be divided; the one shall be stronger than the other, the elder shall serve the younger." When her time to give birth was at hand, there were twins in her womb. The first came out red, all his body like a hairy mantle; so they named him Esau. Afterward his brother came out, with his hand gripping Esau's heel; so he was named Jacob. Isaac was sixty years old when she bore them. (Gen 25:23–26)

Already at birth we see a struggle between the sons—who are actually already, instructively, called "nations" and "peoples." The reference here to the sons as "nations" prefigures the fact that Jacob will later be renamed as "Israel" (Gen 32:28; 35:10), as in the nation of Israel, and his children will comprise the bulk of the twelve tribes of Israel. The fact that Esau comes out of the womb "out red, all his body like a hairy mantle" gestures toward Edom in two ways: (1) the Hebrew word for "red" in this text, *admoni*, partly sounds like the word "Edom," and may also refer geographically to the red sandstone characteristic of the desert region of Edom; (2) the "hairy" body baby Esau has (Hebrew *se'ar*) invokes another biblical name for the region of Edom, *Se'ir*.

The connection between Esau and Edom becomes completely explicit in the first scene involving the twins as adults:

> Once when Jacob was cooking a stew, Esau came in from the field, and he was famished. Esau said to Jacob, "Let me eat some of that red stuff, for I am famished!" (Therefore he was called Edom.) Jacob said, "First sell me your birthright." Esau said, "I am about to die; of what use is a birthright to me?" Jacob said, "Swear to me first." So he swore to him, and sold his birthright to Jacob. Then Jacob gave Esau bread and lentil stew, and he ate and drank, and rose and went his way. Thus Esau despised his birthright. (Gen 25:30–34)

Esau's apparently hasty request to eat "some of that red stuff" again references the connection among the color red (of the stew), the Hebrew word for red, the word Edom, and the geography of Edom—and the narrator here makes all of this wordplay the source for calling Esau "Edom." Overall, the story does not make Esau look very smart—he sells his birthright for a mere pot of lentils—and, combined with the famous account in Genesis 27 where Jacob steals their father Isaac's blessing of the firstborn (intended for Esau), Esau/Edom seems altogether denigrated from the start. We might compare this phenomenon of origins equaling fate with the Canaanites, Ammonites, and Moabites, all of whom come from ignoble beginnings and all of whom go on to be enemies of Israel. The pattern becomes quite predictable.

In the case of Esau/Edom, however, the Hebrew Bible has a longer and subtler story to tell. The tale of Esau losing the fatherly blessing to Jacob through Jacob's trickery could evoke sympathy for Esau as a character in the narrative—and Jacob does not get off without penalty either, as he gets tricked by his father-in-law Laban in the land of Aram (Gen 29). Isaac's deathbed words to Esau, while negative, also encode an ambiguous promise that Esau would come out from under Jacob's domination:

> See, away from the fatness of the earth shall your home be, and away from the dew of heaven on high.

> By your sword you shall live, and you shall serve your
> brother;but when you break loose, you shall break his yoke from
> your neck. (Gen 27:39–40)

When the two brothers meet again, years after Jacob's initial tricks, Esau seems ready to kill Jacob, perhaps justifiably, and may have done so had Jacob not come to his older brother with a load of gifts and verbal flattery (Gen 32:1–33:17). The brothers then go their separate ways—Esau south on to Seir (Edom), and Jacob north to Succoth, on the way to the land that would later become Israel—without any particular judgment on Esau for traveling where he does. Both Esau and Jacob bury their father, Isaac, in Genesis 35:29. Esau had married Hittite women, who made life bitter for his parents, Isaac and Rebekah (Gen 26:34–35), but then in Genesis 36 Esau receives a very long and detailed genealogy, which begins this way:

> These are the descendants of Esau (that is, Edom). Esau took his
> wives from the Canaanites. . . . Then Esau . . . moved to a land some
> distance from his brother Jacob. For their possessions were too
> great for them to live together; the land where they were staying
> could not support them because of their livestock. So Esau settled
> in the hill country of Seir; Esau is Edom. (Gen 36:1–8, excerpts)

The text renarrates the split between the brothers, citing their numerous possessions as the reason they do not live together—not an explicit theological or moral reason (compare with Abraham and Lot in Gen 13)—and then, again, affirming the identity between Esau and Edom.[16]

---

16. Several details in the Genesis 36 genealogy differ regarding Esau's wives, compared with Genesis 26:34–35; perhaps the material here comes from a separate source? Biblical scholars often attribute variation like this to different underlying source material or different authors contributing to the story; see various kinds of analysis along

The rest of Genesis 36 offers a lengthy list of Edomite clans and kings, the names of which are obscure and difficult to correlate with anything we know from outside the Bible about Edom. In Genesis 36:40–43, the list mentions Esau specifically, and ends with this summary: "these are the clans of Edom (that is, Esau, the father of Edom), according to their settlements in the land that they held." Why did the narrator add this note about Esau's identity as Edom's "father" yet again? It could be that this was a traditional way to "bookend" the genealogy (see also Gen 36:1)—or it could be that some later editor took an existing genealogy and integrated the name of Esau into it, affirming Esau's identity as Edomite. If so, what we see in the Bible here is a complex process, whereby traditional stories and characters get linked with genealogical information by a process of reverse engineering. In other words, authors living long after characters like Jacob and Esau would have lived (presuming they were historical at all) took *their own* experiences during later periods (say, between the tenth and sixth centuries BCE) and read those experiences back into traditional stories about Israel's ancestors, weaving in details and connection that were the result of those later experiences.

Taking a broader view of Edom/Esau in the Torah and the books narrating Israel's settlement in the land (Joshua and Judges), we find a variety of images. In Numbers 20, the Hebrew slaves who had escaped from Egypt approach the land of Edom as part of their journey on the east side of the Jordan River toward their promised land. The Edomites send Moses and the people a message,

these lines and on Edom in general in Diana V. Edelman, ed., *You Shall Not Abhor an Edomite for He Is Your Brother: Edom and Seir in History and Tradition* (Atlanta: Scholars Press, 1995); Bert Dicou, *Edom, Israel's Brother and Antagonist: The Role of Edom in Biblical Prophecy and Story* (Sheffield: JSOT Press, 1994); John F. A. Sawyer and David J. A. Clines, eds., *Midian, Moab and Edom: The History and Archaeology of Late Bronze and Iron Age Jordan and North-West Arabia* (Sheffield: JSOT Press, 1983).

refusing them passage through their territory (Num 20:14–21). Judges 11:17–18 essentially repeats this story, in truncated form. However, Deuteronomy 2 presents a different picture, with a different tone. Apparently recounting the same incident as Numbers 20, Moses now casts the encounter this way:

> You are about to pass through the territory of your relatives the descendants of Esau, who live in Seir. They will be afraid of you, but be very careful. Do not provoke them to war, for I will not give you any of their land, not even enough to put your foot on. I have given Esau the hill country of Seir as his own. You are to pay them in silver for the food you eat and the water you drink. . . . So we went on past our relatives the descendants of Esau, who live in Seir. (Deut 2:1–8, excerpts)

Here we find an attitude similar to the way Moses in Deuteronomy speaks of the Moabites as well—God has given these two neighboring nations their land, and therefore they are not to be harassed. In the case of Edom, God even affirms the identity of Edom as Israel's "relatives." Later, Moses instructs the people, "You shall not abhor any of the Edomites, for they are your kin" (Deut 23:8). The book of Joshua follows the line of thought from Deuteronomy, where Esau's right to possess Seir is again emphasized: "to Isaac I gave Jacob and Esau. I gave Esau the hill country of Seir to possess, but Jacob and his children went down to Egypt" (Josh 24:4).

How might we account for this different tone in Deuteronomy? Most biblical scholars see the book of Deuteronomy as the product of a time period much later than the exodus and wilderness period itself, and perhaps later than many other materials in the Torah. In the classic formulation, scholars suggested that some of the earlier sources in the Torah date to around 1000–800 BCE, while the book of Deuteronomy took shape during the 600s BCE. If this were true, then we could understand the differing views of Edom reflected in different time periods. Perhaps some eras were tense, and that is reflected in the literature of conflict, and other texts came from periods that saw an attempt to honor Edomite identity alongside Israel (e.g., Deut 2).

The books of Samuel and Kings portray the kings of the United Monarchy—Saul, David, and Solomon—as being in constant conflict with Edom, which continues throughout the later monarchic period as well. Saul fights the Edomites (1 Sam 14:47), and commands a man named "Doeg the Edomite" to slaughter Israelite priests (1 Sam 22). David slaughters many Edomites, and sets up military outposts throughout Edom to mark his victory (2 Sam 8). Solomon sets up a fleet of ships at a harbor on the Red Sea, presumably in what had been Edomite territory at Ezion-geber (1 Kgs 9:26). The résumé of King Solomon's legendary wealth in 1 Kings 10 has suggested to some that Solomon had exploited a series of mines—perhaps correlated with the copper mines we know of from the Faynan region—through his domination over Edom. The Bible mentions very little about copper, however, and no connection at all between Solomon and Edomite mines. Perhaps biblical narrators received some tradition about Solomon's wealth and attributed that to commerce with the coastal Phoenicians, with mountains of gold delivered on the "ships of Tarshish" that the king had allegedly procured (1 Kgs 10:14–22). An individual named Hadad the Edomite later rises up against Solomon (1 Kgs 11:14–17), part of a divine punishment against the king for his marital entanglements with foreign women, including Edomites (1 Kgs 11:1). In 2 Kings 3, an anonymous king of Edom joins Israel and Judah in battle against Moab. Amaziah, cited as a righteous king by the narrator, also defeats many Edomites (2 Kgs 14), though the king is chided for his pride associated with the victory. Our assessment of these passages as historians cannot be very certain; many of these events and details seem possible, but we have no evidence for them outside of the Bible. A rather offhanded reference to Edom in 1 Kings 22:47–50, involving a deputy king ruling over Edom during the time of Jehoshaphat, would be quite strange if it were not in fact something that the author thought was reliable and had some basis in a source from the time period in question (around the middle of the ninth century BCE).

Other texts present Edom in a state of revolt or victory over Israel, particularly from later periods of Israel's existence as a nation with a king. Edom's rebellion against Judah, recorded in 2 Kings 8:20–22, may reflect Isaac's words to Esau in Genesis 27.[17] 2 Kings 16:6 presents a situation where, during a time of civil war between the northern and southern parts of Israel, the Edomites recover territory they had previously lost (Elath), driving out the Judeans (from the southern part of the country). The narrator then notes that the Edomites live in Elath "to this day," presumably in the contemporary time of the author (sixth century BCE?). Thus, it seems reasonable to assume that the political dynamic between Israel/Judah and Edom moved in various directions, and that during the period of Assyrian imperial domination in the region (reflected in 2 Kgs 16), the Edomites would have benefited since they allied themselves with the empire—a fact we know from sources outside of the Bible. Even a snippet of material in Chronicles—which is otherwise parallel to the information in Samuel–Kings—preserves a picture of conflict with Edom involving Assyrian involvement: "At that time King Ahaz sent to the king of Assyria for help. For the Edomites had again invaded and defeated Judah, and carried away captives" (2 Chr 28:16–17).

Prophetic voices from the eighth century BCE heaped abuse upon the Edomites. Isaiah 34 speaks of God's sword descending upon Edom, and compares a great slaughter there to a religious sacrifice—"her land shall become burning pitch" (Isa 34:9). Amos enigmatically speaks of other neighbors of Israel (Philistia, the Phoenicians) delivering captives over to Edom, and specifically cites the ideal "brotherly" relationship between Jacob/Israel and

17. John Bartlett, "Edom in the Nonprophetical Corpus," in *You Shall Not Abhor an Edomite for He Is Your Brother: Edom and Seir in History and Tradition*, ed. Diana V. Edelman (Atlanta: Scholars Press, 1995), 13–21, here 16–17.

Esau/Edom as grounds for anger at the fact that the brotherhood had been violated by a lack of mercy from Edom (Amos 1:11). Amos also castigates the Moabites for a transgression against Edom: "because he burned to lime the bones of the king of Edom" (Amos 2:1). Which king, and what this lime burning signifies, are unclear. However, at the end of the book, Amos seems to predict that "the remnant of Edom" may be included in "all the nations who are called by my name" (i.e., the Lord's name), provided that the fallen "booth of David" is repaired and Israel retakes whatever was allotted to them among the Edomites (Amos 9:11–12). Later voices from the late seventh and early sixth centuries BCE, particularly Jeremiah and Ezekiel, mention strife between Israel and Edom, and predict calamity for Edom because of their actions (e.g., Jer 49:7–20).

Of particular interest for biblical authors in the sixth century BCE are the events surrounding some perceived involvement Edom had in the destruction of Jerusalem and the Temple there in the year 586 BCE. Outside of the Bible, the Arad ostraca—fragmentary inscriptions from a fortress in the Negev desert bordering on Edom from the years leading up to Babylonian incursion—refer to an Edomite threat and presence in the region even before the events of 586 BCE, suggesting the collision with the Edomites was not merely an invention of biblical authors after 586 BCE.[18] Though the Babylonians, directly, destroyed the Temple and took captives to Babylon, biblical authors saw Edom playing some role. Ezekiel speaks of Edom acting "revengefully against the house of Judah" (Ezek 25:12–14), and later refers to Edom acting "with wholehearted joy and utter contempt," taking "my land as their possession, because of its pasture, to plunder it" (Ezek 36:5). Though a very short book, Obadiah is entirely devoted to reporting the transgressions of Edom in this infamous

18. Dennis Pardee, "Arad Ostraca," in *The Context of Scripture III: Archival Documents from the Biblical World*, ed. W. W. Hallo and K. L. Younger (Leiden: Brill, 2003), 81–85, esp. letters 24 and 40.

event. However, in Obadiah, the crime seems to be a *lack* of doing something, failing to help, of "standing aside" as the Babylonians plundered (vv. 9–11). Psalm 137:7 directly cites the Edomites for their words: "Remember, O LORD, against the Edomites the day of Jerusalem's fall, how they said, 'Tear it down! Tear it down!'" Writing in an indeterminate period—but presumably reflecting a period in the wake of Jerusalem's destruction—Malachi recalls the brotherhood story of Jacob and Esau to make a stunning declaration:

> I have loved you, says the LORD. But you say, "How have you loved us?" Is not Esau Jacob's brother? says the LORD. Yet I have loved Jacob but I have hated Esau; I have made his hill country a desolation and his heritage a desert for jackals. If Edom says, "We are shattered but we will rebuild the ruins," the LORD of hosts says: They may build, but I will tear down, until they are called the wicked country, the people with whom the LORD is angry forever. (1:2–4)

The book of Job seems to occur squarely within Edom, featuring all Edomite characters (including the main character, Job himself). The area may have been renowned for its wisdom traditions and writing, though none of that exists in native form today. The fact that the wisdom of Job's friends falls flat in light of the divine speech that closes out the book (Job 39–42) may cast doubt on Edom's claim to wisdom, but Israel's religious connection with the region comes in the form of poetic references scattered throughout the Hebrew Bible. In these poems, sometimes thought to be linguistically archaic, Israel's God is said to have marched forth from the region of Edom/Seir (Deut 33:2; Judg 5:4; and Isa 63:1). Indeed, some of the earliest references to the deity YHWH ("Yahweh," the name rendered as "the LORD" in contemporary Bible translations) appear in Egyptian documents from the fourteenth century BCE, and refer to a region or deity (or both combined) that probably can be identified with the area that later became Edom and the land of Midian (overlapping with Edom). Some scholars have come up with a "Midian hypothesis," a theory to explain how an earlier religious tradition about Yahweh from this Edomite or Midianite region spread, through Moses's father-in-law, the Midianite priest Jethro/Reuel (Exod 3:1; 18:1), on to Israel.[19] If there were any credence to this theory, then the close relationship between Israel and Edom that the Bible reflects would have very ancient and deep roots.

WHAT HAPPENED TO THE EDOMITES?

All of Israel's neighbors continued to exist, as land and people in some form, after the biblical period—though some, along with Israel, lost their name and whatever sense of national identity they may have had during the first millennium BCE. The Edomites stand as one exception here insofar as the name "Edom," transformed into Greek as "Idoumaia" and Latin as "Idumaea/Idumea," survived well into the Hellenistic period (beginning in the fourth century BCE) and beyond into Roman times.[20] Though the territory of Idumea did not overlap perfectly or entirely with the former Iron Age entity of Edom, the term "Idumea" described land directly to the south of Judah—though not so far to the east and southeast, hence the lack of overlap with Edom. The cultural and religious identity of Edom continued on into Idumea in some sense, though certainly not completely or even in a major way. Thus, we must not simply conflate

19. See newer essays in Jürgen van Oorschot and Markus Witte (eds.), *The Origins of Yahwism* (Berlin: Walter de Gruyter, 2017).

20. But see Bradley L. Crowell, "Nabonidus, as-Sila', and the Beginning of the End of Edom," *Bulletin of the American Schools of Oriental Research* 348 (2007): 75–88.

"Idumea" with the "Edomites," despite the fact that the names seem connected and the territory overlaps.[21]

Some sources (such as the first century CE Jewish historian Josephus) suggest that a Jewish leader named John Hyrcanus forcibly "converted" the residents of Idumea to Judaism during the middle of the second century BCE, though others have pointed to natural affinities between Idumea and Judah that would have made the two regions natural allies (not requiring conversion). The royal line of Herod the Great—the king of Judea in the New Testament (Matt 2) who tries to kill the baby Jesus—came from the Idumean region, beginning with Antipater ("Antipater I the Idumean"). Whether the family was truly Jewish by birth or converted during the time of John Hyrcanus is unclear, but Herod the Great cherished elements of his Jewish identity, working to greatly expand the Second Temple structure in the first century BCE. The surviving Western Wall or Wailing Wall in Jerusalem today, the only part of the Second Temple still standing and accessible to visitors, is a remnant of this project.

Distinct from both the Edomites and Idumeans is yet another group that occupied the southern desert region once occupied partly by Edom: the Nabateans. They were a nomadic, desert-dwelling people who capitalized on regional trading routes to amass great wealth, and occupied (at maximum) a large region extending to the southeast of Israel, all the way down the eastern coast of the Red Sea into the northwestern corner of what is now Saudi Arabia. Nabatean political prominence began probably in the fourth century BCE and continued on into the Roman period, ending in 106 CE when the Romans took direct control of the region. The Nabataeans had a distinctive artistic and religious tradition that in some ways mirrors the approach in early Judaism: they held to a prohibition on "graven images" of certain kinds and

---

21. John R. Bartlett, "Edom and Idumaeans," *Palestine Exploration Quarterly* 131.2 (1999): 102–114.

participated in some type of emerging monotheistic expressions.[22] They were skilled stone carvers, leaving behind monumental tombs and structures, including the most famous Nabatean structure at Petra (their capital): Al-Khazneh, a temple or grave edifice carved into orange sandstone. Readers may recognize this structure for its role in the climax of the 1989 film *Indiana Jones and the Last Crusade*, where it was used for filming the site of the location of the Holy Grail.

In Jewish literature from the Hellenistic period and the Christian New Testament, whatever ambiguity the Hebrew Bible may have accorded to the Esau/Edom tradition gave way to a one-dimensional view of Esau/Edom as the absolute bad guy. In a writing called 1 Esdras (4:45), the Edomites—and not the Babylonians!—are accused of burning down the Temple in 586 BCE. At least on a symbolic level, the connection between the Edomites and Babylonians lived on in Jewish interpretation, as Esau/Edom became a cipher for Rome.[23] In the Maccabean wars of the 160s BCE, at least as recorded in the book of 1 Maccabees, the Jewish patriot Judas Maccabeus routed the Idumeans as part of his reconquest of the land (1 Macc 5:3, 65). In the Christian book of Romans, perhaps written in the 60s CE, the author takes up the statement about God's hatred of Esau in Malachi (compare with Sir 50:25–26) and develops the notion of divine choice as a theological theme; God shows mercy on some (Jacob), and others (Esau) he rejects. The author of Hebrews likewise takes up Esau, using him as an example to the audience of an "immoral and godless person, who sold his birthright for a single meal" (12:16). The theological

---

22. John F. Healey, *The Religion of the Nabataeans: A Conspectus* (Leiden: Brill, 2001); Joseph Patrich, *The Formation of Nabataean Art: Prohibition of a Graven Image among the Nabataeans* (Jerusalem: Magnes Press, 1990).

23. James L. Kugel, *The Ladder of Jacob: Ancient Interpretations of the Story of Jacob and His Children* (Princeton, NJ: Princeton University Press, 2006), 20–21.

theme of God's rejection of Esau in favor of Jacob also appears in 2 Esdras 3 and 6, Jewish texts written later than Paul's letter to the Romans, in language that resembles Paul's usage (2 Esdr 3:15–16; 6:8–9). Thus, the primordial conflict between the brothers continued on with a new life, as a symbol of the deepest and most consequential division between people.

7

The Philistines

IN A POLITICAL AND MILITARY sense, none of Israel's neighbors loom as large in the biblical imagination as the Philistines. Indeed, the Bible depicts the Philistines as inextricably involved with Israel's early experience with the monarchy, threatening the existence of the new nation. Throughout 1 Samuel—most famously in the story of David and Goliath—the Philistines antagonize Israel. Though they already play a potentially sympathetic role toward Sarah and Abraham in the ancestral narratives of Genesis (through Abimelech), the Philistines overwhelmingly appear as a site of conflict and destruction. In Judges 14–16, Samson's relationship with Philistine women serves for the narrator to problematize Samson's status as a "hero." First Samuel 5 contains a tale of the Israelite ark in the temple of Dagan, a Philistine deity, with speculation on Philistine priestly customs. Even though David seems to finally defeat the Philistines in 2 Samuel 5, they are back as foes in 2 Samuel 21 and then again for Solomon as subjects in 1 Kings 4. The picture gains more complexity when we read that David takes refuge with a Philistine king, Achish, on two occasions (1 Sam 21; 27). The biblical narratives probably reflect real alliances with and battles against the Philistines, as the two groups sought to carve out land in roughly the same place at the same time, probably with continual conflict at the edge of the coastal plain. Despite all of this, the Philistines do appear once as recipients of God's divine guidance in Amos 9:7, where the prophet uses the Philistine migration from Caphtor (Crete) as a historical example for chastising Israel's behavior.

Ancient Israel's Neighbors. Brian R. Doak, Oxford University Press (2020). © Oxford University Press.
DOI: 10.1093/oso/9780190690595.001.0001

Though the adjective "Philistine" has entered the English language as a slur against those of boorish attitude and cultural backwardness, the last several decades of archaeological research have given us an independent view of the Philistines—as a refined, cultured people who were a contingent of the so-called Sea Peoples who migrated east after the collapse of the Late Bronze Age political system in the Mediterranean world. Unlike any of Israel's other neighbors, the Philistines seem to be the only group that had large-scale origins entirely outside of the Levant. The question of how cohesive Philistine identity really was is complicated by the fact that they probably operated independently out of key cities, each with its own ruler. Like the Arameans, then, the Philistines occupied a cluster of cities that could cooperate but that did not constitute a nation called Philistia with a singular king or political structure. Though we have no substantial native Philistine literary culture (or even a script) to speak of, archaeological work at sites along the coastal plain has given us rich examples of a distinctive Philistine pottery tradition, iconography, and glimpses into their religious practice.

THE ARCHAEOLOGY OF PHILISTIA AND THE PHILISTINES

The region designated "Philistia" stretches down the central part of the coastal plain, encompassing cities at least as far south as Gaza (in the contemporary Gaza Strip), and then, moving north up the coast, Ashkelon, Ashdod, and Tel Qasile, with the sites of Ekron (Tell Miqneh) and Gath (Tell es-Safi) about 10 miles/15 km inland (Fig. 7.1). As the coastal region transitions into the central hill country farther east from the coast, sites such as Tel Zayit and Tel Burna (the latter sometimes identified with the biblical city of Libnah) on the border between what might have been Philistia and Judah cannot be easily identified as belonging to a particular nation or group. Thus, as with so many other political entities we've

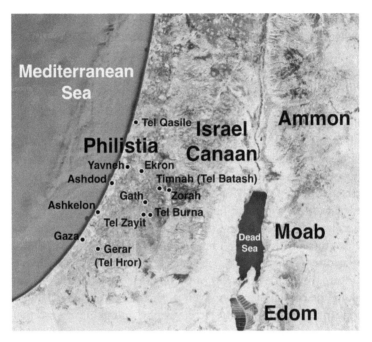

FIG. 7.1 Map of Philistia and selected cities; Map data ©2019 Google, with text added by the author.

discussed in this book, we need to exercise hesitancy about confidently declaring territorial boundaries.

The geographical region of the coastal plain, bordering the Mediterranean Sea, is quite narrow at its northern extreme but widens out in the south. The region offered access to an international trade route that brought great wealth to those who could control major cities along its path. Good soil, combined with ample availability of water, made the plain a rich agricultural zone. For these reasons, people in the region greatly prized the land.[1]

1. Yohanan Aharoni, *The Land of the Bible: A Historical Geography*, rev. and enlarged ed., trans. Anson F. Rainey (Philadelphia: Westminster Press, 1979), 21–22, 25.

The arrival of the Philistines to the Levant constitutes an exciting area of study for those interested in the ancient Near Eastern and Mediterranean worlds. Through this group, we have strong evidence of a population that migrated from one area of the world to a very different, distinct area, and then were able to carve out a significant space for themselves in the new homeland and act as a political force. Sometime during the thirteenth and twelfth centuries BCE, perhaps in waves, what had been a stable political and economic system in the ancient Mediterranean world fell apart.[2] The cause of this collapse of the Late Bronze Age system has been debated for decades; it is likely that some confluence of events, perhaps natural disasters or climate issues, forced a reevaluation of land and leadership across the region. What emerged on the other side of this shake-up, in the Levant, was a mixture of continuity with the previous arrangement and also a system of smaller, independent entities—groups with which we are now familiar, such as the Moabites, Ammonites, Edomites, Philistines, and Israelites.

Archaeologists are confident that the Philistines were one contingent of a broader group, often called "Sea Peoples."[3] We do not

2. Eric H. Cline, *1177 B.C.: The Year Civilization Collapsed* (Princeton, NJ: Princeton University Press, 2014).

3. For sources on the emergence and identity of the Philistines, on which I rely for the presentation below, see Ann E. Killebrew and Gunnar Lehmann (eds.), *The Philistines and Other "Sea Peoples" in Text and Archaeology* (Atlanta: Society of Biblical Literature, 2013); Ann E. Killebrew, *Biblical Peoples and Ethnicity: An Archaeological Study of Egyptians, Canaanites, Philistines, and Early Israel, 1300–1100 B.C.E.* (Atlanta: Society of Biblical Literature, 2005); Assaf Yasur-Landau, *The Philistines and Aegean Migration at the End of the Late Bronze Age* (Cambridge: Cambridge University Press, 2014); Amihai Mazar, *Archaeology of the Land of the Bible, 10,000–586 B.C.E.* (New York: Doubleday, 1992), 300–328; Ephraim Stern, *Archaeology of the Land of the Bible*, volume 2: *The Assyrian, Babylonian, and Persian Periods, 732–332 BCE* (New York: Doubleday, 2001), 102–129; Lawrence E. Stager, "Forging an Identity: The Emergence of Ancient

possess any native story from any of these groups explaining their homelands, identity, or motives. However, we do have a lengthy inscription from an Egyptian king, Ramses III, on the walls of a temple at Medinet Habu in Egypt (around the year 1175 BCE), detailing his fight against an invasion of the Sea Peoples on several occasions.[4] Some of the Sea Peoples attacked by land, and others came by sea. Accompanying a massive wall-relief image of the battle, in which the pharaoh looms large against his enemies with a bow, an accompanying text dramatizes the battle:[5]

> Year 8 under the majesty of Ramses III . . . The foreign countries [i.e., the Sea Peoples] made a conspiracy in their islands. All at once the lands were removed and scattered in the fray. No land could stand before their arms, from Hatti, Kode, Carchemish, Arzawa, and Alashiya on, being cut off at one time. A camp was set up in one place at Amor. They desolated its people, and its land was like that which has never come into being. They were coming forward toward Egypt, while the flame was prepared before them. Their confederation was the Peleset, Tjeker, Shekelesh, Denyen, and Weshesh, lands united. They laid their hands upon

Israel," in *The Oxford History of the Biblical World*, ed. Michael D. Coogan (Oxford: Oxford University Press, 1998), 90–131, esp. 113–128; Lawrence E. Stager, "The Impact of the Sea Peoples in Canaan (1185–1050 BCE)," in *The Archaeology of Society in the Holy Land*, ed. Thomas E. Levy (New York: Facts on File, 1995), 332–348. Note also the summation of pioneering work by Trude Dothan in Trude Dothan and Moshe Dothan, *People of the Sea: The Search for the Philistines* (New York: Macmillan, 1992).

4. Donald B. Redford, *The Medinet Habu Records of the Foreign Wars of Ramesses III* (Leiden: Brill, 2018), esp. 25–30, 117–120.

5. Translation from John A. Wilson (trans.), in *Ancient Near Eastern Texts Relating to the Old Testament*, 3rd ed., ed. James B. Pritchard (Princeton: Princeton University Press, 1969), 262–263.

the lands as far as the circuit of the earth, their hearts confident and trusting: "Our plans will succeed!"

Ramses III goes on to describe, in bombastic terms, his utter annihilation of the Sea Peoples. In several other inscriptions, the list of these Sea Peoples appears in various groupings, though the five mentioned as the "confederation" in the portion from the Medinet Habu inscription quoted above are among the most frequent.[6] Some of these names are ambiguous, but one stands out for our inquiry here: "Peleset" is almost certainly a cognate term for what the biblical authors and others called "Philistines."

There is room for reasonable suspicion regarding whether the Peleset/Philistines of Egyptian texts were the exact ethnic and historical Philistines whom the biblical authors and other ancient Near Eastern authors (such as royal scribes from Assyria) mention. Perhaps later authors used blanket terminology for a group that the native members of that same group would not have used for themselves. However, in this case we do know, through the light of native archaeological evidence from major Philistine cities, that the coastal settlers of Philistia were indeed almost certainly migrants from the Aegean and were likely a contingent of the fearsome Sea Peoples who left their Mediterranean homes in the thirteenth century BCE and engaged with populations in Egypt and the Levant. The major Philistine sites where excavations have occurred are sometimes referred to as the Philistine "pentapolis," a confederation of five cities that functioned independently but may have had some shared identity and goals: Gaza, Ashkelon, Ashdod, Gath (Tell es-Safi), and Ekron (Tell Miqneh). Other sites,

---

6. Matthew J. Adams and Margaret E. Cohen, "The 'Sea Peoples' in Primary Sources," in *The Philistines and Other "Sea Peoples" in Text and Archaeology*, ed. Ann E. Killebrew and Gunnar Lehmann (Atlanta: Society of Biblical Literature, 2013), 645–664

such as Tell Haror (ancient Gerar), also show evidence of Philistine occupation.

In summary, the material evidence for Philistine identity comes from several fronts. Most prominently in the archaeological record, Philistine sites have been identified by their distinctive pottery, called "Mycenaean IIIC," as well as other variations (such as "Philistine bichrome"). Comparisons to this pottery come from Cyprus, as well as from the Aegean world and even mainland Greece farther west in the Mediterranean.[7] By the standards of other Levantine pottery of the era, Philistine vessels were finely wrought and nicely decorated, sometimes with intricate bird motifs, communicating the wealth and sophistication of their users.

Philistine sites also have specific architectural features, such as hearths, of styles similar to those at Mycenaean Greek sites as a focus of home and religious life. Moreover, they seem to have brought with them distinctive animal husbandry techniques and dietary habits. Though pigs were relatively rare in the central highland area putatively occupied by early Israel in the thirteenth–tenth centuries BCE, the early period of Philistine settlement along the coast saw a marked increase in pork consumption.[8]

The period of Assyrian domination in the region during the eighth century BCE brought encounters at varying levels of violence and local compliance as the empire campaigned west all the way to the Mediterranean Sea. Already during the reign of Adad

7. Penelope A. Mountjoy, "The Mycenaean IIIC Pottery at Tel Miqne-Ekron," pp. 53–75; Ann E. Killebrew, "Early Philistine Pottery Technology at Tel Miqne-Ekron: Implications for the Late Bronze–Early Iron Age Transition in the Eastern Mediterranean," pp. 77–129; and Gunnar Lehmann, "Aegean-Style Pottery in Syria and Lebanon during Iron Age I," pp. 265–328, all in *The Philistines and Other "Sea Peoples" in Text and Archaeology*, ed. Ann E. Killebrew and Gunnar Lehmann (Atlanta: Society of Biblical Literature, 2013).
8. Stager, "Impact," 344.

Nirari III, an Assyrian king who ruled during the early ninth and late eighth centuries BCE, an inscription boasts of the king forcing the submission of the Philistines generally (among other coastal groups, as well as the Israelites and Edomites). Frequent Assyrian incursions into the region occurred during 734–701 BCE; even so, evidence suggests that Philistine sites flourished, despite the fact that local Philistine rulers rebelled against the Assyrians. Assyrians fortified the region with numerous building projects and political reorganizations, which included importing thousands of people taken from nearby areas, such as the northern Phoenician coast. Some of the cities, most notably Ekron, grew considerably—a very small settlement before the eighth century BCE, with perhaps only a few dozen residents, after Assyrian involvement Ekron reemerged as a carefully plotted urban center, divided into four districts and encompassing some eighty-five acres, with a large defensive wall and a thriving economy based on olive oil production.

The case of Assyrian involvement with the city of Gaza during the reign of Tiglath-pilesar III provides a fascinating case study for understanding the complexity of Philistine politics in the eighth century BCE. Consider the following inscription of Tiglath-pilesar III on his campaign against a certain Hananu, ruler of Gaza:[9]

As for Ḥanūnu of the city of Gaza, who fled before my weapons and escaped to Egypt—I conquered the city Gaza, his royal city, and I carried off his property and his gods. I fashioned a statue bearing images of the gods, my lords, and my royal image out of gold, erected it in the palace of the city Gaza, and I reckoned it among the gods of their land; I established their *sattukku* offerings.

9. Adapted from Hayim Tadmor and Shigeo Yamada, *The Royal Inscriptions of Tiglath-pilesar III (744–727 BC), and Shalmaneser V (726–722 BC), Kings of Assyria*, The Royal Inscriptions of the Neo-Assyrian Period, vol. 1 (Winona Lake, IN: Eisenbrauns, 2011), 105–106.

There seems to have been some level of Assyrian symbolic and religious coercion that went along with their political dominance—though the extent of fidelity to the Assyrian system that would have been required remains a topic of debate. Whatever the case, Gaza's status under Assyrian rule may have been quite a bit more ambiguous than the Assyrian inscription presents the situation.[10] Though the city was designated an "Assyrian customs station," the empire did not convert it into a full-blown province, and repeated rebellions in the years to follow (under the Assyrian king Sargon) reveal that imperial control was not absolute. Similarly, at Ashdod, two local kings ruled over the city despite the fact that under Sargon (c. 712 BCE) the Assyrians had previously imported and deported citizens from the region and attempted to install an Assyrian administrator in the city.

At some point, possibly as early as the tenth century but presumably before the eighth or seventh century BCE, the Philistines adopted a variant of the northwest Semitic language and script used by their neighbors (Israel and Phoenicia). The language they initially wrote in and spoke before migration to the area remains a mystery—some assume it must have been some Indo-European language, though detailed evidence remains elusive. At Ashkelon, a series of inscriptions in a (proposed) Cypro-Minoan script have been found, suggesting, at least to some scholars, that early Philistine settlers in the region could in fact read and write in a non-Semitic language. These inscriptions could indicate that the Sea Peoples, including the Philistines, brought a system of writing

---

10. See Mordechai Cogan, "Judah under Assyrian Hegemony: A Reexamination of Imperialism and Religion," *Journal of Biblical Literature* 112.3 (1993): 403–414, and Brian R. Doak, "Religion between Core and Periphery in Ancient Syria-Palestine," in the *Oxford Handbook of Religions in the Ancient Near East*, ed. Tawny L. Holm (Oxford: Oxford University Press, forthcoming).

with them, or that they rapidly adopted the Cypro-Minoan writing system that was used at nearby Cyprus.[11]

The most significant and lengthy Philistine inscription we possess thus far is the so-called Ekron inscription. Etched on stone in the seventh century BCE, the text comes from a temple context and serves a dedicatory role. The script appears to be similar to the Phoenician writing system, while some of the spellings more closely resemble conventions used in Hebrew. The full translation reads as follows:[12]

> The house which Akayus son of Padi son of YSD [an undecipherable personal name] son of Ada son of Ya'ir, ruler of Aqqaron [Ekron] built for PTGYH [the name of a goddess] his lady. May she bless him and may she keep him and may she lengthen his days and may she bless his land.

Notably, the name of the king who dedicates the structure in question, Akayus, is not Semitic—rather, it is probably Indo-European, reflecting Philistine origins from the Aegean world. The other names (Padi, Ada, Ya'ir) are all probably Semitic; one interpreter suggests that the name Akayus may reflect a "revival" of pride in Philistine origins.[13] We also know that some of the names, particularly Akayus and Padi, are known from other sources dating from the same time period—the Assyrian King Esarhaddon listed "Ikausu" (= Akayus) in an official document, and the annals of king Sennacherib mention Padi.[14] Another inscription, from Tell

---

11. Frank Moore Cross and Lawrence E. Stager, "Cypro-Minoan Inscriptions Found in Ashkelon," *Israel Exploration Journal* 56.2 (2006): 129–159.

12. Shmuel Ahituv, *Echoes from the Past: Hebrew and Cognate Inscriptions from the Biblical Period* (Jerusalem: Carta, 2008), 335–340.

13. Ahituv, *Echoes*, 338.

14. Some had claimed to find the probably non-Semitic biblical name Goliath (spelled *alwat*; biblical *golyat*) on an inscribed potsherd from Goliath's biblical hometown Gath (Tell es-Safi), though the reading is

Jemmeh (just south of Gaza), contains a list of names—some of them are Semitic, while many are not (particularly those ending in -s, such as Adonis, Papas, etc.).[15] The Philistines produced a rich artistic tradition compared with what we have preserved from Israel or Israel's other neighbors.[16] One particularly distinct motif is the so-called Ashdoda figurine, an image of what many have assumed is a goddess figure found primarily at Ashdod but also at Ekron and all along the Philistine coast (see Fig. 7.2). This piece fuses together the body of a female figure, with stylized breasts, to a chair or couch, a style also attested in Mycenaean art from the Aegean world. Perhaps Ashdoda represents the fusion of a throne with the image of a popular goddess in the region as a symbol of the meaning of whatever political power was in place where the object was utilized, or perhaps it played some kind of fertility function,[17] linking a goddess associated with procreative powers and a bed.

Images of male lyre players were also prominent, sometimes alone or sometimes in musical groups, and female figures can

disputed (Cross and Stager, "Cypro-Minoan," 151–152). See Aaron Meir, Stefan J. Wimmer, Alexander Zuckerman, and Aaron Demsky, "A Late Iron Age I / Early Iron Age II Old Canaanite Inscription from Tell eṣ-Ṣâfī/Gath: Palaeography, Dating, and Historical-Cultural Significance," *Bulletin of the American Schools of Oriental Research* 351 (2008): 39–71 (esp. pp. 57–58, where the authors question the identification with Goliath).

15. Ahituv, *Echoes*, 346.
16. David Ben-Shlomo, *Philistine Iconography: A Wealth of Style and Symbolism* (Fribourg: Academic Press, 2010); Othmar Keel and Christoph Uehlinger, *Gods, Goddesses, and Images of God in Ancient Israel*, trans. Thomas H. Trapp (Minneapolis: Fortress Press, 1998), 122–124.
17. Keel and Uehlinger, *Gods*, 122. See also Assaf Yasur-Landau, "The Mother(s) of All Philistines? Aegean Enthroned Deities of the 12th–11th Century Philistia," in *Potnia: Deities in the Aegean Bronze Age*, Aegeum 22, ed. R. Laffineur and R. Hägg (Liège: Université de L'Etat, 2001), 329–343.

FIG. 7.2 Philistine "Ashdoda" figure; after drawing in Othmar Keel and Christoph Uehlinger, *Gods, Goddesses, and Images of God in Ancient Israel*, trans. Thomas H. Trapp (Minneapolis: Fortress Press, 1998), 124 illus. 148.

frequently be found in positions of mourning (with hands on head), particularly on vessels often associated, as they were in the Greek world, with burial and mourning ritual. Philistine pottery often features lavish painted scenes, such as those featuring birds (see Fig. 7.3). Indeed, the Philistines must have viewed these birds as quite significant, as they appear in many different forms from the region—perhaps they signified a deity, or they were auspicious for traveling at sea, or they were decorative and reminded their viewers of the ancient Philistine homeland in the Aegean world.[18]

18. Ben-Shlomo, *Philistine Iconography*, 132–142, 180.

FIG. 7.3 Examples of Philistine pottery (kraters/mixing bowls) and bird motif on pottery; at left and center (kraters), after drawings in Penelope A. Mountjoy, "The Mycenaean IIIC Pottery at Tel Miqne-Ekron," in *The Philistines and Other "Sea Peoples" in Text and Archaeology*, ed. Ann E. Killebrew and Gunnar Lehmann (Atlanta: Society of Biblical Literature, 2013), 53–75, here figs. 3:22 and 4:25; at right (bird image), after drawing in David Ben-Shlomo, *Philistine Iconography: A Wealth of Style and Symbolism* (Fribourg: Academic Press, 2010), 133, fig. 3.74.3.

We know unfortunately little about Philistine religion from native sources. Most scholars agree that one primary deity worshiped along the Philistine coast was Dagan, whose Semitic name possibly indicates "grain" (or agriculture more generally) or "fish," though no completely satisfactory etymology has emerged.[19] The Hebrew Bible identifies Dagan specifically as the deity of Ashdod, though evidence suggests that Dagan remained popular throughout the Mesopotamian world for a long time. Nevertheless, we have no direct or native Philistine literary evidence identifying any specific role for Dagan. Preserved Philistine personal names often contain the element Baal ("Lord," or the proper name of a deity, Baal), such as "Baalshama," "Silbaal," which could indicate that Baal was used as an epithet of another deity (such as Dagan), or that Baal was a popular deity in his own right. Perhaps the "Baal" element was vestigial and popular for other reasons. Some seventh century BCE Philistine jars from Ekron bear the inscription *qodesh le'asherat*, "holy/sacred to Asherat" (Asherat = a form of

19. Jeffrey F. Healey, "Dagon [DGWN]," in *Dictionary of Deities and Demons in the Bible*, ed. Karel van der Toorn, Bob Becking, and Pieter W. van der Horst (Leiden: Brill, 1999), 216–219.

the popular Semitic goddess's name Asherah), and it is likely that a goddess like Asherat played a role in the Philistine pantheon.[20] Various sacred spaces in Philistia have been excavated (perhaps some "temples"), though as of yet they offer no evidence of a singular "Philistine cult" or sacred architectural program. The seventh century BCE Ekron inscription served to dedicate a particular "house" (temple) to a goddess named PTGYH; some vocalize the name as "Pitgiah," though others read the name as Potnia, a divine title known from archaic Greece that may serve as a sign connecting the Philistines to an Aegean homeland.[21] Another aspect of Philistine religious practice with connections to the Greek world are intramural infant burials—that is, the practice of burying babies or very young children beneath the floor of one's house. We have evidence of this practice from several Philistine sites, including prominently at Ashkelon, where an infant was buried in a jar incised with Egyptian funerary symbols (probably indicating the Philistine adaptation of Egyptian popular religious imagery).[22] Another recent discovery bearing upon Philistine religion at Yavneh, a site about 16 miles/25 km north of both Ashdod and Ekron and thus very possibly within the Philistine orbit, revealed thousands of objects buried together, which scholars have called a *genizah* (or favissa, a space where sacred objects were stored or put out of commission in a special way after they were worn out).[23] These objects included intricate

---

20. Stern, *Archaeology*, 118.
21. Stern, *Archaeology*, 120.
22. Kathleen Birney and Brian R. Doak, "Funerary Iconography on an Infant Burial Jar from Ashkelon," *Israel Exploration Journal* 61 (2011): 32–53.
23. Raz Kletter, Irit Ziffer, and Wolfgang Zwickel, "Cult Stands of the Philistines: A Genizah from Yavneh," *Near Eastern Archaeology* 69.3–4 (2006): 146–159; *Yavneh I, The Excavation of the "Temple Hill"*

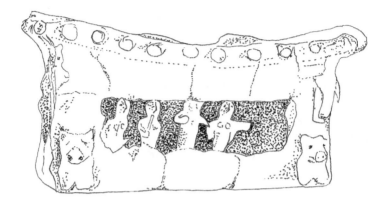

FIG. 7.4 Philistine clay "musicians stand" from Yavneh; after photo in Raz Kletter, Irit Ziffer, and Wolfgang Zwickel, *Yavneh I, The Excavation of the "Temple Hill" Repository Pit and the Cult Stands* (Fribourg: Academic Press, 2010), plate 13, CAT44.

clay houselike structures, perhaps models of temples, as well as bowls and other items used in religious practice, such as small altars, sacrificial vessels, and other implements. The objects in this group could be from different time periods, but seem to be from the tenth through eighth centuries BCE. One of the more intricate clay models shows a series of musicians standing in the windows of an oval-shaped house structure (Fig. 7.4). We cannot be sure how these objects were used, but they could have served as miniature cosmic models to facilitate worship through small offerings of food or incense, placed in a strategic ritual location for worshipers.

Repository Pit and the Cult Stands (Fribourg: Academic Press, 2010), and *Yavneh II, The "Temple Hill" Repository Pit Fire: Pans, Kernos, Naos, Painted Stands, "Plain" Pottery, Cypriot Pottery, Inscribed Bowl, Dog Bones, Stone Fragments, and Other Studies* (Fribourg: Academic Press, 2015).

PHILISTIA AND THE PHILISTINES
IN THE HEBREW BIBLE

The Philistines appear in the Hebrew Bible at several key junctures, often in an adversarial role to Israel. Indeed, one could make the argument that the Philistines became one of the primary others to Israel, as real historical conflict with the Philistines during the period of Israel's settlement and establishment of a monarchy (c. twelfth–tenth centuries BCE) served to define Israel.[24] The biblical story of the Philistines begins in the book of Genesis, in two locations. First, in the so-called Table of Nations in Genesis 10 (also 1 Chr 1), the genealogist presents the Philistines as descendants of Noah's least favorite son, Ham, who bore the ancient ancestors of Cush, Egypt, Put, and Canaan (Gen 10:6); from Egypt then came several groups, including the "Kasluhites," "from whom the Philistines came" (Gen 10:13) as well as the "Caphtorites." Though we cannot be sure what the biblical author's intentions were regarding the location of either Kasluh or Caphtor (the latter is commonly identified with the island of Crete), it is at least clear that the author recognizes the Philistines' nonnative origins. The prophet Amos associates the Philistines with Caphtor, in a passage suggesting that Israel's God controls the fates of all nations (compare with Deut 2:23):

> "Are not you Israelites the same to me as the Cushites?" declares the Lord. "Did I not bring Israel up from Egypt, the Philistines from Caphtor and the Arameans from Kir?" (Amos 9:7)

However, in other texts, authors present the Philistines as living in the land far before Israel as a nation arrives—or at the very

24. Peter Machinist, "Biblical Traditions: The Philistines and Israelite History," in *The Sea Peoples and Their World: A Reassessment*, ed. Eliezer D. Oren (Philadelphia: University of Pennsylvania Press, 2013), 53–83, and Stager, "Forging an Identity."

least, they are already there when Israel arrives to conquer their promised land, along with other Canaanite groups (see Josh 13:1–2; Exod 15:17). Genesis 21 and 26 also present an oddity on this front. Even though we know that the Philistines (by that name) founded their cities along the coast no earlier than the late thirteenth or early twelfth centuries BCE, in Genesis the narrator unabashedly has Israel's ancestors living in a putative time period many centuries earlier and interacting with Philistines by name. Abraham encounters a military commander named Phicol, from "the land of the Philistines," and after making a treaty Abraham goes on to live "in the land of the Philistines for a long time" (Gen 21:32–34). Perhaps the phrase "land of the Philistines" was a way to denote geography, not the Philistine ethnicity? Genesis 26, however, narrates an extended interaction Isaac has with Abimelek, "king of the Philistines," and Isaac proceeds to have a conflict with the Philistines about water and herding rights. In these passages it would be harder to deny that the biblical author engages in anachronism. Though the Philistines in general do oppose Isaac's family and tamper with his wells, the two groups are not presented as complete enemies or on violent terms. Moreover, the (presumably) Philistine king Abimelek of Gerar does not harm Abraham's wife, Sarah, when he has the chance, but rather obeys the voice of God and returns her to Abraham, having been lied to in the first place about her identity. (In Gen 26, another Abimelek has the same type of encounter with Isaac and his wife, Rebekah.)

The names of what would later become key Philistine cities—Gaza, Ashdod, Ashkelon, Gath, and Ekron—appear throughout the books of Joshua and Judges (particularly in Josh 13 and 15), and Philistines appear as enemies of the newly settled Israelites in the book of Judges, among other regional enemies. The Israelites illicitly worship the "gods of the Philistines," resulting in God handing them over to the oppression of the Philistines (Judg 10:6–7). The story of the judge Samson, in Judges 13–16, narrates the first elongated encounter any character has with Philistines. Samson's family home is Zorah (Judg 13), a site in a region approaching what may have been a contested territory between Israel and Philistia; later action in the story (Judg 14) has Samson and his family traveling to Timnah, a site only about 25 miles/40 km east of Ashdod. Samson marries a Philistine woman; in the process, he engages in a game of riddles with the Philistine, goes into a rage, and slaughters Philistines in Ashkelon. The narrator gives a theological rationale for why Samson, an Israelite hero, would want to marry a Philistine woman: "the LORD . . . was seeking an occasion to confront the Philistines; for at that time they were ruling over Israel" (Judg 14:4). It is quite possible that real intermarriage issues between the two groups flared up, as questions of identity loom large between competing neighbor groups. Samson ends up slaughtering count-less further Philistines, visits a Philistine prostitute, and eventu-ally falls in love with a woman named Delilah. She cuts Samson's hair, which had been the source of his enormous strength, and the Philistines take him captive, forcing him to perform for them as a sort of circus animal. However, once his hair had grown back, Samson performs one final act of vengeance against the Philistines, pushing down the pillars of their temple at Gaza and killing untold numbers of Philistines in the process.

Through all of this, it is not exactly clear what we are to learn about the real, historical Philistines—except, perhaps crucially, that already in the period of Joshua and the Judges the Philistines were considered regional competitors, vying for dominance in some of the same regions as Israel. Granted, the books of Joshua and Judges may have been written much later than the events they purport to describe. Even so, Israelite memory and storytelling en-code pivotal contact between the two groups during the earliest period of settlement in the land.

Now for the main event: the Philistines come back in the book of 1 Samuel and engage in a long series of conflicts with Israel—beginning just before Israel's first king, Saul, emerges on the scene and extending through the era of David's rise to power. In 1 Samuel 4–5, the Philistines come out of nowhere and steal the ark, pre-sumably taking advantage of the overall leaderless state of Israel at the time. They pay for the theft, however, as the ark carries with it the power of Israel's God. The mere presence of the ark in the temple of Dagan at Ashdod causes the statue of Dagan to topple over on its face (1 Sam 5:1–5), and further travels of the ark cause panic to break out among the Philistine populace (1 Sam 5:6–11). The stories have a clear theological point: Israel's God dominates the Philistine gods, even when Israel is not strong enough to defend themselves. The Israelites later ask for a king, a presumably rational move after seeing that they cannot protect their most sacred objects from neighboring enemies (see 1 Sam 7, when the Philistines return to route Israel in battle again). King Saul thus emerges as a credible military leader to keep the nation safe.

However, war against the Philistines continues, leading to one of the most famous stories in the entire Bible (1 Sam 17). A Philistine giant named Goliath comes out to confront Israel, proposing a one-on-one battle to determine who should win the day. Goliath's height in the traditional Hebrew text is listed as "six cubits and a span," which could measure something like nine and a half feet tall. However, probably an older (and more reliable) textual tradition from the Dead Sea Scrolls and the Septuagint (an early Greek translation of the Hebrew Bible) has his height at a more realistic but still reasonably imposing *four* cubits and a span, reducing his height by some three feet. The lavish description of Goliath's heavy armor and the notion of one-on-one combat—a fighting style otherwise rare in the Hebrew Bible—has provoked comparisons with the Greek *Iliad*, perhaps providing yet another point of contact between the Philistines and their Aegean homeland. At the very least, the name Goliath (Hebrew *golyat*) is very likely non-Semitic and has an Indo-European origin.[25] Goliath taunts Israel, and the Israelites cower in fear.

---

25. See the discussion in Brian R. Doak, *The Last of the Rephaim: Conquest and Cataclysm in the Heroic Ages of Ancient Israel* (Boston: Ilex Foundation, 2012), 101–109.

A young shepherd named David rises up to fight the giant, famously killing him with a single slingshot to the head. This victory is David's first major political moment in the spotlight, and combined with further victories against the Philistines, cements his legend and propels him to the kingship. The story of David's opposition to the Philistines gains complexity when we read that David takes refuge with a Philistine king, Achish, on two occasions (1 Sam 21; 27). David lies to Achish in order to secure his place as a refugee, however, and in the end David thrives and the Philistines look gullible.

Even though David seems to finally defeat the Philistines in 2 Samuel 5 and 8, they are back as foes in 2 Samuel 21, and then again for Solomon as subjects in 1 Kings 4. In 2 Kings 1, during the time of the divided kingdom, an Israelite king in the north, Ahaziah, seeks out medical advice from "Baal Zebub, the god of Ekron." The prophet Elijah intercepts the message, however, and assures the king that he will indeed die soon. By the time of Hezekiah's reign in Judah, near the end of the eighth century BCE, 2 Kings 18 has the righteous king again defeating the Philistines—perhaps suggesting that the defeat of the Philistines is a biblical trope applied to kings of whom God approves. The fact that the Philistines occupy this role so prominently, for such a long stretch of narrative, suggests that Philistines loomed large in Israelite memory. Moreover, the biblical sense of Philistine military and political organization seems historically credible, and probably reflects knowledge about Philistines during repeated contacts throughout the Iron Age.[26] The Philistine city leaders are called *seranim* (rulers) in Hebrew (a term not typically used of Israel's leaders), and are always presented as a group, suggesting a larger identity of cooperation in Philistia—a fact that could at least be inferred from archaeology and nonbiblical materials as well. Their military exploits, for example, mastering metallurgy and weaponry (1 Sam 13:19–22)

---

26. Machinist, "Biblical Traditions," 57–59.

and Goliath's heavy bronze armor (1 Sam 17:5–7), also set them apart, and such details would be strange to invent if they were not based in ancient reality. This is *not* to suggest that we read every aspect of Israel's encounter with the Philistines as historically accurate. Rather, the biblical presentation of the Philistines appears to broadly reflect real historical alliances with and battles against the Philistines, as the two groups sought to carve out land in the same time and place, probably with continual conflict at the edge of the coastal plain.[27]

In the prophetic corpus, the Philistines are an object of complete derision. The eighth century BCE prophet Amos, in a series of oracles against nations neighboring Israel, singles out all five of the Philistine Pentapolis cities:

> Thus says the LORD: For three transgressions of Gaza, and for four, I will not revoke the punishment; because they carried into exile entire communities, to hand them over to Edom. So I will send a fire on the wall of Gaza, fire that shall devour its strongholds. I will cut off the inhabitants from Ashdod, and the one who holds the scepter from Ashkelon; I will turn my hand against Ekron, and the remnant of the Philistines shall perish, says the Lord God. (Amos 1:6–8)

The prophet Isaiah rails against Philistia for rejoicing that King Ahaz has died: "Wail, O gate; cry, O city; melt in fear, O Philistia,

---

27. Elizabeth Bloch-Smith, "Israelite Ethnicity in Iron I: Archaeology Preserves What Is Remembered and What Is Forgotten in Israel's History," *Journal of Biblical Literature* 122.3 (2003): 401–425. Bloch-Smith points to differentiation that developed between the two groups, such as circumcision for Israel and not for Philistines, Philistines had long beards vs. Israelites with short beards, Philistine pork consumption vs. Israelite prohibition on pork, and the Philistines' superior military compared with Israel's varied success on the battlefield.

all of you!" (14:31). The sixth-century BCE prophet Jeremiah proclaims that

> the day has come to destroy all the Philistines who could help Tyre and Sidon. The LORD is about to destroy the Philistines, the remnant from the coasts of Caphtor. Gaza will shave her head in mourning; Ashkelon will be silenced. You remnant on the plain, how long will you cut yourselves? (Jer 47:4–5)

Contemporary to Jeremiah, Ezekiel cites Philistia's malice toward Judah and proclaims that the Lord is "about to stretch out [his] hand against the Philistines, and I will wipe out the Kerethites and destroy those remaining along the coast" (Ezek 25:16). The prophets Zephaniah (see ch. 2) and Zechariah (see ch. 9) likewise predict and celebrate the end of Philistine power.

WHAT HAPPENED TO THE PHILISTINES?

After the destruction of most of the region during the Babylonian onslaught of the 580s BCE, the Philistines—or at least residents from formerly Philistine cities—continue to antagonize Israel in the Bible. The newly formed Jewish community, returned from exile and attempting to rebuild the walls of Jerusalem in the mid-fifth century BCE under the guidance of Nehemiah, encounter residents of Ashdod (among other towns) who oppose their building project (see Neh 4:7–8). Moreover, Nehemiah himself upbraids his fellow Jews for intermarrying with foreign women—including those from Ashdod

> In those days also I saw Jews who had married women of Ashdod, Ammon, and Moab; and half of their children spoke the language of Ashdod, and they could not speak the language of Judah, but spoke the language of various peoples. And I contended with

them and cursed them and beat some of them and pulled out their hair. (Neh 13:23–25)

Such an encounter shows how the power of boundaries continued to play a vital role for national identification. In books like Sirach, 1 Maccabees (particularly chs. 3–5), 2 Esdras, and 4 Maccabees, the Philistines are remembered primarily as David's vanquished foes, and the category of "Philistine" became a stereotype for the land of Israel's enemies (see 1 Maccabees)—even to the present-day aspersion "Philistine" for those who are uncultured and ignorant (a usage that runs against the grain of the sophistication of ancient Philistine art and culture).

The title "Philistine" seems to have faded as a real, living people group during the Hellenistic period.[28] Already before this, however, the Philistines were destroyed (in several of their major cities, like Ashkelon) by the Babylonians in the 580s BCE and were then integrated into the Persian imperial structure after 539 BCE. Even so, the major cities continued to function in various ways—Gaza, Ashdod, and Ashkelon still exist today at or near their original sites in Palestine and Israel. Due to extensive excavation, we know that Ashkelon, to choose one example, flourished throughout the classical and Byzantine periods, all the way through the time of the advent of Islam and the Crusades, continuing on as a well-populated town in the Ottoman period (beginning c. 1300) and then into the twentieth century (the city hosts a population of nearly 130,000 people today). The contemporary political term "Palestine"/"Palestinians" originates

---

28. Lawrence E. Stager, "Biblical Philistines: A Hellenistic Literary Creation?" in *"I Will Speak the Riddle of Ancient Times": Archaeological and Historical Studies in Honor of Amihai Mazar on the Occasion of His Sixtieth Birthday*, vol. 2, ed. Aren M. Maier and Pierre de Miroschedji (Winona Lake, IN: Eisenbrauns, 2006), 375–384.

from the term "Philistia"/"Philistines," by process of etymological generalization probably beginning in the classical period (the Romans designated a large region along the coast as "Syria Palaestina" after the Bar Kochba revolt of 135 CE). This does not imply, of course, that contemporary Palestinians have any genealogical or cultural connection to ancient Philistines—even though the name survives.

8

The Phoenicians

OFTEN REVILED IN THE BIBLE as overly wealthy traders and
false worshipers, the Phoenicians appear in the biblical accounts
under the label of their principal cities, Tyre and Sidon. We learn
little about the actual, historical Phoenicians from the Bible, except
to note that the perception of their wealth—accurately perceived
from what we know from other sources—marked them as arrogant in the biblical narrators' eyes. Additionally, however, the
Phoenicians play an important role in one of the most important moments in the Hebrew Bible: the building of the Solomonic
Temple in 1 Kings 5–7.

From native inscriptions and new archaeological efforts at
key sites, we learn of Phoenician royal politics, religion, and colonial ambitions as far west as the south of Spain and the far northwestern African coast. We first hear the name "Phoenicians"
from the Homeric corpus in the eighth century BCE (and then
later in other Greek sources), though it is never clear that any
particular group called themselves "Phoenicians" during the
Iron Age. Nevertheless, the cities of Sidon, Tyre, Byblos, and
others (situated along what is currently the Lebanese coast)
constitute a coherent group of city-states that comfortably fit
under the Phoenician label. Though excavation has been sparse
at key sites, new efforts during the past two decades have revealed a plethora of data on Phoenician burial customs, art, and
architecture.

Ancient Israel's Neighbors. Brian R. Doak, Oxford University Press (2020). © Oxford University Press.
DOI: 10.1093/oso/9780190690595.001.0001

THE ARCHAEOLOGY OF PHOENICIA
AND THE PHOENICIANS

Our word "Phoenician" functions as a broad description for the people who lived in a series of related cities on the northern coast of the Levant (now mostly in contemporary Lebanon), and also for an elaborate system of colonial settlements throughout the Mediterranean Sea basin—along the northern African coast (most famously at Carthage), in Greece, some Italian islands (e.g., Sardinia, Malta, and Sicily), and even as far west as southern Spain and the Strait of Gibraltar. The Phoenician mainland in the Levant spans a 62 miles/100 km north-to-south and 12–31 miles/20–50 km east-to-west strip of land, with its eastern border roughly at the Lebanon mountain range. At the far northern end were the cities of Arvad and Tell Sukas, while major sites such as Byblos, Sidon, and Tyre formed the core of Phoenician territory and identity. Other cities, including Sarepta, Akko, Dor, and Akhziv, were also prominent in this cultural orbit (Fig. 8.1).[1]

Scholars also sometimes use the term "Punic" to describe settlements in the western Mediterranean established by the

1. The content in this section on religion is based upon my work in *Phoenician Aniconism in Its Mediterranean and Ancient Near Eastern Contexts* (Atlanta: Society of Biblical Literature, 2015), 8–19. See also the essays in the *Oxford Handbook of the Phoenician and Punic Mediterranean*, ed. Carolina López-Ruiz and Brian R. Doak (Oxford: Oxford University Press, 2019). For major survey works, see Josephine Quinn, *In Search of the Phoenicians* (Princeton, NJ: Princeton University Press, 2017); Mark Woolmer, *A Short History of the Phoenicians* (London: I. B. Tauris, 2017); Maria E. Aubet, *The Phoenicians and the West: Politics, Colonies, and Trade*, 2nd ed., trans. Mary Turton (Cambridge: Cambridge University Press, 2001); Glenn E. Markoe, *The Phoenicians* (Berkeley: University of California Press, 2000).

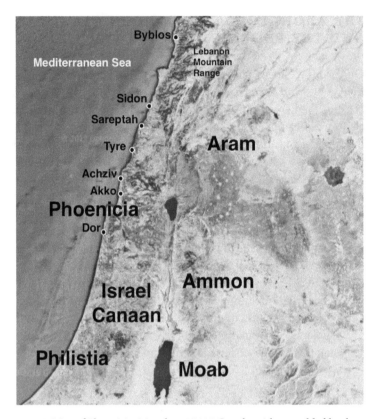

FIG. 8.1 Map of Phoenicia; Map data ©2019 Google, with text added by the author.

Phoenician cities, and for the Semitic language used in those places, especially in the era after the sixth or fifth century BCE.

Although the term is broad, and could encompass a number of different settlements in the Iron Age, the word "Phoenician" is not purely artificial. Greek and Roman authors both identified Phoenicia with at least the northern coastal region in the Levant, extended also to the Mediterranean colonies. The etymology of the term "Phoenicians," from the Greek word *phoinikes/phoenix*, tells us something about their perception at least by the eighth century BCE among the Aegean authors (such as Homer, in the *Iliad* and *Odyssey*) who first used the term: *phoenix* probably refers to a dye color, dark red or purple, produced by the murex snail and used for trade goods throughout the Mediterranean world.[2] Thus, the most notable Phoenician identity was for sailing and trade. Even so, our evidence does not suggest that Phoenicians called themselves by that name before the Roman provincial system. Rather, residents of particular Canaanite cities—most prominently Tyre, Sidon, and Byblos—identified with their city.

Another way of identifying Phoenicians is to investigate the question of the Canaanites (see chapter 2 in this book). Why? Because we could say that the Phoenicians were northern-coastal Canaanites of the first millennium BCE, whereas the non-Semitic and non-Canaanite Philistines settled along the southern coast (see chapter 7 in this book).[3] Why not simply call these northern coastal residents "Canaanites"? If the people living in these affiliated cities along the northern coast did not call themselves "Phoenicians" at all, and if later historians and archaeologists have grouped together artifacts, artwork, and other items under this label "Phoenician" for the purposes of mere convenience of categorization, then perhaps we should discard the term altogether![4] While it is true

2. Paul Wathelet, "Les Phéniciens et la Tradition Homerique," in *Redt Tyrus / Sauvons Tyr: Histoire phénicienne / Fenicische Geschiedenis*, ed. E. Gubel and B. Servai-Sayez (Leuven: Peeters, 1983), 235–243; Aubet, *Phoenicians*, 6–25; Jonathan R. Prag, "*Phoinix* and *Poenus*: Usage in Antiquity," in *The Punic Mediterranean: Identities and Identification from Phoenician Settlement to Roman Rule*, ed. J. C. Quinn and N. C. Vella (Cambridge: Cambridge University Press, 2014), 11–23.

3. Aubet, *Phoenicians*, 13; Nadav Na'aman, "The Canaanites: A Rejoinder," *Ugarit Forschungen* 26 (1994): 397–418; Niels Peter Lemche, *The Canaanites and Their Land: The Tradition of the Canaanites* (Sheffield: JSOT Press, 1991).

4. Quinn, *In Search*; Nicholas C. Vella, "The Invention of the Phoenicians: On Object Definition, Decontextualization, and

that many of the groups we've been examining in this book face similar problems regarding their identity, it is still the case that Edom, Aram, Moab, Philistia, Canaan, Ammon, Israel, and others were referred to in the inscriptions of larger empires (mostly the Assyrians, but also the Babylonians and Persians), thus indicating that they were recognized by their names for political purposes. The Phoenicians, on the other hand, receive no such clear recognition as "Phoenicians" in the Iron Age outside of Homer, but rather the major cities (Sidon, Tyre, and Byblos) are singled out by name (this is the practice of the biblical authors as well).

Still, the issue has broader implications than just one name. If we were to discard the title "Phoenician" as too sweeping or misleading, then we should also consider discarding "Edomite," "Israelite," "Moabite," and so on—not to mention terms like "Greek" or any number of other imprecise labels from the ancient Near Eastern and Mediterranean worlds. And perhaps we should. Scholars will continue to debate these issues, and yet, for purposes of using a common reference to a body of scholarship, most are likely to continue using the term "Phoenician" in the traditional way, but perhaps, going forward, with great care to distinguish the traits they see as determinative in a given context. Until a stronger consensus emerges, Phoenicia will take a normal place alongside other first-millennium groups in the Levant. Still, keep in mind that scholars increasingly question the ambiguity of the term "Phoenicians" and use it as a shorthand—a term more specific than calling them "Canaanites" but less annoying than having to call them "Canaanites living in a set of cities along the northern Levantine coast who shared a language and material culture in the Iron I–II period and who also developed an organized system of colonies in the western Mediterranean world."

Display," in *The Punic Mediterranean: Identities and Identification from Phoenician Settlement to Roman Rule*, ed. J. C. Quinn and N. C. Vella, 24–41 (Cambridge: Cambridge University Press, 2014).

In the Homeric *Iliad* and *Odyssey*, the Phoenicians and Sidonians appear as merchants, slave traders, kidnappers, and "tricksters" (see the *Odyssey* XIV.300; XV.388–484).[5] Though these depictions are exaggerations and racial stereotypes that Homer set up in order to present an exotic other for his stories of the heroic Greeks, they do tell us something about the way Phoenicians were perceived in the Greek-speaking world. Moreover, we do get confirmation on some basic aspects of Phoenician activity: they were a seafaring group, famous for trading in elite objects such as the silver bowl from the king of Sidon mentioned in the *Odyssey* (IV.614–19). Homer's Phoenicians may be a negative foil to the Greeks, the (fictional) Phaeacians, and Odysseus, but these conflicts undoubtedly symbolize real, historical conflicts and adventures Phoenician traders in the Mediterranean truly had.

Given such scattered evidence and, for the most part, a lack of native sources, can we speak of the history of Phoenicia in a coherent way? Most of the information we have is episodic and anecdotal.[6] We do know that some Phoenician cities, such as Tyre, had roots as early as the third millennium BCE.[7] During the second millennium, broadly, Egyptians controlled the coastal region (and much of the Levant), especially during a period of heavy trading action in the fourteenth century BCE; at the collapse of the Bronze Age, around 1200 BCE, the region entered something of a "dark age," and then

---

5. Joseph E. Skinner, *The Invention of Greek Ethnography: From Homer to Herodotus* (Oxford: Oxford University Press, 2012), 86–89.

6. Echoing the subtitle of Brian Peckham, *Phoenicia: Episodes and Anecdotes from the Ancient Mediterranean* (Winona Lake, IN: Eisenbrauns, 2014).

7. E.g., H. J. Katzenstein, *The History of Tyre from the Beginning of the 2nd Millennium B.C.E. until the Fall of the Neo-Babylonian Empire in 538 B.C.E.*, 2nd rev. ed. (Jerusalem: Ben Gurion University of the Negev Press, 1997); Éric Gubel, Edward Lipiński, and Brigette Servais-Soyez (eds.), *Redt Tyrus / Sauvons Tyr: Histoire phénicienne / Fenicische Geschiedenis* (Leuven: Peeters, 1983).

during the eleventh–ninth centuries BCE emerges with some written sources of significance and a clearer sense of native political rule. Even so, while some regions in the Levant experienced great population shifts and clear changes between the collapse of the Bronze Age system and the emergence of new groups in the Iron Age, the key Phoenician cities seem to have passed through the period with relatively little disruption and certainly no significant record of destruction (contrasted with major cities like Ugarit and Hazor).[8]

With some notable exceptions, we've learned remarkably little about the Phoenicians from archaeological excavations on the Levantine mainland—key sites, such as Byblos, remain largely unexplored, due to politics, lack of access (continuous human occupation at a site), insufficient funding, and other problems. However, renewed excavations at Tyre (starting in 1997) uncovered a large cemetery, offering us a glimpse of the way ancient residents of the city buried their dead (often with accompanying stelae, that is, vertical stone monuments, sometimes with short inscriptions). At Sidon, excavations renewed in 1998 called into question older interpretations of the site and yielded fascinating finds, such as a fragmented, life-sized sculpture of a male figure (perhaps a priest)—a discovery that made its way into news headlines and provided hope of more to come.[9]

We have noticed throughout our study of Israel's neighbors that the fate of these small Levantine entities profoundly felt the impact of the large empires to the east—particularly the Assyrians, but also

8. Aubet, *Phoenicians*, 20–25; R. R. Stieglitz, "The Geopolitics of the Phoenician Littoral in the Early Iron Age," *Bulletin of the American Schools of Oriental Research* 279 (1990): 9–12.

9. "Ancient Phoenician Relics Unearthed in Lebanon," NBC News, May 21, 2014, at https://www.nbcnews.com/science/science-news/ancient-phoenician-relics-unearthed-lebanon-n110361; Claude Doumet-Serhal, *And Canaan Begat Sidon His Firstborn . . . A Tribute to Dr. John Curtis on His 65th Birthday*, in collaboration with A. Rebate and A. Resek (eds.) (Beirut: Lebanese British Friends of the National Museum, 2011); Claude Doumet-Serhal, *Sidon: 15 Years of Excavations* (Beirut: Lebanese British Friends of the National Museum, 2013).

Egypt, the Babylonians, and the Persians. The region of Phoenicia was no different. For example, a particular goal of Assyrian military campaigns was to reach the coast of the Mediterranean Sea, and in some cases this included reaching Phoenician sites such as Sidon, Arvad, and Byblos (Gubal) as early as the eleventh–tenth centuries BCE by Tiglath-pilesar I. In the middle of the eighth century BCE, Tiglath-pilesar III swept through the region, plundering tribute and particularly taking note of obeisance he received from Hiram of Tyre and Sibitti-bi'ili of Byblos, two local kings. In the next generation, Sennacherib marched through the region in the late eighth and early seventh centuries BCE, again collecting tribute and forcing the king of Sidon, Luli, to take refuge at Cyprus.[10] From these repeated conquests and the tribute taken, we can at least infer the great wealth of these cities.

From the Phoenicians themselves, we have precious few written sources to tell us of politics and history in the region, though we have enough evidence to identify the Phoenician language in a range of sources.[11] Probably the earliest native Phoenician inscription from an "official" source is the sarcophagus of a king named Ahiram, which dates from the tenth century BCE. The coffin itself is intricate, and the clear letters on the inscription present a wonderful example of the Phoenician writing system:[12]

> The sarcophagus which Ethba'l son of Ahiram king of Byblos made for Ahiram, his father, when committing him to eternity.

10. James B. Pritchard (ed.), *Ancient Near Eastern Texts Relating to the Old Testament*, 3rd ed., with supplement (Princeton, NJ: Princeton University Press, 1969), 274–288.
11. Jo Ann Hackett, "Phoenician and Punic," in *The Cambridge Encyclopedia of the World's Ancient Languages*, ed. Roger D. Woodward (Cambridge: Cambridge University Press, 2004), 265–285.
12. See Christopher B. Rollston, "Epigraphy: Writing Culture in the Iron Age Levant," in *The Wiley Blackwell Companion to Ancient Israel*, ed. Susan Niditch (Malden, MA: Wiley Blackwell, 2016), 131–150, from which this translation is adapted (here p. 142), as well as Rollston's

> And if a king among kings or a governor among governors, or an army commander should come up to Byblos and expose his sarcophagus, may the scepter of his rule be overturned, and may the throne of his kingdom be in tumult, and may rest flee from Byblos. And as for him, may his royal records be erased from Byblos.

Though the inscription tells us little about the inner workings of tenth century BCE Byblos, we do get insight into Phoenician royal religion—the king's son attempts to enact a curse on anyone who would disturb his father's legacy by dishonoring the grave.

Many shorter inscriptions were produced in the Phoenician script between the tenth and sixth centuries BCE at mainland sites[13]—not to mention from the broader Mediterranean world where Phoenicians traveled. In this latter category, the most famous and enigmatic is the so-called Nora Stone, a short narrative from the ninth or eighth century BCE inscribed on a large stone from the island of Nora, located in southern Sardinia off the coast of Italy. Most think the inscription refers to a battle fought by Phoenician explorers at the site. Though the reading is disputed, one plausible translation reads:[14]

> He fought with the Sardinians at Tarshish, and he drove them out. Among the Sardinians he is now at peace, and his army is at peace. Milkaton son of Shubna, general of king Pummay.

Writing and Literacy in the World of Ancient Israel: Epigraphic Evidence from the Iron Age (Atlanta: Society of Biblical Literature, 2010), esp. 19–41.

13. Rollston, *Writing*, 19–41; J. C. L. Gibson, *Textbook of Syrian Semitic Inscriptions*, vol. 3: *Phoenician Inscriptions, Including Inscriptions in the Mixed Dialect of Arslan Tash* (Oxford: Oxford University Press, 1982).

14. Frank Moore Cross, "An Interpretation of the Nora Stone," *Bulletin of the American Schools of Oriental Research* 208 (1972): 13–19.

The Phoenician writing system made its way far and wide across the Mediterranean world, in diverse contexts, such as in thousands of dedicatory inscriptions at the Phoenician settlement at Carthage, in northern Africa.[15] Beyond these inscriptions, and perhaps more important than all of them combined for historical and cultural interest, is the very script with which the Phoenicians wrote: their innovation with the Canaanite alphabet system paved the way not only for many other writing systems in the Levant (including Israel's) that borrowed the basic Phoenician script, but also westward into the Mediterranean Sea, as the Greeks adapted the writing system for their own alphabet (beginning around the eighth century BCE). This Phoenician-influenced Greek system then influenced the Romans, and thus some basic shapes and their corresponding letter sounds from the earliest Phoenician alphabet still persist into the Roman alphabet used in so much of the world today (Fig. 8.2).

Regarding Phoenician material culture: the Phoenicians were renowned producers of elite trade objects and art; a trip to any major art museum with selections on the ancient world will feature many creations from Phoenician artisans (Fig. 8.3).[16] Their style was heavily international, freely borrowing motifs from Egypt and Mesopotamia. They were famous crafters of ivory, and their art sometimes trended toward a type of realism, such as the intricately wrought bodies and faces on their sphinx figures (a Phoenician specialty motif).[17]

Pottery from the Phoenician mainland (especially Sarepta) reveals a reasonably clear picture, such as bichrome pottery and

15. Shelby Brown, *Late Carthaginian Child Sacrifice and Sacrificial Monuments in Their Mediterranean Context* (Sheffield: Sheffield Academic Press, 1991).

16. For a broad selection, see Sabatino Moscati (ed.), *The Phoenicians: Under the Scientific Direction of Sabatino Moscati* (New York: Abbeville, 1988).

17. Glenn E. Markoe, "The Emergence of Phoenician Art," *Bulletin of the American Schools of Oriental Research* 279 (1990): 13–26; Irene J.

＋ω	ꟼ		) ○ ₮ ﻉ	﴾ ∠	ᴠᴢ	◉	日工 Ƴ╕	⊿1	ᧃ	ĸ
T Σ	P		Π	N	M Λ	K		Z H	ΔΓ	B	A
T S	R		P	N	M L	KY		Z H	DG	B	A

FIG. 8.2 Phoenician alphabet, compared with Greek and Latin alphabets (capital letters); Phoenician alphabet as represented by the Ahiram sarcophagus (c. 1000–975 BCE), modeled on the script chart from Frank M. Cross, "The Arrow of Suwar, Retainer of 'Abday," in *Leaves from an Epigrapher's Notebook: Collected Papers in Hebrew and West Semitic Palaeography and Epigraphy* (Winona Lake, IN: Eisenbrauns, 2003), 195–202, here 197, Fig. 29.3.

FIG. 8.3 Three examples of Phoenician iconography. From left to right: (at left) Phoenician-style sphinx plaque; Nimrud; ninth century BCE; (center) silver and gold bowl from Kourion (Cyprus; date unknown); d. 16.8 cm; (right) front and side view of a small clay throne with ovoid object; Sidon; second–first century BCE (?); h. 6–7 cm. Drawings by Nora Clair, in Brian R. Doak, *Phoenician Aniconism in Its Ancient Near Eastern and Mediterranean Contexts* (Atlanta: SBL Press, 2015), figs. 2.3, 4.1, and 5.43, respectively.

specific types of vessels (globular jugs and side-spouted strainers). As one archaeologist put it, the sequential development and types

Winter, "Is There a South Syrian Style of Ivory Carving in the Early First Millennium B.C.?," vol. 1, 101–30, and "Phoenician and North Syrian Ivory Carving in Historical Perspective: Questions of Style and Distribution," vol. 1, 187–224, both in Winter's collected essays, *On Art in the Ancient Near East*, 2 vols. (Leiden: Brill, 2010).

of pottery at major Phoenician sites (particularly with reference to Tyre) is "linear and clear," and "the diverse stages of its evolution can be recognized with a great degree of certainty."[18] Scholars who study the Phoenician religion are quick to point out that we know so little, and that we have no singular, monolithic, or official Phoenician religion.[19] Worshipers at Phoenician sites participated in religious rituals and engaged in belief that seems to have been shared by many groups in the region: there are multiple deities, both male and female, in a polytheistic system; there were formal temples and less formal cultic sites; a particular male deity was often called "Ba'al," a somewhat generic Semitic term meaning "lord"; and worshipers engaged in rituals involving dead ancestors and spoke incantations against demons and other cosmic forces. By name, different cities seem to have highlighted specific deities, often in a "pairing" of a male and female. At Byblos, Baal Shamem ("lord of heaven") and Baalat Gubal ("lady of Byblos," possibly identified with the goddess Anat); at Tyre, Melqart (who would later be equated with

---

18. Francisco Núñez Calvo, "Phoenicia," in *Beyond the Homeland: Markers in Phoenician Chronology*, ed. Claudia Sagona (Leuven: Peeters, 2008), 19–95, here at 69. See also William P. Anderson, "The Beginnings of Phoenician Pottery: Vessel Shape, Style, and Ceramic Technology in the Early Phases of the Phoenician Iron Age," *Bulletin of the American Schools of Oriental Research* 279 (1990): 35–54 and Patricia M. Bikai, "The Phoenician Pottery," in *La nécropole d'Amathonte, Tombes 113– 367, vol. 2: Céramiques non chypriotes*, ed. Vassos Karageorghis, Oliver Picard, and Christiane Tytgat (Nicosia: Leventis, 1987), 1–19, as well as updates in López-Ruiz and Doak (eds.), *Handbook*.

19. See attempts at a synthesis by Markoe, *Phoenicians*, 115–42; Richard J. Clifford, "Phoenician Religion," *Bulletin of the American Schools of Oriental Research* 279 (1990): 55–64; Sergio Ribichini, "Beliefs and Religious Life," in *The Phoenicians: Under the Scientific Direction of Sabatino Moscati*, ed. Sabatino Moscati (New York: Abbeville, 1988), 104–125.

the Greek Hercules) and Astarte (a popular regional goddess); and at Sidon, Eshmun (a healing deity) and Astarte. We also know that the Phoenicians took these religious traditions with them to their western colonies. Melqart, for example, was also the principle deity at Gadir, an important Phoenician colony in southern Spain. Phoenicians produced images of their deities in normal ways for their context, but may have also engaged in "aniconic" worship (i.e., without images), a move that can be compared with an alleged Israelite practice for not making images of their deity.[20]

PHOENICIA AND THE PHOENICIANS IN THE HEBREW BIBLE

In its so-called Primeval History, in Genesis 1–11, the Hebrew Bible sketches out the origins of various people groups around Israel. Scholars typically do not take these materials as historical in the sense that they would represent actual bloodlines and migration patterns, but these materials do have value for telling us how ancient Israelite authors thought of their identity vis-à-vis their neighbors.[21] How do these stories represent the Phoenicians?[22] Not in very clear ways, though there are suggestions. Genesis 10 offers a genealogy for Canaan, one of

---

20. Doak, *Phoenician Aniconism*.
21. Providing a date for the materials in Genesis 1–11 has been a notorious problem in biblical scholarship. Regarding the Phoenicians, see Yu. B. Tsirkin, "Japheth's Progeny and the Phoenicians," in *Phoenicia and the Bible*, Proceedings of the Conference held at the University of Leuven, March 15–16, 1990 (Leuven: Peeters, 1991), 117–134.
22. The contents of this portion of the chapter have been re-written from my essay "Phoenicians in the Hebrew Bible," in *The Oxford Handbook of the Phoenician and Punic Mediterranean*, ed. Carolina López-Ruiz and Brian Doak (Oxford: Oxford University Press, 2019), 657–670.

Noah's grandsons—in fact, Canaan is the son of Ham, who "saw his father's nakedness" (whatever that means) at the end of Genesis 9, thus incurring a curse on his entire line, including, directly, Canaan. These Canaanites are categorized in various ways throughout the Bible; they are often associated with groups such as Jebusites, Amorites, Girgashites, Hivites, and others (see Gen 10:15–20, and chapter 2 of this book). In the vision of Genesis 10, Canaanite territory extends from Sidon, as a northern coastal boundary, all the way south to around the Dead Sea. The Canaanite territory is thus larger than the thin coastal strip of Phoenician cities, yet it includes not only Sidon but also Tyre, Dor, and Sarepta (but notably not Byblos and Arvad, to the north of Sidon; see the reference to Arvad in Gen 10:18).

Genesis 49 and Deuteronomy 3 mention Sidon in prominent ways, but again, not Tyre or Byblos. And then later, Joshua and Judges invoke Sidon as an important site and boundary marker, calling Sidon "Mighty Sidon" and "Sidon the Great" (in Josh 11:8 and 19:28; see also Josh 13:4). This may reflect a political situation where Sidon was perceived as strong—as one of the oldest and most powerful Phoenician cities, nailing down an exact era would be difficult. Tyre's prominence began in the eighth century BCE, but Tyre does not appear alongside Sidon in the Bible until at least the sixth century BCE and the alleged encounter between Israelite kings (David and Solomon) and the Tyrian king Hiram. Some biblical authors, all during the sixth century BCE and later, saw Tyre and Sidon as a pair, perhaps invoking the power of the Phoenician coast generally (Joel 3:4; Zech 9:2; Jer 47:4).

Despite playing no major role in Genesis, the exodus from Egypt and wilderness wanderings (Exodus, Numbers, and Deuteronomy), or settlement traditions in Joshua or Judges, Phoenicians appear at several critical moments in the story of Israel's monarchy in the books of Samuel and Kings (as well as some parallel and nonparallel stories in Chronicles). The construction of the Israelite Temple features a Phoenician king from Tyre, Hiram, in a prominent role of partnership alongside Israel.

Upon rising to undisputed kingship, David receives validation from Hiram: "King Hiram of Tyre sent messengers to David, along with cedar trees, and carpenters and masons who built David a house. David then perceived that the LORD had established him as king over Israel" (2 Sam 5:11–12). Hiram then disappears from the scene until David's son, Solomon, takes the throne. Hiram again interacts with the Israelite king through messengers (1 Kgs 5); citing the Sidonian craftwork with wood—even though he is talking to a Tyrian king?—Solomon requests building materials for the Temple, while Hiram asks for food provisions. Solomon and Hiram make a treaty (1 Kgs 5:12) and proceed to work together to build the Temple. A separate Tyrian individual, confusingly named Hiram from Tyre (i.e., not Hiram the "king" of Tyre), pitches in his specialized labor to help Solomon build his personal residence and also various items for the Temple (1 Kgs 7).[23]

Long after the Temple has been built, Hiram and Solomon engage in a quarrel about land:

> King Hiram of Tyre having supplied Solomon with cedar and cypress timber and gold, as much as he desired, King Solomon gave to Hiram twenty cities in the land of Galilee. But when Hiram came from Tyre to see the cities that Solomon had given him, they did not please him. Therefore he said, "What kind of cities are these that you have given me, my brother?" So they are called the land of Cabul [Good for nothing (?)] to this day. But Hiram had sent to the king one hundred twenty talents of gold. (1 Kgs 9:11–14)

Why narrate an account like this? Perhaps it is truly historical, as the account has an "incidental" nature that would make its

---

23. Note that 2 Chronicles 2:12–14 attempts to explain the problem of the two Hirams (the king and the craftsman) by invoking a letter from King Hiram to Solomon regarding craftsman Hiram. See discussion in Ralph W. Klein, *2 Chronicles*, Hermeneia Commentary (Minneapolis: Fortress Press, 2012), 37.

invention unclear for ideological reasons. On the other hand, perhaps the narrator intends to present Solomon as the more powerful partner in the treaty by having him offer undesirable cities to Hiram as a rude gesture? Or perhaps Solomon's involvement with Hiram and the Phoenicians—who would later be maligned as arrogant false worshipers by the prophets—indicates that we must view Solomon in a negative light (note 1 Kgs 11, where the narrator calls Solomon to account for his sins)? We do know that archaeology confirms the material contact that Israel had with the Phoenicians, as evidenced by the widespread use of Phoenician pottery, timber, and artistic motifs (e.g., the sphinx decorations for the Temple and the Ark of the Covenant; see 1 Kgs 6:23–36; Exod 25:18–22; 1 Sam 4:4; and note also Ahab's "house of ivory" in 1 Kgs 22:39 [compare with Amos 3:15; 6:4; Ps 45:8], which may have been built with Phoenician artistic assistance or material trade for the ivory).[24] The historical status of the Hiram accounts remains a question; presuming the biblical texts were produced in the Iron Age (and in the case of Kings, perhaps finalized in the sixth century BCE), the Hebrew Bible has the earliest reference to Hiram and there are no narratives other than the Bible recounting these stories of alliance with Israel that would have occurred in the tenth century BCE.[25]

Another crucial link to the Phoenician world comes through the narratives involving a princess from the city of Sidon, Jezebel, in 1–2 Kings. Before Jezebel arrives on the scene, we already learn that Solomon participated in Phoenician religion as it was

24. Carly L. Crouch, *The Making of Israel: Cultural Diversity in the Southern Levant and the Formation of Ethnic Identity in Deuteronomy* (Leiden: Brill, 2014), 28–29; Amihai Mazar, *The Archaeology of the Land of the Bible, 10,000–586 B.C.E.* (New York: Doubleday, 1992), 376–379, 464–475, 502–514.

25. A first-century CE Jewish author, Josephus, preserves additional accounts regarding Hiram and Solomon, including a claim that the letters these two kings exchanged are "preserved to this day among the Tyrians." See Josephus's *Jewish Antiquities* 8.146–148 and *Against*

practiced at Sidon: "For Solomon followed Astarte the goddess of the Sidonians . . . he has forsaken me [God], [and] worshiped the goddess of the Sidonians" (1 Kgs 11:5, 33). By 1 Kings 16, the Sidonian influence problem appears in a more extreme form. A king named Omri takes control of the northern part of the country, continuing the breakaway from the Davidic line of kings God had appointed to rule over Israel forever in 2 Samuel 7. The narrator casts Omri in a negative religious light (1 Kgs 16:25–26), and his son, Ahab, continues in his father's ways, adding a new problem to the mix:

> [Ahab] took as his wife Jezebel daughter of King Ethbaal of the Sidonians, and went and served Baal, and worshiped him. He erected an altar for Baal in the house of Baal, which he built in Samaria. Ahab also made a sacred pole. Ahab did more to provoke the anger of the LORD, the God of Israel, than had all the kings of Israel who were before him. (1 Kgs 16:31–33)

Thus, we are led to presume, the Sidonian Jezebel's introduction into the country exacerbates the existing idolatry problem, linking her presence to increased worship of Baal, a deity rival to Israel's God.

These problems grow more intense in 1 Kings 18, when Jezebel confronts the prophet Elijah. The prophet had called a drought upon the nation, and then defeated a group of Jezebel's Baal prophets at a famous battle upon Mount Carmel—these prophets, of Baal and also of the goddess Asherah, were said to "eat at Jezebel's table" (1 Kgs 18:19), that is, she supported them,

Apion 1.17–20 (the latter for the quote about letter preservation), in J. M. G. Barclay (translation and commentary), *Flavius Josephus. Translation and Commentary*, vol. 10: *Against Apion*, ed. S. Mason (Leiden: Brill, 2007).

even though the prophets themselves are not exactly designated as Phoenician imports. The contest potentially refers to an enigmatic aspect of Phoenician religion in that Elijah taunts the Baal prophets with the words, "perhaps he [Baal] is asleep and must be awakened," after Baal does not respond to their rituals (1 Kgs 18:27). Some native ancient Phoenician sources speak of something like an "awakening" ritual, when a deity is buried and then brought back to life in some way, and this text may be read as a mockery of that ritual.[26] Elijah personally slaughters the Baal prophets after he defeats them in the contest, invoking Jezebel's wrath and subsequent (failed) promise to kill Elijah. Sandwiched in the middle of all of this drama involving Sidon, in 1 Kings 17 we read of an unnamed widow living in Zarephath, situated between Tyre and Sidon but "which belongs to Sidon" (1 Kgs 17:8). This widow fears she will die because of the drought the prophet had brought upon the land, but nevertheless she shelters Elijah, receives miraculous food, and Elijah raises the woman's son from the dead. "Now I know that you are a man of God, and that the word of the LORD in your mouth is truth," she proclaims (1 Kgs 17:24). Thus, we see that although Phoenician leaders are wicked (note Jezebel in 1 Kgs 21), the common populace can, according to this narrator, be a source of God's provision and confess the power of a true prophet. Jezebel dies a gruesome death in 2 Kings 9—she is tossed from a tower and her body devoured by dogs—thus fulfilling Elijah's earlier pronouncement that she would die and be dishonored in just such a way.

Taken as a whole, the Jezebel narratives help prove an important point for the narration of 1–2 Kings (perhaps compiled after the destruction of Jerusalem in the year 586 BCE): Israel, and particularly the northern kingdom into which Jezebel married, forsook the Lord and earned their own destruction through idolatry.

---

26. Gibson, *Textbook*, 151–159; Corrine Bonnet, *Melqart: Cultes et Mythes de l'Héraclès Tyrien en Méditerranée* (Leuven: Peeters, 1988), 104–112.

Similar to the biblical engagement with the other neighbors of Israel, most of these stories have no corollary in any other literature or material evidence from the Iron Age. Jezebel and the widow of Zarephath appear only in the Bible. Perhaps modern readers will find some stories more historically (or theologically or personally) compelling than others. Whatever the case, we can reasonably assume that in some cases these narratives are based in historical reality. Figures like Omri and Ahab were real, and documented in other sources from outside the Bible with no interest in fabricating the names of Israel's kings (specifically, Assyrian inscriptions). Israelites did worship a variety of deities other than the God the Bible's authors wanted them to exclusively worship; international marriages for political purposes like the one Ahab and Jezebel had are known from the ancient world; and it's reasonable to think that there was competition between religious professionals (such as prophets and priests) in ancient Israel, especially during periods of political unrest or social change. Moreover, we must be reasonable about what we expect from ancient sources—most texts from the ancient world cannot be corroborated in any accepted sense with other sources. The Phoenician inscriptions mentioned earlier in this chapter, at Nora and the Ahiram sarcophagus, also have no parallels or independent attestations for their information. The Bible, however, has received unique scrutiny as a historical source because of its lengthy and passionately motivated presentation—and because of its influence on the lives of its readers.

Ancient Israel's prophets attest to the power and influence of Phoenician cities at many different points. True to form, these prophets often have bombastic and harsh things to say. Take the prophet Amos, for example—if this prophet operated in the eighth century BCE, then we might have access to Israelite views of Phoenicians during an early period of Phoenician colonial and commercial activity. In Amos 1, the prophet spews out judgment upon many of Israel's close neighbors, such as the Philistines, Arameans, Moabites, Edomites, and more, including Phoenician Tyre:

Thus says the LORD: For three transgressions of Tyre, and for four, I will not revoke the punishment; because they delivered entire communities over to Edom, and did not remember the covenant of kinship. So I will send a fire on the wall of Tyre, fire that shall devour its strongholds. (Amos 1:9–10)

These references are obscure. What did Amos mean by saying that Tyre "delivered entire communities over to Edom"? Is this a reference to a slave trade (see also Ezek 27:13; Joel 4:6–7) or to some other treacherous act? What was the "covenant of kinship" Tyre had with Edom? And did a fire devour Tyre's strongholds? (Tyre was besieged by Alexander the Great in the fourth century BCE—is that the reference here?)

Isaiah, another eighth-century BCE prophet—though the dating and editorial layers in the book are quite uncertain—mentions Sidon and Tyre in a critique of Phoenician wealth and arrogance:

The oracle concerning Tyre. Wail, O ships of Tarshish, for your fortress is destroyed. When they came in from Cyprus they learned of it. Be still, O inhabitants of the coast, O merchants of Sidon, your messengers crossed over the sea and were on the mighty waters; your revenue was the grain of Shihor, the harvest of the Nile; you were the merchant of the nations. Be ashamed, O Sidon, for the sea has spoken, the fortress of the sea, saying: "I have neither labored nor given birth, I have neither reared young men nor brought up young women." When the report comes to Egypt, they will be in anguish over the report about Tyre. Cross over to Tarshish—wail, O inhabitants of the coast! Is this your exultant city whose origin is from days of old, whose feet carried her to settle far away? (Isa 23:1–7)

The theme of Phoenician trade and wealth leads the biblical prophetic critics to condemn these coastal cities, predicting their doom (see also, for example, Jer 25:20–23; 27:3–6; 47:4; Joel

3:4; Zech 9:1–4). Of several references in Isaiah 23, the location of Tarshish deserves explanation. Greek and Roman sources speak of a nearly mystical location called "Tartessos" far in the Phoenician western Mediterranean trading world, in what is now southern Spain, famed for its riches and precious metals. Isaiah's Tarshish may be identified with Tartessos, telling us something about the fame of the Phoenician trade network and how Phoenicia's neighbors envied their broad economic and political reach.[27]

Another famous engagement with Phoenicia appears in the prophet Ezekiel in the sixth century BCE. Ezekiel 26–28 contain a long condemnation of Tyre and the "prince of Tyre," its unnamed ruler. The native Semitic term for Tyre in Hebrew, *tsur* (rock), alludes to Tyre's location and original status as an island just off the coast of the mainland, and forms the basis of Ezekiel's imagery at the opening of his set of oracles: "See, I am against you, O Tyre! I will hurl many nations against you, as the sea hurls its waves. They shall destroy the walls of Tyre and break down its towers. I will scrape its soil from it and make it a bare rock" (Ezek 26:3–4).

In Ezekiel 27 the prophet goes on to catalog the great wealth of the city, listing its trading allies, exports, and activities, culminating in the desire that Tyre sink to the bottom of the sea: "So you were filled and heavily laden in the heart of the seas. . . . Your riches . . . with all the company that is with you, sink into the heart of the seas on the day of your ruin" (vv. 26–27, excerpts).

---

27. On Tarshish elsewhere in the Bible, see Genesis 10:4; 1 Kings 10:22; Psalm 72:10; Jeremiah 10:9; Ezekiel 27:12, 25; and Jonah 1:3. For research on Tartessos, see, e.g., Sebastián Celestino and Carolina López-Ruiz, *Tartessos and the Phoenicians in Iberia* (Oxford: Oxford University Press, 2016).

WHAT HAPPENED TO THE PHOENICIANS?

The prophetic condemnations of Phoenicia were realized, even if by chance and only partially, when Tyre was besieged by Alexander the Great in 332 BCE—a military feat often lauded as the Greek king's greatest tactical achievement. The siege worked to connect what had been an island just off the coast to the mainland (ancient Ushu, closely associated with the island), leaving the coastal landscape changed to this day in contemporary Lebanon. References to Phoenician cities continue throughout the Hellenistic and Roman periods, when Phoenicia became a properly named district. Early Jewish works such as 1 Maccabees (5:15), 1 Esdras (5:55), 2 Esdras (1:11), and the Christian New Testament (Matthew, Luke, and Acts) mention Phoenician locations, while further mention of the Phoenician trade in slaves continues as well (1 Macc 3:41 and 2 Macc 8:11). The New Testament in particular mentions Phoenicians in a few prominent locations—Jesus ministers to a "Syro-Phoenician" woman (Mk 7:26) and travels to Sidon and Tyre in a move echoing the prophet Elijah's work there with the widow (Lk 4:26). Archaeological remains and coinage show a continued network of exchange between the upper Galilee region of Israel and Tyre,[28] and the book of Acts mentions Paul journeying through Tyre (Acts 21:3–7; 27:3) and depicts the Roman-sponsored governor Herod Antipas providing food for Tyre and Sidon (Acts 12:20).

In the first–second century CE, an individual named Philo from Byblos wrote a "Phoenician History," supposedly preserving the records of a man named Sanchouniaton (possibly a real

---

28. Jonathan L. Reed, *Archaeology and the Galilean Jesus: A Re-Examination of the Evidence* (Harrisburg, PA: Trinity Press, 2002), 185–186.

person, whose historical records had roots in a much earlier period).[29] Sanchouniaton spoke of Phoenician creation stories, the birth of deities in a bygone era, various cultural inventors among the Phoenicians, and various forms of cult and worship at Tyre and other far-flung locations. Of Phoenicia's many colonies in the Mediterranean world, Carthage was perhaps the most famous. Archaeological evidence may point to a founding of the city by its mainland sponsor, Tyre, in the late ninth century BCE, though the site gained independence and had a long and complex historical development. Phoenician deities were worshiped at the site for centuries, as evidenced by the "Marseilles Tariff" inscription (fourth century BCE?), which possibly refers to practices at the temple of the Phoenician deity Baal-Saphon. Thousands of dedicatory inscriptions at Carthage mark the occasion of dead infants and sacrificed lambs—and debate has raged about whether these infants were sacrificed as part of a grisly ancient ritual or whether the children had already died and were later dedicated to particular deities. The history of Carthage came to a stunning end through the so-called Punic Wars, which lasted about a century (from 264–146 BCE), fought between Rome and Carthage. In the second of these wars (ending around 201 BCE), the Carthaginian general Hannibal famously crossed the Alps with elephants to attack Rome, and in the third and final conflict, Rome utterly destroyed Carthage.

Even today, the great feats of Phoenician seafarers continue to inspire conspiracies and legends about how far away from their homeland Phoenician explorers may have traveled during the first millennium BCE. In 2019 the Travel Channel's hit TV show *America Unearthed* featured an episode attempting to track down a possible Phoenician inscription from the state of Wyoming (which

---

29. Carolina López-Ruiz, *When the Gods Were Born: Greek Cosmogonies and the Near East* (Cambridge, MA: Harvard University Press, 2010), 94–101.

was fake), and throughout the twentieth century several forged Phoenician inscriptions in the United States and South America made headlines and provided fodder for discussion about ancient explorers crossing the Atlantic long before Europeans attempted the feat.[30]

30. E.g., Frank Moore Cross, "The Phoenician Inscription from Brazil: A Nineteenth-Century Forgery," *Orientalia* 37 (1968): 437–460.

Conclusion

History and Identity

THE CONTEMPORARY NATION OF ISRAEL continues to engage its direct neighbors—Egypt, Syria, Lebanon, and Jordan—along many of the same lines as biblical Israel engaged its neighbors: hints of cooperation, fighting, and contentious narratives of betrayal and violence. Indeed, "Israel" today is not even a singular, homogenous, uncontested state, as Palestinians make a claim to the land and nation as their own as well (Palestine). The creation of the state of Israel in 1947 provided a homeland for the Jewish people that has ties to the ancient biblical homeland of the Jews, but could only do so in the face of other national and tribal identities within the same boundaries. The British had a plan and the Americans had a plan and the United Nations had a plan, and there was a war in 1948 (the so-called Arab-Israeli War) and then another in 1967 (the Six-Day War), pitting Israel against Syria, Egypt, and Jordan, and resulting in the Israeli occupation of land formerly controlled by others in the West Bank, Gaza Strip, the Golan Heights, and elsewhere. Some have proposed a "two-state solution," which would grant independent national identities to Palestine and Israel, but complicating factors have time and again stalled progress. Joshua's attempt in the Hebrew Bible to eradicate the Canaanites from the land haunts Israel's history and echoes uncomfortably throughout conversations about Palestinian Arabs forced to flee their homeland in 1948, Jewish settlers attempting to make homes on (disputed) Palestinian lands in the wake of the 1967 war, and even

Ancient Israel's Neighbors. Brian R. Doak, Oxford University Press (2020). © Oxford University Press.
DOI: 10.1093/oso/9780190690595.001.0001

the Holocaust. Political actors periodically make claims to archaic primacy in the land, appealing to the Bible, to archaeology, and to legend.

These sorts of problems can strike home, on a personal level, for our own nation or even the neighborhoods we live in. Neighbors force us into difficult conversations about our own identity, as they did for ancient Israel in its struggle to define itself. Having written this book, I'm left with a new appreciation of the complexity of the topic at hand—questions about what a nation or state really is, whether any political or geographical boundaries are natural, and about what we know and don't know about all of the specific neighbors of ancient Israel treated in this book's chapters. By way of conclusion, then, allow me to reflect back on the categorical divisions I used to organize my research and comment on some challenges and frustrations these categories pose: archaeology, the Bible, and the ongoing history of the people in question after the biblical period.

I had started out this project hoping that in each chapter I could offer a discussion of each neighbor that would be fully integrated with the biblical data from the start. I soon realized this would be difficult—impossible, actually—in a study that endeavored to provide not so much new and consensus-altering original research but rather what I hoped would be an engaging summary of current views. Sometimes, as it turned out, we just don't know very much about a particular neighbor—and all that the Hebrew Bible has to say, in many cases, is that the neighbor was an enemy and had forbidden and horrible religious practices. To be blunt, I felt frustrated, many times, when finishing the "archaeology" section for a given group and then seeing how this research transitioned into the discussion of the Bible. Having learned something about a particular group's pottery, iconography, art, language, and history, and then starting on the "biblical representation" sections, I discovered a similar pattern almost every time: *the neighbor has shameful origins; they have a bad religion; they fought with Israel; and the prophets hate them, predicting doom.*

What I ended up doing was trying harder to present each of the neighbors on its own terms and then trying to show what the biblical authors were doing on their own terms. Where these two perspectives meet is not always clear. At times, we could see how the biblical texts converged with archaeology and other materials. The book of Genesis presents the Edomites (through Esau) as the ancient brother of Israel, and in fact some of the earliest references to the specific name of Israel's deity, YHWH, come from Edomite territory. The book of Kings remembers the Phoenicians as artisans and traders in timber, and indeed we know that Phoenician craftsmanship was one of their defining features in the ancient Mediterranean world. In the case of the Arameans, we even have a tantalizing native inscription (the Tel Dan Stele) that mentions characters and events also known from the Bible, albeit with different claims. And so on. Still, so much more cannot be easily correlated. The effect, for me at least, is to begin to understand more deeply how the biblical authors were not disinterested historians, scientists, or archaeologists. They were not journalists or scholars, and they were not concerned with presenting multiple viewpoints or upholding the fairness or extolling the beauty of diversity in a fractured world. Rather, they were people, perhaps like us, with intense political views, ideological commitments, and religious conviction.

Viewed through the lens of a progressive political project, we may feel moved to reject the othering of Israel's neighbors in the Bible, and thus we can only see much of the Bible's presentation of its neighbors as a lamentable mistake. Indeed, from this perspective, the Bible can be considered the primal source of and ongoing justification for the West's triumphal attitude toward its neighbors and the world at large. Viewed from a conservative theological or spiritual lens, we would probably be persuaded to take what the Bible says at face value—the Philistines and Edomites and Ammonites were truly as horrible as the biblical authors say they are. In this view, those who inherit the mantle of "spiritual Israel" inherit the blessing of the biblical God, and those who participate in the ways of the Canaanites are doomed to perish in their iniquity. Others may see a middle way between these extremes of total rejection and total embrace of the Bible's ancient message about its neighbors. Whether one likes it or not, it's hard to deny the fact that these neighbors have been indelibly marked by the biblical authors, and the Bible continues to set the research and interest agendas to a very large degree, despite laudable attempts by scholars to remain neutral or chart an independent course.

It is possible to achieve some level of historical context, if not some sympathy, for the way biblical authors wrote about their neighbors by considering the circumstances under which ancient Israel settled its land in the early Iron Age (around 1200–1100 BCE). Israel entered a space where new identities were blooming; the Late Bronze Age system had collapsed, and new opportunities arose for smaller groups to emerge. Israel was one of these groups—and the land they first settled, in the rugged hill country, needed to be literally and physically carved out, for terracing and capturing water and for clearing brush and stones to make inhabitable space. These were no doubt very intense times. And simultaneously, all around them, other groups sought to carve out their own space: Moabites, Edomites, Philistines, Ammonites, Canaanites, and others. This early period of intense competition for resources echoed out into Israel's story of itself in the Bible. Biblical authors represented one vision—or rather, as many visions as there were authors and distinct sources—but we are left in the dark regarding how "average Israelites" (i.e., not the biblical authors) would have viewed these neighboring groups.

In the concluding section to each chapter, "What Happened to the . . .," I found bewildering complexity and was forced to cut many of these sections shorter than I would have liked. The problem is not as simple as saying, "Well, when the Babylonians or Persians or Greeks or Romans rolled in, this or that group simply ceased to exist." True, under a national label, the Ammonites probably ceased to exist during the Persian period or at least by the time of the Greek conquest of the ancient Near East. But does this mean that people living in this region simply vanished into thin air? Or ceased thinking of themselves with familial or tribal identities that had long histories quite independent of the Bible or any empire? No, they did not. To be sure, many of these areas remain occupied today, after a centuries-long process of migration, hybridization, war, continuity, and many other dizzying levels of imperceptible change. Nevertheless, though I was not always able to track in great detail the ways these identities played out after the Iron Age, this area of research is ripe for more work, and students looking to break new ground might do well to pursue questions of local identity for particular groups during the Hellenistic and Roman periods—and beyond.

Ultimately, we are thrown back upon the problem of history, memory, and interpretation I raised in the first chapter of this book: Are we bound to see Israel's neighbors as Israel saw them—filtered through the Hebrew Bible—or should we use the Bible as but one (flawed) source among many others we can use to reconstruct the reality of these other nations "as they really were," giving them their rightful place in history as independent entities who wanted the same things ancient Israelites wanted (safety, autonomy, success, fertility, etc.)? Has the Bible been more of a hindrance than a help for reconstructing the history of the region? Or does the Bible show us what we truly need to see on some other level, transcending history, in the realms of religion or spirituality? Whatever the case, hopefully readers have caught my many cues and cautions about making simplistic judgments about complex issues of the history, archaeology, language, and geography of the neighbors covered in this book, as well as Israel. There is so much that we do not know—so much left to learn.

SOURCES AND RESEARCH TOOLS

The following resources (listed reverse chronologically) will help readers continue their study of ancient Israel's neighbors in a number of different ways. Some of these sources listed below are cited in the footnotes for particular chapters, and some are not—but all of these publications will give readers ample ideas for further study.

Other Books that Treat Israel's Neighbors and Immediate Geographical Context

Jonathan S. Greer, John W. Hilber, and John H. Walton, *Behind the Scenes of the Old Testament: Cultural, Social, and Historical Contexts* (Grand Rapids: Baker Academic, 2018)

Bill T. Arnold and Brent A. Strawn (eds.), *The World around the Old Testament: The People and Places of the Ancient Near East* (Grand Rapids: Baker Academic, 2016)

Ann E. Killebrew, *Biblical Peoples and Ethnicity: An Archaeological Study of Egyptians, Canaanites, Philistines, and Early Israel, 1300–1100 B.C.E.* (Atlanta: Society of Biblical Literature, 2005)

Alfred J. Hoerth, Gerald L. Mattingly, and Edwin M. Yamauchi (eds.), *Peoples of the Old Testament World* (Grand Rapids: Baker Academic, 1998)

D. J. Wiseman, *Peoples of Old Testament Times* (Oxford: Oxford University Press, 1973)

Archaeological resources

Ephraim Stern, *Archaeology of the Land of the Bible*, vol. 2: *The Assyrian, Babylonian, and Persian Periods, 732–332 BCE* (New York: Doubleday, 2001)

Thomas E. Levy (ed.), *The Archaeology of Society in the Holy Land* (London: Leicester University Press, 1995)

Ephraim Stern (ed.), *The New Encyclopedia of Archaeological Excavations in the Holy Land*, 4 vols. (Jerusalem: Israel Exploration Society and Carta, 1993)

Amihai Mazar, *Archaeology of the Land of the Bible, 10,000–586 B.C.E.* (New York: Doubleday, 1992)

Historical Geography

Anson F. Rainey and R. Steven Notley, *The Sacred Bridge*, Carta's Atlas of the Biblical World (Jerusalem: Carta, 2006)

Gershon Galil and Moshe Weinfeld (eds.), *Studies in Historical Geography and Biblical Historiography, Presented to Zechariah Kallai* (Leiden: Brill, 2000)

Yohanan Aharoni, *The Land of the Bible: A Historical Geography*, illustrated and revised, trans. A. F. Rainey (Philadelphia: Westminster Press, 1979)

For Inscriptions, Texts, and Language

Holger Gzella, *A Cultural History of Aramaic: From the Beginnings to the Advent of Islam* (Leiden: Brill, 2015)

Christopher B. Hays, *Hidden Riches: A Sourcebook for the Comparative Study of the Hebrew Bible and the Ancient Near East* (Louisville, KY: Westminster John Knox, 2014)

Christopher Rollston, *Writing and Literacy in the World of Ancient Israel: Epigraphic Evidence from the Iron Age* (Atlanta: Society of Biblical Literature, 2010)

Shmuel Ahituv, *Echoes from the Past: Hebrew and Cognate Inscriptions from the Biblical Period* (Jerusalem: Carta, 2008)

Frank M. Cross, *Leaves from an Epigrapher's Notebook: Collected Papers in Hebrew and West Semitic Paleography and Epigraphy* (Winona Lake, IN: Eisenbrauns, 2003)

Dennis Pardee, *Ritual and Cult at Ugarit* (Atlanta: Society of Biblical Literature, 2002)

William W. Hallo and K. Lawson Younger Jr. (eds.), *The Context of Scripture*, 3 vols. (Leiden: Brill, 2002)

Simon B. Parker (ed.), *Ugaritic Narrative Poetry* (Atlanta: Scholars Press, 1997)

Joseph Naveh, *Early History of the Alphabet: An Introduction to West Semitic Epigraphy and Palaeography*, 2nd rev. ed., reprinted (Jerusalem: Magnes Press, 1997)

J. C. L. Gibson, *Textbook of Syrian Semitic Inscriptions*, 3 vols. (Oxford: Oxford University Press, 1975–1982)

J. Hoftijzer and G. van der Kooij (eds.), *Aramaic Texts from Deir 'Alla* (Leiden: Brill, 1976)

James B. Pritchard (ed.), *Ancient Near Eastern Texts Relating to the Old Testament*, 3rd ed. with Supplement (Princeton, NJ: Princeton University Press, 1969)

Major Sources on the Canaanites

Brendon C. Benz, *The Land before the Kingdom of Israel: A History of the Southern Levant and the People Who Populated It* (Winona Lake, IN: Eisenbrauns, 2016).

K. L. Noll, *Canaan and Israel in Antiquity: A Textbook on History and Religion*, 2nd ed. (London: Bloomsbury, 2013)

Jonathan M. Golden, *Ancient Canaan and Israel: An Introduction* (New York: Oxford University Press, 2009)

Beth Alpert Nakhai, *Archaeology and the Religions of Canaan and Israel* (Boston: American Schools of Oriental Research, 2001)

Jonathan N. Tubb, *Canaanites* (Norman: University of Oklahoma Press, 1998)

Major Sources on the Arameans

Angelika Berlejung, Andreas Schüle, and Aren M. Maeir (eds.), *Wandering Aramaeans: Aramaeans outside Syria. Textual and Archaeological Perspectives* (Wiesbaden: Harrassowitz, 2017)

K. Lawson Younger, *A Political History of the Arameans: From Their Origins to the End of Their Polities* (SBL Press: Atlanta, 2016)

Gotthard G. G. Reinhold, *The Rise and Fall of the Aramaeans in the Ancient Near East, from Their First Appearance until 732 BCE* (Frankfurt: Peter Lang, 2016)

Herbert Niehr (ed.), *The Aramaeans in Ancient Syria* (Leiden: Brill, 2014)

P. M. Michèle Daviau, John William Wevers, and Michael Weigl (eds.), *The World of the Aramaeans*, 3 vols. (Sheffield: Sheffield Academic Press, 2001)

Edward Lipiński, *The Aramaeans: Their Ancient History, Culture, Religion* (Leuven: Peeters, 2000)

Major Sources on the Ammonites

Craig W. Tyson, *The Ammonites: Elites, Empires, and Sociopolitical Change (1000–500 BCE)* (London: Bloomsbury, 2014)

Benjamin W. Porter, *Complex Communities: The Archaeology of Early Iron Age West-Central Jordan* (Tucson: University of Arizona Press, 2013)

Burton MacDonald and Randall W. Younker (eds.), *Ancient Ammon* (Leiden: Brill, 1999)

Ulrich Hübner, *Die Ammoniter. Untersuchungen zur Geschichte, Kultur und Religion eines transjordanischen Volkes im 1. Jahrtausend v. Chr.* (Wiesbaden: Harrassowitz, 1992)

Major Sources on the Moabites

Benjamin W. Porter, *Complex Communities: The Archaeology of Early Iron Age West-Central Jordan* (Tucson: University of Arizona Press, 2013)

Erasmus Gass, *Die Moabiter—Geschichte und Kultur eines ostjordanisches Volkes im 1. Jahrtausent v. Chr* (Wiesbaden: Harrassowitz, 2009)

Bruce Routledge, *Moab in the Iron Age: Hegemony, Polity, Archaeology* (Philadelphia: University of Pennsylvania Press, 2004)

Piotr Bienkowski (ed.), *Early Edom and Moab: The Beginning of the Iron Age in Southern Jordan* (Sheffield: J. R. Collis Publications, 1992)

Andrew Dearman (ed.), *Studies in the Mesha Inscription and Moab* (Atlanta: Scholars Press, 1989)

A. H. van Zyl, *The Moabites* (Leiden: Brill, 1960)

Major Sources on the Edomites

Burton MacDonald, *The Southern Transjordan Edomite Plateau and the Dead Sea Rift Valley: The Bronze Age to the Islamic Period* (3800/3700 BC–AD 1917) (Oxford: Oxbow Books, 2015)

Thomas E. Levy, Mohammad Najjar, and Erez Ben-Yosef (eds.), *New Insights into the Iron Age Archaeology of Edom, Southern Jordan*, 2 vols. (Los Angeles: Cotsen Institute of Archaeology Press, 2014)

Diana V. Edelman (ed.), *You Shall Not Abhor an Edomite for He Is Your Brother: Edom and Seir in History and Tradition* (Atlanta: Scholars Press, 1995)

Bert Dicou, *Edom, Israel's Brother and Antagonist: The Role of Edom in Biblical Prophecy and Story* (Sheffield: JSOT Press, 1994)

Piotr Bienkowski (ed.), *Early Edom and Moab: The Beginning of the Iron Age in Southern Jordan* (Sheffield: J. R. Collis Publications, 1992)

John R. Bartlett, *Edom and the Edomites* (Sheffield: JSOT Press, 1989)

Itzhaq Beit-Arieh and Pirhiya Beck, *Edomite Shrine: Discoveries from Qitmit in the Negev* (Jerusalem: Israel Museum, 1987)

John F. A. Sawyer and David J. A. Clines (eds.), *Midian, Moab and Edom: The History and Archaeology of Late Bronze and Iron Age Jordan and North-West Arabia* (Sheffield: JSOT Press, 1983)

Nelson Glueck, *The Other Side of the Jordan* (New Haven, CT: American Schools of Oriental Research, 1940)

Major Sources on the Philistines

Assaf Yasur-Landau, *The Philistines and Aegean Migration at the End of the Late Bronze Age* (Cambridge: Cambridge University Press, 2014)

Ann E. Killebrew and Gunnar Lehmann (eds.), *The Philistines and Other "Sea Peoples" in Text and Archaeology* (Atlanta: Society of Biblical Literature, 2013)

Eliezer D. Oren (ed.), *The Sea Peoples and Their World: A Reassessment* (Philadelphia: University of Pennsylvania Press, 2013)

David Ben-Shlomo, *Philistine Iconography: A Wealth of Style and Symbolism* (Fribourg: Academic Press, 2010)

Trude Dothan and Moshe Dothan, *People of the Sea: The Search for the Philistines* (New York: Macmillan, 1992)

Major Sources on the Phoenicians

Carolina López-Ruiz and Brian R. Doak (eds.), *The Oxford Handbook of the Phoenician and Punic Mediterranean* (Oxford: Oxford University Press, 2019)

Josephine Quinn, *In Search of the Phoenicians* (Princeton, NJ: Princeton University Press, 2017)

Mark Woolmer, *A Short History of the Phoenicians* (London: I. B. Tauris, 2017)

Sebastián Celestino and Carolina López-Ruiz, *Tartessos and the Phoenicians in Iberia* (Oxford: Oxford University Press, 2016)

Brian R. Doak, *Phoenician Aniconism in Its Mediterranean and Ancient Near Eastern Contexts* (Atlanta: Society of Biblical Literature, 2015)

Brian Peckham, *Phoenicia: Episodes and Anecdotes from the Ancient Mediterranean* (Winona Lake, IN: Eisenbrauns, 2014)

Josephine C. Quinn and Nicholas C. Vella (eds.), *The Punic Mediterranean: Identities and Identification from Phoenician Settlement to Roman Rule* (Cambridge: Cambridge University Press, 2014)

Maria E. Aubet, *The Phoenicians and the West: Politics, Colonies, and Trade*, 2nd ed., trans. Mary Turton (Cambridge: Cambridge University Press, 2001)

Glenn E. Markoe, *The Phoenicians* (Berkeley: University of California Press, 2000)

H. J. Katzenstein, *The History of Tyre from the Beginning of the 2nd Millennium B.C.E. until the Fall of the Neo-Babylonian Empire in 538 B.C.E.*, 2nd rev. ed. (Jerusalem: Ben Gurion University of the Negev Press, 1997)

Sabatino Moscati (ed.), *The Phoenicians: Under the Scientific Direction of Sabatino Moscati* (New York: Abbeville, 1988)

Other Resources

Christine Helmer, Steven L. McKenzie, Thomas Chr. Römer, Jens Schroeter, Barry Dov Walfish, and Eric Ziolkowski (eds.), *The Encyclopedia of the Bible and Its Reception*, 30 vols. (Berlin: De Gruyter, 2009–; and online at www.degruyter.com/view/db/ebr).
Mary Ann Beavis and Michael J. Gilmour (eds.), *Dictionary of the Bible and Western Culture* (Sheffield: Sheffield Academic Press, 2012)
Karel van der Toorn, Bob Becking, and Pieter W. van der Horst (eds.), *Dictionary of Deities and Demons in the Bible*, 2nd ed. (Leiden: Brill, 1999)
David N. Freedman (ed.), *The Anchor Bible Dictionary* (New York: Doubleday, 1990–1992)

INDEX

For the benefit of digital users, indexed terms that span two pages (e.g., 52–53) may, on occasion, appear on only one of those pages.

Readers looking for broad information for any of Israel's neighbors treated in this book can consult the appropriate chapter and then look under the uniform headings for each chapter: *The Archaeology of the Neighbor* (what do we know about the neighbor outside of the Bible); *The Neighbor in the Hebrew Bible* (what does the Hebrew Bible say about the neighbor); *What Happened to the Neighbor* (what do we know about the continued existence of the neighbor and its people after the Iron Age and on into the Common Era). Some other selected terms are indexed here below.

Figures are indicated by *f* following the page number

Abram/Abraham, 4, 63–64, 67, 74, 86–87, 111–12, 132, 135, 146
Ahaz, 69–70, 139, 166–67
Ahiram, 177, 187–88
'Ain Dara, 57–58
alphabet, 30–31, 32*f*, 179, 180*f*
Amarna letters, 23, 30–31
Amman (Rabbath-Ammon), 75–77, 78–79, 80, 89, 93, 94, 95
Amman Citadel Inscription, 79*f*, 83
'Amminadab (Ammonite king), 81

Amos (book of), 67, 70, 94, 119, 139–40, 146, 161, 166, 184–85, 188–89
Aramaic (language), 51–52, 57, 58–59, 60–61, 65–66, 70–73, 78, 81–82
art, artistic traditions
    Ammonite, 77–78, 84–85
    Aramean, 61–62
    Canaanite, 30, 45
    Edomite, 36–39

art, artistic traditions (*Cont.*)
  Moabite, 109–10
  Philistine, 156, 168
  Phoenician, 170, 179
  Asherah, 19, 29, 42–43,
    158–59, 186–87
  Assyria, Assyrians, 2, 7–8, 16, 19–20,
    51–52, 53–57, 60–62, 69, 70–
    71, 72–73, 76–78, 81, 82–83,
    84–85, 90, 94–95, 97, 101–2,
    122–26, 139, 151–53, 154, 155–
    56, 173–74, 176–77, 187–88

Baal (deity), 19, 33, 57–58, 113,
    158–59, 165–66, 181–82,
    186–87, 191–92
Babylon, Babylonians, 2, 20–21,
    36, 37, 51–52, 70–71, 72–73,
    77–78, 82–83, 94–95, 97,
    119–20, 122, 125–26, 140–41,
    144–45, 167, 168–69, 173–74,
    176–77, 197–98
Balaam, 65–66, 78, 83, 112–13, 114,
    116–17, 119–20
Balu'a Stele, 109–10, 110*f*
Bloch-Smith, Elizabeth, 34–35,
    165–66n.27
burial customs, 26–27, 29–30,
    84, 143–44, 156–57, 159–60,
    170, 178
Byblos, 7–8, 11, 170–71, 172–74,
    176–78, 181–82, 183, 191–92

Carthage, 171, 178, 191–92
Chemosh/Kemosh, 57, 91–92,
    102–4, 105, 107–10, 114–15,
    117, 118, 119
child sacrifice, 19, 42–43, 91–92,
    93–94, 118, 191–92
Chronicles (books of), 62–63, 94–
    95, 117, 139, 183–84n.23

copper (mines), 123–26, 138–39
Cross, Frank Moore, 30–31

Dagan, 14, 146, 158–59, 163–64
Damascus, 7–8, 51–52, 53–55, 56–
    57, 67–68, 69
David (king), 3, 15–16, 37, 67–68,
    69, 90, 93, 98, 102, 103, 115,
    117, 122, 125–26, 138–40, 146,
    163–66, 168, 183–84, 185–86
Deir 'Alla, 65, 78, 83
Deuteronomy (book of), 3, 16–17,
    18–19, 22–23, 36–37, 38, 39–
    40, 41, 43–44, 45, 66, 67, 88,
    89, 91–92, 96, 112–14, 120–21,
    122, 136–37, 183
Dhiban/Dibon, 99, 102, 105–6

Eglon, 114–15
Egypt, Egyptians, 2, 3, 6–8, 20–
    21, 23–24, 26–27, 29–30,
    31–33, 36, 39–40, 45, 60–
    61, 63–64, 66, 70, 72–73,
    81, 82–83, 84–85, 88, 91–
    92, 96, 100–1, 112–13, 114,
    125–26, 128–29, 136–37,
    141–42, 149–50, 151–52,
    153, 159–60, 161, 175–77,
    179, 183–84, 189, 194–95
Ehud, 114–15
Ekron, 7–8, 147–48, 151–53, 156,
    159–60, 162–63, 165–66
Ekron inscription, 155–56, 159–60
Elephantine, 30, 72–73
Elijah, 68, 165–66, 186–87, 191
Emim, 114
En Hatzeva, 122–23, 124*f*, 129–32
Esau, 4, 88–89, 122, 123, 133–37,
    139–41, 144–45, 196
Exodus (book of), 16–17, 19, 48,
    122, 183–84

Ezekiel (book of), 11, 19, 22–23, 44–45, 46, 119, 139–40, 167, 190
Ezra (book of), 45, 70–71, 72–73, 96, 117

Faust, Avraham, 25–26
Finkelstein, Israel, 34–35

Genesis (book of), 3, 4, 16–17, 22, 36, 39–40, 62–65, 74, 85–88, 89, 98, 111–13, 122, 133, 134, 135–36, 139, 146, 161–62, 182–83, 196
Goliath, 40, 146, 155–56n.14, 164–66
Gomorrah, 85–87, 111
Gottwald, Norman, 31–33

Hadad (deity), 58–60, 61–62, 69
Hadad (Edomite king), 138–39
Hadad-ezer (Hadadezer), 56–57, 67–68
Hamath, 51–52, 53–54, 56–57, 61–62
Hanun (Ammonite king), 74, 93
Hazael, 67, 68–69
Hazor, 27–29, 28f, 34–35, 44, 175–76
Hebrew, Hebrews (as group), 3, 63, 113, 120–21, 136–37
Hebrew (language), 35–36, 39–40, 41, 64–65, 67, 70, 86–87, 104–5, 111–12, 134, 155, 165–66, 190
herem/haram (warfare), 41, 43–44, 45, 50
Hesban/Heshbon, 87–88, 99, 100–1
Hiram of Tyre, 176–77, 183–85
history (definition, method), 3, 7, 11–18, 89–90
Hittites, 2, 22–23, 36–39, 44–45, 54–55, 61–62, 65, 96, 135
Horvat Uzza, 126–27, 128–29

Huizinga, Johann, 12
Hyksos, 29–30

Isaac, 63–64, 133, 134, 135, 137, 139, 161–62
Isaiah (book of), 16, 67, 69–70, 118–19, 139–40, 166–67, 189–90
Israel (modern), 6–7, 49, 194–95

Jacob, 63–65, 67, 133, 134, 135, 136, 137, 139–41, 144–45
Jeremiah (book of), 16–17, 67, 94–95, 118–19, 139–40, 166–67
Jerusalem, 3, 6–7, 19–20, 27–29, 37, 68–69, 94–95, 140–41, 143
Jews, Judaism, 19–20, 30, 45, 46–47, 70–71, 72–73, 94–95, 96, 115–16, 117, 143, 144–45, 167–68, 191, 194–95
Jezebel, 185–88
Job (character and book), 62, 98, 141–42
Jordan (modern nation), 6–7, 51–52, 75–77, 80, 95, 119–20, 123, 194–95
Jordan River, 6–7, 24, 38, 39–40, 65, 75–76, 84, 113–14, 136–37
Joshua (character and book), 18–19, 22–23, 39, 41, 43–44, 136–37, 162–63, 183–84, 194–95
Judges (book of), 43–44, 90–91, 106, 114–15, 136–37, 146, 162–63, 183–84
Judith (book of), 97

Killebrew, Ann, 26–27
Kings (books of), 3, 4, 19–20, 22–23, 42–43, 67, 68–69, 91–92, 93–95, 106, 117–18, 122, 138–39, 146, 165–66, 170, 183–88, 196

Laban, 63–65, 134
Lebanon, 6–7, 24, 51–53, 171,
    191, 194–95
Lévi-Strauss, Claude, 12
Lot (Abraham's nephew), 4, 74, 86–
    87, 88, 111–12, 114, 135

Megiddo, 27–29, 30, 30*f*, 34–35
Mendenhall, George, 31–33
Mesha (Moabite king); Mesha
    Stele, 98–99, 102, 104–8,
    114–15, 117–18
Midian, Midianites, 44,
    112–13, 141–42
Milcom/Milkom (deity), 80,
    83, 93–117
Moabite Stone. *See* Mesha Stele
Molech, 42–43, 93–94
Moses, 16–17, 40, 66, 88, 113–14,
    116, 136–37, 141–42

Nabateans, 46, 143–44
Nahash, 74, 92–93
nation (definition), 9–11
Native Americans / First Nation,
    18–19, 49
Nehemiah (book of), 45, 72–73, 94–
    95, 96, 115–17, 167–68
New Testament, 19–20, 46, 115,
    119–20, 143, 144–45, 191
Nora Stone, 178, 187–88
Numbers (book of), 40, 65,
    87–88, 89, 91–92, 112–13,
    115–16, 117, 119–21, 122,
    136–37, 183–84

Palestine, Palestinians (modern),
    6–7, 49, 168–69, 194–95
Pekah, 69–70
Peleset, 150–52

Persia, Persians, 16, 51–52, 70–71,
    95–96, 125–26, 168–69, 173–
    74, 176–77, 197–98
Phinehas, 113
pottery, 15
    Ammonite, 78–79, 95–96
    Canaanite, 26, 34–35
    Edomite, 132*f*
    Philistine, 152, 158*f*
    Phoenician, 179–81, 184–85

Qitmit, 122–23, 129–32
Qos (deity), 57, 122–23, 126–30

Ranke, Leopold von, 11–12
Rebekah, 63–64, 133, 135, 161–62
Rephaim, 88–89, 114
Rome, Roman Empire, 70–71, 79,
    142–45, 168–69, 172–73, 179,
    189–90, 191–92, 197–98
Ruth, 3, 98, 115–17, 119–20, 121

Samaritans, 19–20
Samson, 146, 162–63
Samuel (prophet; books of), 4, 22–
    23, 67–68, 92–93, 106, 117, 122,
    138–39, 146, 163–64, 165–66,
    183–84, 185–86
Sea Peoples, 147, 149–51, 155
Seir, 88–89, 123, 135, 137, 141–42
Shechem, 27–29
Shihan Warrior Stele, 109–10, 110*f*
Sidon, 4, 7–8, 11, 36, 46, 167, 170,
    171, 172–74, 175, 176–77, 181–
    84, 185–87, 189, 191
Sodom, 85–87, 111–12
Solomon (king), 57–58, 90, 93–94,
    117, 122, 125–26, 138–39, 146,
    165–66, 170, 183–86
State (definition), 9–11

Syria (modern nation), 6–7, 23, 29,
    33, 52–53, 71–72, 194–95

Table of Nations (Genesis ch. 10),
    36, 62, 111, 133, 161
Tell Dan Stele, 68–69
Tell Siran Bottle
    Inscription, 80, 83
temples, 2, 19–20, 27–29, 57–58,
    80, 94–95, 104, 122, 140–41,
    143–45, 146, 149–50, 155,

159–60, 162–64, 170, 181–82,
    183–85, 191–92
Tiglath-pilesar III, 53–54, 55–57, 69,
    77–78, 153, 176–77
Tribe (definition), 10
Tyre, 4, 7–8, 11, 46, 167, 170, 171,
    172–74, 175–77, 179–81, 182–
    84, 186–87, 188–92

Ugarit, Ugaritic (language, culture),
    29, 33, 175–76

CPSIA information can be obtained
at www.ICGtesting.com
Printed in the USA
BVHW031949121222
654048BV00009B/166